BY THE SAME AUTHOR

*Special Delivery: The Complete Guide to Informed Birth*
*Pregnant Feelings* (co-authored with Terra Palmarini)

*You Are Your Child's First Teacher*

# You
# Are Your
# Child's First
# Teacher

RAHIMA BALDWIN

*Photographs by Harriette Hartigan*

**CELESTIALARTS**
*Berkeley, California*

CELESTIAL ARTS
P.O. Box 7327
Berkeley, California 94707

Cover and interior photographs Copyright © by Harriette Hartigan
Design photography for cover by George Post
Author photo by Paula Christensen
Cover design by Ken Scott
Text design by Nancy Austin
Editorial production by Judith Johnstone
Composition by Recorder Typesetting Network

Library of Congress Cataloging-in-Publication Data

Baldwin, Rahima, 1949–
    You are your child's first teacher / Rahima Baldwin.
        p.    cm.
    Bibliography: p.
    Includes index.
    ISBN 0-89087-519-7
    1. Child rearing—United States. 2. Child development.
3. Education, preschool—United States—Parent participation.
4. Parenting—United States.    I. Title.
HQ769.B3125    1988
649'.1—dc19                                                  88-3983
                                                            CIP


Manufactured in the United States of America


2    3    4    5    6    –    91    90    89

# Contents

# Preface

Parents today are bombarded by contradictions when they look for advice about how to act with their children. We need, not another authority or set of rules by which to raise children, but a new way of seeing and understanding the human being. If we can enlarge our understanding of child and adult development to encompass the whole human being—body, mind, emotions and spirit—then we will be best equipped to make our own decisions based on a combination of cognitive and intuitive knowledge.

One dilemma of parents today is how best to support their child's development in the early years—the years in which they are their child's first teachers. Parents hear about ways to "build a better baby" and to "hothouse" preschoolers on the one hand and, on the other hand, warnings of the dangers of hurrying children and "miseducation" by child psychologists like David Elkind. Parents who have come to realize the risks involved in treating their children like little adults still don't feel satisfied just playing tea party or making sand castles together. What can parents do with and for their children from birth to age six that will enhance their development without having negative effects at a later age? How can we help our children to develop the skills needed for life in the twenty-first century?

These and other questions led me to an in-depth exploration of early childhood and parenting. After more than a decade as a childbirth educator and midwife who continually asked, "How can children be born in a way that is best for them physically, emotionally and spiritually?," I felt I knew something about birth. But, though I had three children, I knew that somewhere there *had* to be greater wisdom available about children than I had yet discovered. My question about birth was transformed into a similar question about parenting these children who had such wonderful births.

My search led me to study the work of Rudolf Steiner, an Austrian educator and visionary who founded the first Waldorf School in 1919. (See Appendix B for further information on Steiner and Waldorf education.) I studied for two years at the Waldorf Institute, then located in Southfield, Michigan, and then taught kindergarten and preschool for four years with the Rudolf Steiner School of Ann Arbor. I was also fortunate to attend the International Waldorf Kindergarten Association conferences in Germany, where work with parents and children from birth to age three is much more developed than in this country.

I found that using the insights into human development provided by Steiner enabled me to see children in a new way. I was suddenly able to relate better to children and found more creative things to do with them. My home life became more harmonious; I was able to become an early-childhood teacher—and the children flourished! In this book I want to share some of these new ways of seeing, so that we as parents, childcare providers and early-childhood teachers will gain an appreciation of the magical years of early childhood and the special needs of the young child. The complexity and stressfulness of life today make it even more urgent that we honor the laws of early childhood, for the health of human beings and society are at stake.

Although this book makes many concrete suggestions of things you can do with your children, it is not offered as a formula for raising children! Rather, I hope that some of these new ways of seeing and understanding the child between birth and age six will provide fertile ground for your own creativity and will help to increase your own perceptions and confidence in what you are doing.

As a midwife, I came to see myself as a guardian of normal birth, providing a tremendous amount of support but intervening only as needed. This comes from a fundamental respect for women and their ability to birth normally. Now I also see myself as a guardian of normal childhood, speaking up for a new common sense about raising children, one which helps children be children while enabling us to recognize our important role as parents. Our task is to understand the child's development and allow that new knowledge to strengthen our intuition about our own children. Through this we may come to see the value in the simple things we do, as well as the spiritual in even the most mundane. In the small world of the developing child we can see the recapitulation of humanity's development and even have intimations of the divine functioning of the cosmos.

In addition to enlivening your life with your children, I hope this book will serve as a bridge leading to further discovery of the richness of Rudolf Steiner's work as it applies to education, medicine, biodynamic agriculture, adult development and a wealth of other fields.

In wrestling with the gender difficulties of the English language, I finally decided to attempt balance by usually referring to the child under three as *she* and to the older child as *he*. Because this is a personal and a practical book, I have also addressed *you* at many places throughout the book. I hope that you will find it a helpful guide on the path of parenting.

—*Rahima Baldwin*
August, 1988
Ann Arbor, Michigan

# Acknowledgments

Both this book and my work as a parent and early-childhood educator take their greatest inspiration from the work of Rudolf Steiner, an Austrian philosopher and educator who founded the first Waldorf School in Stuttgart, Germany in 1919. Steiner's understanding of child development and his reverence for life have enabled me to be with young children in ways that complement the natural unfolding of their capacities. I would also like to thank Werner Glas, co-director of the Waldorf Institute, for inspiring me to undertake the task of making the wisdom of Rudolf Steiner more accessible to parents so they can apply it in home life.

I would also like to acknowledge the work of Burton White, founder and director of the Center for Parent Education in Newton, Massachusetts. While director of the Harvard Preschool Project and the Brookline Early Education Project, he observed mothers in their homes to see what parenting practices were being used on siblings of "wonderful children" rather than starting from some theoretical or laboratory base. His observations and conclusions about the first three years of life strongly support many of the principles set down by Rudolf Steiner a half-century earlier. His book *The First Three Years of Life* and his "New Parents as Teachers" project, which was so successful in Missouri, have encouraged me in writing this book and developing ways of working with parents and children during these vital years.

I have found similar support from the work of David Elkind, Professor of Child Study at Tufts University, who has described the current crisis in education and parenting in *Miseducation: Preschoolers at Risk* and *The Hurried Child*. Characteristic of Waldorf education are activities that are developmentally appropriate and take into account the whole child—in mental, emotional, physical and spiritual development. Our rapidly changing society needs more than ever to protect early childhood and to assure children's healthy development of inner resources so they may successfully assume their places as adults.

I would like to thank my own children, Seth (14), Faith (12) and Jasmine (8), for leading me on this path through parenting and for being so cooperative while I wrote yet another book. My husband, Agaf Dancy, also deserves hugs and kisses for his continual support in all areas and for his editorial skills. Thanks also to Katherine Czapp, Susan Howard, Wahhab Baldwin, Mary Lynn Channer, Ann Pratt, Joan Almon, Barbara Stern and others who have read and commented on the manuscript. Special thanks also go to Judith Johnstone and David Hinds at Celestial Arts for their help in making this book available for parents.

# 1 | *You Are Your Child's First Teacher*

## A UNIQUE OPPORTUNITY

The time between birth and age six is a time of growth and learning unparalleled in later life. Tremendous physical growth and learning occur between birth and age three. The four-year-old continues learning about the world through his play, imitating all that goes on around him and expressing his own unique personality and approach to the world. The first-grader evokes in us a picture of a grinning child with missing teeth who is well-oriented in time and space and eager to exercise his emerging skills in reading and writing. From first grade on we assume that the child will do his or her primary learning at school, but we cannot forget that what the child has learned in the home forms the necessary and irreplaceable foundation for all that comes later.

The formative power of children's experiences in the early years has been recognized by thinkers and educators throughout history. However, the importance of the first three years gained scientific backing in America only since the 1960s. Follow-up studies on the Head Start Program that arose during that decade for three- and four-year-olds showed that it was necessary to start much younger if children were going to be helped to achieve their full potential; increasing interest in Piaget's work and in the maternal deprivation studies from the 1940s convinced researchers and educators that the first years were critical for building social and emotional foundations and for the development of intelligence.[1]

While many researchers were focusing on programs for poorly-developing preschool children, Burton White and his associates at Harvard undertook a thirteen-year study of how all children develop in the first six years of life. White states:

> In our studies we were not only impressed by what some children could achieve in the first years, but also by the fact that a child's own family seemed so obviously central to the outcome. Indeed, we came to believe that the more informal education that families provide for their children makes more of an impact on a child's total education than the formal educational system. If a family does its job well, the professional can then provide effective training. If not, there may be little a professional can do to save a child from mediocrity. This grim assessment is the direct conclusion from the findings of thousands of programs for remedial education, such as the Head Start and Follow Through projects.[2]

In the Brookline Early Education Project, White continued his studies by focussing on the question of what helps children to develop into "wonderful" people. First he found "great" six-year-olds—children who were not only intelligent and well-developed, but well-balanced and a pleasure to be with. To try to determine what parental factors and experiences in the early years had helped to make them that way, he involved their families in the study when a new baby was expected so he could observe the ways these parents interacted with their children before the age of three. White's work is especially interesting because he truly *observed* and learned from mothers and babies in their own homes, and he was concerned with the children's overall balance, not just intellectual development.

White discovered that most families get their children through the first six to eight months of life reasonably well in terms of overall development. Unless a child was part of the small percentage of children who are born with a significant handicap or acquire one within the first year, there was little measurable difference in development among babies in their first eight months. But White and others have shown the period that begins at eight months and ends at three years is uniquely important in the development of a human being. White feels that perhaps no more than ten percent of American families get their children through the ages of eight to thirty-six months as well educated and developed as they might be.[3]

White also observed that "raising a bright three-year-old is much easier than raising a pleasant unspoiled three-year-old."[4] Therefore, he developed educational programs for new parents that emphasize more than just intellectual development. One such program based on White's work, the Missouri Project, was offered to couples from before birth until the children turned three. Group sessions for parents were supplemented by home visits in which trained workers answered parents' questions and offered suggestions from what they observed. Not only was parent satisfaction with the program ninety-nine percent, but studies done after the three years of the pilot program showed a positive impact of parent education on children's development in many spheres.[5]

Another educator who recognized the importance of the early years in the development of the human being was Rudolf Steiner. Steiner, a scientist and visionary as well as an educator, founded the first Waldorf School in Stuttgart, Germany in 1919. Albert Steffen, who attended many of Steiner's lectures, reports, "Many times in his writings Dr. Steiner has shown that it is in the earliest years of childhood that things happen which are the deciding factors in later life. Whatever is done well or ill to a child in its earliest age will reappear in the grown person as faculties or failings, health or disease. On this account we should feel it our duty at the outset to gain an understanding of the whole course of life."[6]

## PARENTS' DILEMMA TODAY

All parents want to do what is best for their children, to give them the best possible start in life. But what *is* best? Many parents feel that they ought to be doing more with their eight-month-old. But what? Or parents want to spend "quality time" with their child, but find it boring to sit and do puzzles together. That we are plagued with so many questions, doubts and guilt about how to raise our children is the result of living in a time of tremendous changes. Our culture no longer provides a strong and unified message about how children should be reared. In addition, most of us live separated from our own parents or other extended family who traditionally provided wisdom, help and continuity in rearing children. The art of mothering was replaced by the science of parenting, yet many parents have come to question the values their own parents embraced in such practices as bottle feeding every four hours and letting the child "cry it out."

As members of modern Western society, it is appropriate that we question everything, that we bring things to consciousness and go on to create something whole and nourishing. For example, we found, in questioning modern practices of technological intervention in birth, that there is no such thing as "natural childbirth." All childbirth is influenced by the culture in which it takes place. It is not possible to just do it "naturally"; rather, we have to re-educate ourselves and try to bring our minds, bodies and feelings into a new harmony, a new integration that will allow us to birth as complete human beings, with body, mind and emotions working together.

The same is true of parenting. It is appropriate that we question what we are doing and that we discuss our attitudes and intentions with one another—but not in front of the children! It is beneficial for children to think we know what we are doing, even if we aren't so sure ourselves. They don't need to be involved in the intricacies of adult considerations and thought processes. Rather, they need to feel that mother and father are united in what they are doing.

Being in a state of "not knowing" and "questioning" can be very positive, but it can also be frustrating because children don't wait until we have it all figured out! They demand constant interaction and decisions that will influence them in both the present and the future. Just as babies don't wait until the world and our lives are in perfect order before they are born, children don't wait until we are "perfect parents." Indeed, we will be better off if we can give up the idea of perfection in regard to parenting. Parenting is a process of mutual growth, in which parents and children grow on different levels through their interactions and through the elements they bring into one another's lives.

Because everything has come into question, many of us find ourselves as new parents in a real quandary about what to do in various situations. And we often find we have no way of foreseeing the effects of our actions on our children—especially the first child! Should we encourage our child to express all of his emotions and perhaps end up as a little tyrant, or yell at him and risk producing a repressed and resentful adult? Neither alternative is very inviting! Should we start teaching our nine-month-old to read or swim? Does our three-year-old need to be computer literate in order to get ahead in today's world? We don't seem to have any way of judging, and therefore find ourselves at the mercy of whatever notion comes along. We need to listen to our own inner knowing. And we need to acquire knowledge about how the young child develops so we can make choices with confidence and receptivity. Many of us as new parents have no knowledge of child development, and we haven't even been around children since we grew up. Many of us have forgotten what children are like and find ourselves on the path of parenting without any knowledge of the landscape.

## CULTURAL DILEMMAS

We need to begin to see the child in a new way, one which takes into account physical, emotional and mental development, as well as the less tangible spiritual dimension of the human being. Once we begin to perceive the whole child and how he or she unfolds, then our choices will begin to have coherence. No longer wanting a cookbook of "how to's," we will trust our own decisions, based on our understanding of the developing child and observation of the resultant flowering of our own children.

We need to realize that there are many cultural norms working against seeing the child in such a way. First of all, our society tends to regard children as little adults, so we are encouraged to reason with them as if they were grown-ups and to teach them with techniques appropriate for much older children. Despite years of studies by Piaget and neurophysiologists, educational politicians determine curricula and textbooks seemingly without any regard to the way children actually think and learn. The "new math" fiasco of the early 1960s illustrates how professors and book companies tried (and ultimately failed) to introduce an approach which was far too abstract for elementary-school students.

We also need to recognize that our society values intellectual development above all else and tends to ignore other aspects of development, both as to their own value and the impact they have on learning. In an attempt to produce more intellectual and literate students and adults after Sputnik in 1957, the American elementary-school curriculum has been pushed earlier and earlier, so that kindergarteners are now doing what used to be taught in first grade. The fact that many children are now failing kindergarten and functional illiteracy continues to rise in this country has only led to starting "reading readiness" with four-year-olds in an increasing number of school systems. The fact that there is a difference between kindergarteners and first graders—that is, that there is a major developmental change that goes on around age six or seven—is being ignored as parents and educators begin to "hot house" preschoolers into academic channels.

This disregard for the natural development of children has resulted in what David Elkind calls "miseducation," or practices that put preschoolers at risk and have no real benefit. His books *The Hurried Child*[7] and *Miseducation: Preschoolers at Risk*[8] detail the forces in our culture that are jeopardizing the healthy development of our children.

We have lost touch with natural processes in child development, convinced that we have to "do something" rather than allowing the child's own inner process of unfolding. Pediatricians try to reassure mothers that each child has his own timetable with regard to walking early or late, but educators do not reassure parents or try to maintain the self-esteem of a child who does not learn to read until age nine. Rather, he is labelled "learning disabled" and put into remedial classes, in which the basics are drilled to the point where he loses out on the richness and excitement of learning.

Rudolf Steiner had tremendous confidence in the natural processes of development and reminded us that "That which is asleep will awaken."[9] That doesn't mean we do *nothing*—it means the things we do need to be consonant with the child's own developmental stages as they unfold. It is unhealthy to skip stages or to rush the child through various phases. While it is sometimes possible to do so, just because something *can* be done doesn't mean that it *should* be done! Again, we need an understanding of the development of the human being to be able to judge what is in harmony with a child's development and what violates it.

In summary, many of the factors working against our knowing how to parent are a result of our unique position in time and culture. We are not part of a culture that dictates the way things are done. We question many things as we look for value and meaning in our lives. And we live in isolation from children and more experienced parents who can share with us what children are like. We are also influenced by our culture's distrust of nature and the desire to control nature with the mind. We tend to be unaware of the fact that children have a completely different consciousness from adults.

## THE CHANGING FAMILY

Compounding the dilemmas faced by parents today is the changing nature of family life. Many men have changed their attitudes about fathering over the past decade. While change is always stressful, most men who have increased their involvement with their children feel positive about it. On the other hand, the rise of the two-income family has led to more and more children being placed in fulltime daycare at younger and younger ages. If both parents have careers, they may share concern about finding quality daycare and what is happening with their child in their absence. A survey of executives reported in *Fortune* found that concern about their children was the biggest problem facing both men and women executives—perhaps with good reason![10] Despite the changing role of fathers today, primary responsibility for the children still remains with the mother in our society, whether she stays at home or works outside the home. Many mothers cannot stay at home with their children, either because of being a single parent or because the family needs a second income. Even without economic necessity, some women prefer to work for relatively low wages *and* pay childcare rather than be home day after day with their child or children. Why has it become so difficult for many women to be with children? The answer lies partly in the changing nature of our society. In rural yesteryear, life for women centered around survival tasks that took most of the day—gardening and canning, washing and ironing, baking and cooking, sewing, chopping wood or other farm chores. The children tagged along, helping their parents as soon as they were able, but life never centered around them.

To expect a thirty-seven-year-old Ph.D. candidate, or a woman who has had an exciting career, to be fulfilled spending her days in an apartment with a two-year-old is idyllic but hard to find in reality. In the nuclear or subnuclear family, far too much energy gets focussed on the child because he or she is the most interesting subject around (try getting excited about waxing the kitchen floor!). But after a time many mothers find themselves getting cabin fever. It becomes increasingly difficult, both emotionally and intellectually, to be home day after day with this child because there is a lack of adult stimulation.

Some women find it perfectly delightful to stay home after so many years of working. Generalities never apply! But no matter what a mother does, there isn't much support or value placed on mothering in our society. Whether she finds it the most wonderful thing in the world to stay home with the children, whether she is struggling to make a go of it, or whether she is trying to juggle a work schedule with a child's needs when he is sick, she doesn't get much support from any quarter for her mothering.

## A WAY OF SEEING CHILDREN'S DEVELOPMENT: CHILDREN ARE NOT TINY ADULTS!

One of the keys to avoiding many of the problems that accompany parenting today is to have an understanding of children's development. If we can understand the nature of the young child as it unfolds, we will be able to meet the child's real needs for balanced development of mind, body and emotions.

Although children are obviously very different from grown-ups, our culture tends to treat them as privileged but miniature adults and to rush them through childhood. Many problems arise when we fail to realize how different a three-year-old is from a nine-year-old, a teenager or an adult. That sounds obvious, but many parents take all their children to the same movie in an effort to be fair, or they reason with their five-year-old as if his ease with words ought to translate into control of his actions in the future.

The hurried-child syndrome is apparent in all spheres of activity today. It is obvious physically that children's bodies are not mature, yet we try to speed up their development with baby walkers and baby gymnastics. Designer jeans and Barbie dolls for young children contribute to the ever younger entry into the teen-age world of makeup and clothes consciousness. A recent issue of *The New York Times Magazine* contained fourteen pages of features and ads for preschoolers' fashions, culminating in the "Children's Fashion Marketplace." One ad for a wooden climbing frame said, "Tomorrow's Corporate Climbers . . . Have To Start Somewhere!" Another two-page ad for clothes by Healthtex had drawings of preschoolers and carried the title, "Why Should I Exercise?" The text began, "Just for the fun of it. Besides, how do you think those athletes, dancers and acrobats you love to watch on your TV screen got that way?" It recommended that children walk briskly and ride their bicycles as "ways that will keep you from huffing and puffing when you're chugging down to first base or trying to keep up with mom's aerobics."[11] Whom are they kidding? Anyone who has turned off the television set will know that young children don't need encouragement to move. In fact, it's difficult to have them stay still long enough for the fashion photographs!

It is also obvious that children are not *emotionally* the same as adults. A young child can smile through his tears when given the simplest distraction. The basically happy four-year-old stands in sharp contrast to the brooding adolescent. How does the one turn into the other? It is clear that the emotional inner life only gradually develops the complexity and texture with which we are familiar as adults. Yet many parents try to develop their children's emotions and their awareness of emotions by naming, expressing and even practicing emotions with them. And we tend to expose young children to situations that are far too powerful for them emotionally—notice the unhappy children in the theatre at the next movie you attend!

It is obvious that children do not reason as adults do. They are able to come up with amazing statements, both about how the world works and about how something they shouldn't have done managed to happen. Logical thought and problem-solving ability are slow to develop. Very young toddlers lack "object permanence" and will look for an object where they have repeatedly found it hidden rather than in the place where they have just seen you put it. Children before the age of six lack the ability for what Piaget calls "concrete operational thinking." Rational thinking does not develop until age ten or eleven as observed in Piaget's studies. So it has long been documented that the ability to reason and to think logically is a gradually unfolding power that children grow into. As adults we have forgotten what it was like to live in a nonlinear, nonsequential world. We expect to be able to reason with our children as soon as they are verbal. We reason with them about everything from their behavior and its consequences to why the sea is salty. And indeed, some five-year-olds show great ability to conduct such conversations with their parents—but they have learned it through *imitating* years of that type of interaction with their parents. Young children do not yet think rationally, and reason has little impact on changing their behavior.

Similarly, we offer lengthy scientific explanations as answers to children's questions, when a direct experience of something similar or an image that can live and work in their imaginations would be much more satisfying to them. Rational explanations are like giving a hungry child stones instead of bread. Elkind points out that when young children ask questions like, "Why does the sun shine?" they are really asking about *purpose* rather than mechanics and are much more nourished by an answer like, "To keep us warm and to make the grass and the flowers grow" than a lecture on thermodynamics.[12]

# THE CHILD'S CHANGING CONSCIOUSNESS

Differences in physical, emotional and mental capacities between children of various ages and adults are easy to recognize, though they are often ignored. Differences in consciousness are equally apparent when we observe different-aged children's awareness of themselves and their surroundings. For example, the infant has what can be called "participatory consciousness," with no differentiated sense of self and other. Between the second and third years a major change in consciousness occurs with the development of memory and first saying of the word "I." This change is the reason most people can't remember very much before the age of three. Most young children are fairly dreamy, living in a stream-of-consciousness state that follows whatever comes into awareness without adult concern about intentionality and "task completion." If you send a four-year-old to get ready for bed by himself, you can expect to find him playing with the toothpaste or the water when you join him. Young children have a completely different orientation to time and space. They live in the present, without adult perceptions of the past and future. Hence they find waiting so hard, and don't understand "ten minutes" or "three days" when told they must wait that long.

The achieving of adult consciousness is a gradual process. It does not happen at birth or age eight or even age fifteen. The preschool child, elementary-aged child, adolescent and adult are very different—they perceive the world differently, think, learn and feel differently. We can call the gradual process of achieving adult consciousness *incarnating*, which literally means "coming into the body" or into earthly life. This incarnating process is an important one, for if it does not occur the person remains child-like, not fully able to seize hold of life on this earth. This process unfolds according to its own natural order and time and should not be either rushed or hindered.

If we recognize that the process of incarnation is a gradual one, we will interact with and teach children differently at different ages. For example, the preschool-aged child is centered in the will and in the limbs, in movement. The tremendous growth of the first seven years is accompanied by nearly constant movement as muscles and bones grow and coordination is gradually achieved. During these years the child learns primarily through repetition and movement and by imitating everything around her. Sitting still for long periods is unhealthy if not impossible for the young child, who desires to experience everything through her body.

The elementary-school-aged child is obviously still growing physically, but his "center of gravity" is shifting to the feeling sphere. As the emotions mature between ages seven and fourteen, the child learns with the greatest enthusiasm when a picture is given of what life was like in ancient Greece or on the American frontier. Artistic or imaginative presentations of topics taught in school appeal to this child and make them easy to learn and to remember. Instead of being centered in the movement of the limbs, as was the young child, the child between seven and fourteen is centered in the "rhythmic system" of the breathing and the heartbeat. This means that music, which always involves rhythm and often involves the breath (as in singing or playing a wooden recorder) is especially important for the child in the middle years. The breath and heart are also associated with emotions, which we can see in the way our breathing and heartbeat change when we are excited or afraid.

Not until puberty is the child really centered in the head, in the sense of exercising his newfound capacities to analyze and criticize the world. Certainly major changes are still going on in the body with the maturing of the sexual organs, and the adolescent's emotions can also seem overwhelming at times. But rational and abstract thinking is the exciting new element, which now needs to be engaged by subjects such as the proofs of analytical geometry or the laws of physics. Similarly, an ability to see causes and patterns emerges for the first time, so that courses such as "Trends in Western Civilization" are also vital to the high-school student. It is during these years that independent judgment begins to be born.

With the gradual maturing of the body, emotions and thinking, the vehicle is ready for the person to assume the responsibilities of adult life. The traditional age of twenty-one as the age of majority coincides with Rudolf Steiner's perception that the will (movement, imitation) dominates development between birth and age seven, the feelings between ages seven and fourteen, and the thinking from ages fourteen to twenty-one. At age twenty-one the body, emotions and thinking are ready for further stages of adult development.

Steiner was one of the first to share this perception that the human being is threefold in nature, consisting of thinking, feeling and willing. If we are truly to understand the growing child, we must understand how these three aspects shift in dominance and how they influence the child's consciousness during different stages of development.

## WHOSE CONSCIOUSNESS IS CHANGING?

Steiner also discussed the incarnating process in terms of *who* or *what* is ready to be responsible at age twenty-one (not that twenty-one-year-olds always behave responsibly!). Once the body, emotions and thinking have reached a certain level of maturity, what Steiner called the *Ego* can live out its own biography without guidance from the parents. Steiner does not use the term *Ego* as Freud did, but uses it to mean our unique individuality, or *I*. He perceived the human being as having an individuality which is capable of breaking the bounds of stimulus-response mechanisms and manifesting the unpredictable: free behavior and the possibility of fulfilling a particular destiny on earth.[13] This individuality has been variously described and named by the great religions and by psychology as the *self, I, ego, spirit, observer,* or *consciousness.* By whatever name, it is this *presence* that is felt so strongly in the newborn child and that evokes feelings of awe and wonder in all but the most jaded souls.

Rudolf Steiner speaks of this presence as the spirit, or *I*, of the human being and asserts that it is in a continuing process of incarnating (coming into the physical body) which is only in its beginning stages at birth. The spirit at birth is, in a sense, hovering around the body, loosely connected with it, and gradually, over the course of development to maturity, becomes more and more the master of (and slave to) the body. Perhaps you have had the experience of walking into a room where a newborn is sleeping and wondering how the room can feel so filled by such a tiny creature sleeping over in the corner. This individuality is present from before birth, which explains the feeling many parents have of a child wanting to come to them around the time of conception, or the perception that a pregnant woman has that this second baby is certainly going to be different from the first. Perhaps the glow that we experience around a pregnant woman is really the being of the child that we are vaguely sensing?[14]

Steiner believes that the child is a knowing, spiritual being. Whether or not you have ever thought of children (or yourself) in this way, you have no doubt had the feeling that your children are their own people, not copies of siblings or extensions of you. Often it is not until parents have more than one child that they experience how different children can be. They seem to bring their uniqueness with them when they come, and we have to adjust our parenting accordingly. Perhaps you have had a sense of your own individuality at important moments of decision when you needed to be "true to yourself."

Even if the language of this discussion doesn't match your vocabulary, the phenomena of the incarnating process are still observable: the progressive mastery of physical processes as they come under the young child's control and the simultaneous narrowing and focussing of the child's initially diffuse consciousness. These phenomena will be explored further in the next chapter.


## HOW CHILDREN LEARN
## IN THE FIRST SEVEN YEARS

The child between birth and age seven experiences the world primarily through her body. The senses are completely open, without filters or buffers, beginning with the moment of birth. The newborn continues to experience each sensation with her entire body and being. This is easy to see in the infant, who is *all* hunger or the pain in her stomach, or *all* the blissful sensations of nursing which cause her eyes to roll back and her toes to curl. The three-year-old is also much more open to impressions of the world coming through the senses than is an adult. We can even observe that children's eyes stay open longer between blinking than do an adult's.

Two things are happening through sense impressions from birth through age seven. One is that the child's growth and development are being shaped by the impressions she takes in, just as a sculptor might work with clay. This phenomenon does not occur very often with adults, who are less open and responsive to the environment than young children, but we can see a similar phenomenon in the molding of the features which the elements of light and weather etch into the face of a seaman or farmer.

The second thing the child is doing through sense impressions is learning about the world. Through the body the baby learns about near and far, attainable and unobtainable, as when she learns that the wooden ring can be grasped, but the brightly shining moon cannot. As she begins to learn the names of things, memory, language and thinking develop so she can give expression to her own and the world's emerging complexity. When the child reaches age three and beyond, what is taken in with the senses is also transformed and comes out again in the creative play and imagination of the young child.

The child's major task in the first years is taking control of the body. Sitting, crawling and walking are quickly followed by running, jumping, climbing and other feats of dexterity as fine and gross motor coordination increase. Everything is done for the first time—using a shovel, sewing with a needle, cutting with a scissors—the list is infinite—and then it is done over and over again. The child loves to move and to imitate, learning through doing something along with someone else or after seeing it done. And the young child loves repetition, hearing the same story over and over or playing the same circle game, no matter how simple or boring it may seem to an adult.

The young child is also learning about the world emotionally, learning the fundamental lessons about trust and attachment, and later lessons about sharing and consequences. The baby *is* love. Bonding is less a process of babies loving their parents, because children will love even parents who abuse them, but of parents establishing the connection that will enable them to make room in their busy lives for another being who needs attention twenty-four hours a day! Children enter the world with a great deal of love and trust. They are not yet able to perceive good and bad, but take everything as good and appropriate to absorb and unconsciously imitate.

## OUR TASK AS FIRST TEACHERS

One of our primary tasks as our children's first teachers is to provide them with impressions of the world that are appropriate for them to copy. This means guarding and protecting them from sensory overload in a world of urban frenzy, and surrounding them with experiences that teach them about the world in a gentle way by letting them do things directly themselves and later act them out in their play.

We also need to strive ourselves to model appropriate behavior—that our emotions are under control with our children, that we don't spank them while admonishing, "Don't hit!," and so forth. Our actions speak louder than our words with the young child, who cannot help but imitate. Through us, children learn whether or not their initial love and trust in the world was well founded.

Another of our main tasks is to understand our children's physical, emotional and mental development so we can guard it and let it unfold without hindrance. No one would want to stop a child from walking, but it is also something we don't have to worry about teaching the child. The child will walk when she is ready, as an expression of her mastery of her own body—an achievement of verticality in the face of gravity that has kept her horizontal for so many months. There *is* a task for us—to guard, to protect, to understand, to share and to enjoy with the child the unfolding of his or her abilities. We can also do things to enhance abilities by providing an example and allowing the young child to express them freely from out of his own being. We can also note discrepancies in development and areas at risk and take gentle steps to help assure balance. But with the young child much more is achieved indirectly through example and imitation than head-on through lessons.

No matter what our family situation or lifestyle, we as parents are our children's first teachers. The importance of what they learn in the home and through their relationship with us cannot be underestimated. By understanding how children develop and some things we can do to help their balanced and healthy growth—physically, mentally, emotionally and spiritually—we will not only help our children, but also increase our own enjoyment and growth as parents.

## TRUSTING OURSELVES

Sometimes we can become overwhelmed as parents when we contemplate the momentous nature of the task before us. Contradictory advice from books and friends can leave us feeling frustrated or annoyed. Becoming painfully aware of the times we fall short of our own ideals can be downright discouraging!

As a first-time mother, I fell into most of the pitfalls of mothering today. Although I had prepared myself for labor and delivery and my first child's birth went smoothly enough, parenting (and boys) were a gigantic mystery to me. Fortunately, children are resilient, and my son has developed into a fine young man despite my confusions and shortcomings. But I've realized through the years that much frustration and grief could be avoided by keeping in mind a few basic principles:

*1. We need to accept who we are and build up the support we need.* Today there are as many lifestyles and possibilities as there are people. Not working outside of the home when your children are young, managing a home business, working flexible hours, having your mate be a househusband, living communally, inviting grandma to live with you, going back to work when the baby is six weeks or six months old—all of these approaches have their difficulties and rewards. No matter what you do, you will find you need and deserve support.

The real difficulty comes when we are doing something that we don't want to be doing. For example, if we must work when we want to be home or if we are staying home when it is driving us crazy, then our parenting will tend to be influenced by guilt, resentment and a whole range of other emotions. We need to make our best choices at each moment. We can't always have what we feel would be ideal, but we can actively do the best with the options as we see them.

In my own life, I ran Informed Homebirth out of my home and lived with other adults and children when my children were young, so I had support to be a midwife or to write *Special Delivery* without overly disturbing my children's lives. This situation brought other complications along with it, but I am grateful for the parenting support I received.

**2. *We need fathers to become actively involved with children.*** Fathers need support for their *fathering*, not for babysitting while mother steps out for a few hours. When *both* parents assume responsibility for care of the children, everyone benefits—especially the children.

In addition to developing their own nurturing aspect and becoming more active with the children, fathers need to support mothers in their mothering. This support is partly financial, but it is also emotional. Fathers need to be sure they are actively involved with and in harmony with their wives concerning basic issues of discipline and parenting styles. This includes actively supporting the mother with trite-but-true statements such as, "You heard your mother," or, "Don't talk back to your mother," when necessary.

In single-parent families, support needs to come from a wider circle of friends and social agencies. The parent (most often the mother) not only needs other significant people in the child's life, but needs the perspective that another adult can provide for her parenting and relationship with the child. Perhaps the most important thing a single parent can do is to find or create those connections with other adults that can keep her (or him) from being so *single* in her parenting. Single parenting is a momentous task and involves special stresses and needs.

**3. *We need a true understanding of children and their world.*** When we have an understanding of children's real developmental needs, we can respond to them in ways appropriate for their age level that can lead to their balanced development. In my own floundering as a first-time mother, I turned to Effective Parenting courses, but found that they were really geared to the child who was six or older. The instructor said, "Well, try these things with the younger child as well to start building up good habits." But it was clear to me that parenting a two-year-old was of a completely different order of magnitude and required something entirely different.

When I began studying Rudolf Steiner's indications for Waldorf education and child development, lights began to go on. For example, I had three children but still hadn't realized that up to the age of six they learn primarily through imitation! It seemed so obvious once I had read it. Why hadn't I thought of that? I found in Steiner many things of that nature—and many other things that made no sense whatsoever on first reading. But I approached the ideas with an open mind and in a pragmatic way. Could I observe the same things? Did this new approach improve the situation? I found that Steiner's understanding of the developing human being provided me with ways of seeing children that made a difference. When I *saw* children in those ways, suddenly everything worked: home life became more harmonious; I was able to enjoy young children and relate to them more confidently; I was even able to become an early childhood teacher, something that I never would have foreseen under other circumstances.

**4. We need to trust the natural process of development and not interfere with it.** By understanding a child's physical, mental, emotional and spiritual development, we will be able to avoid doing things that are appropriate for a child at one stage of development but can possibly be damaging for a younger child. Just as children need to crawl before they walk (to establish the neurological patterning), so we need to let children be children and unfold according to their own inner timetable, which always demonstrates both pattern and individual differences. If we see each child as a unique individual, we will be able to do things to enhance gifts and to work on weaknesses with a view toward a balanced development of thinking, feeling and physical abilities.

**5. We need to trust ourselves and our children and to let go of guilt.** Because we usually live isolated from young children and other families before starting our own, we don't have much knowledge about parenting. The discrepancies between expectations and reality are often shocking to new parents. I know when I was pregnant for the first time I felt that I would never put my child in preschool because no one could possibly do as good a job as I would. So I was discouraged when I found my two-year-old and I at constant odds at home and so put him in preschool where he was the model child. At that point it seemed that *anyone* could do a better job than I!

As mothers we tend to feel that "it's all our fault." Naturally, I did things differently with my third child than with my first, based on my increased experience as a mother and my increased understanding of young children. If I hadn't done things differently, maybe I could be accused of not having grown. But it is fruitless to feel guilty for what I did earlier—because I was doing the best I could at the time! If we can see parenting as part of our own inner growth and development and see our children as unique individuals with their own personalities and lives to live, we will be less likely to fall into feelings of guilt. The problem with guilt, aside from being bad for your health, is that it takes you out of the present moment where your child lives and where you need to see and act clearly.

**6. We need to trust our children as individuals.** We are not the only ones participating in our children's development. They also have something to say about it, albeit not consciously! If this were not so, how could children growing up in the same family be so radically different? Each child is unique, neither merely the sum of its experiences in the family, nor the product of our skill as parents. Sometimes it is only when they have a second child that parents realize how different children can be and how they help create what happens to them.

You can neither take all the credit nor all the blame for how your child turns out. We cannot consciously choose the children who come to us, which is no doubt a blessing. Our task is to do our best, and trust in the best. We need to trust our children to be resilient, to be able to heal, to be terrific people despite our flawed efforts and our most regretted actions. We can, however, strive to help each child's experience (and our own) be as positive and rewarding as it will be varied.

**7. *We need to value our parenting.*** There is a way in which no one *can* do a better job than you of raising your child. No paid caregivers, however skillful and loving, can feel as much excitement as you do over your baby's every accomplishment. Parents have a unique involvement with their offspring that is nourishing to the child. Especially in the first year, the child's connection with the mother is so strong that she needs to be close to the mother and frequently held. Taking a child under three out of the home and putting her in a group situation is stressful for the child— and many children will have been in several such situations by the time they are three.

Not everyone can stay home with their children in the first three years, and childcare options are discussed in Chapter 6. But we need to reject the notion that it's all the same. What the child experiences before the age of three has a tremendous effect on him. "Quality time" is not the same as the everydayness of being together. Let's neither glorify nor undervalue it.


## RECOMMENDED READING

(Because many of these titles may be difficult to find, the letters in parentheses indicate mail-order book services listed in Appendix A.)

*Born Dancing* by Evelyn B. Thoman and Sue Browder. (B) A guide to help parents develop trust in themselves and become more relaxed about parenting. Excellent!

*Conception, Birth and Early Childhood* by Norbert Glas (AP, IBP). Written thirty years ago by a doctor working out of Steiner's indications. Spiritual and practical.

*Conscious Conception* by Jeannine Parvati Baker, et al. (IBP). Subtitled "Elemental Journey through the Labyrinth of Sexuality," this remarkable book is well worth your time.

*Cradle of Heaven* by Murshida Vera Justin Corda (IBP). An exploration of the psychological and spiritual dimensions of conception, pregnancy and birth. Corda works out of the Sufi tradition and founded the "Seed Center" early childhood programs.

*The Incarnating Child* by Joan Salter (IBP, SG). An excellent, up-to-date book covering conception through age two by the founder of the Gabriel Baby Centre in Australia. Steiner-oriented. Highly recommended.

*Miseducation: Preschoolers at Risk* by David Elkind (IBP). Discusses the personal and cultural reasons parents and preschools "miseducate" young children and what is age-appropriate for them. A must.

*The Recovery of Man in Childhood* by A. C. Harwood (AP, IBP). A very readable explanation of Steiner's view of the developing child through adolescence.

## Journals for Aware Parenting

*Childhood*, quarterly journal about Waldorf curriculum and spiritual parenting, from Nancy Aldrich, Rt. 2, Box 2675, Westford, VT 05494.

*The Compleat Mother*, excellent quarterly journal on pregnancy, birth and breastfeeding. From Box 399, Mildmay, Ontario, Canada N0G 2J0.

*Mothering*, outstanding magazine published quarterly. From Mothering Publications, Box 1690, Santa Fe, NM 87504. Everyone needs *Mothering*.

*New Families*, quarterly publication dedicated to the exploration of new ways to combine parenting and career into an integrated, enjoyable whole. From Next Step Publications, Box 41108, Fayetteville, NC 28309.

*Parents Bulletin*, quarterly publication by the Parents' Theosophical Research Group, 336 S. Pueblo Ave., Ojai, CA 93023.

*Spiritual Mothering Journal*, quarterly publication dedicated to conscious parenting and spiritual growth. From 18350 Ross, Sandy, Oregon 97055.

*Welcome Home*, newsletter for mothers at home, P.O. Box 2208, Merrifield, VA 22116.

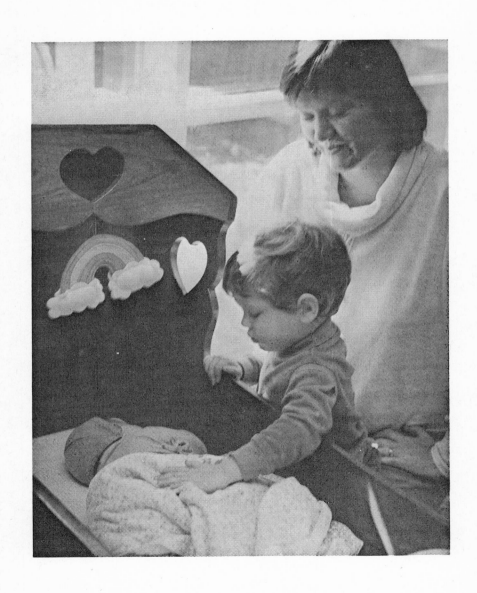

# 2 | *Receiving & Caring for the Newborn*

## WHAT WAS BIRTH LIKE FOR YOUR BABY?

The French obstetrician Frederick Leboyer helped the world to understand the affront to the baby's senses on going from womb to world. Is it possible to gain further insight into the baby's experience of this event, which many psychologists hold to be so primal? In *Birth Without Violence*, Leboyer ironically describes birth as a life-and-death struggle with the mother, who is like a monster needing to be overcome.[1] While this may have been his experience, which he was able to recall through work with an analyst, it is by no means everyone's experience. The birth experience is as individual as we ourselves are, and natural birth is not as traumatic for the baby as doctors have presumed. In fact, research by Lagercrantz and Slotkin has shown that the catecholamines (enzymes associated with stress response) in a newborn's blood are actually part of an adaptive mechanism that helps the baby withstand low levels of oxygen without damage and start to breathe on its own.[2] These studies explain why cesarean babies, who are born without the "stress" of contractions and the passage through the birth canal, often have more trouble breathing and adapting to life outside the womb.

Birth is physiologically sound and all right for your baby. This is even more true the more aware you are of the baby's experience. What can we intuit of his or her experience? Let us envision what life is like in the womb, an environment that protects the baby from many of the influences of ordinary life. The uterus, strongest muscle in the human body, is rounded, and its concave shape serves to concentrate forces so the baby can develop (just as a magnifying glass focusses the rays of the sun). Indeed, a metaphor that has been used to describe the incoming spiritual being is "like a falling star that then becomes a sun glowing in your womb."[3] The baby is surrounded by nine layers of substances, including the waters, membranes, uterus, muscles, tissue, fat and skin. All of these fall away at birth, so that the baby lies naked and unprotected, exposed for the first time to all the influences of earthly life. Thus birth can be seen as an unveiling process, a taking away of the sheaths that have surrounded the developing baby inside the womb.

## The Experience of Space, Time and Gravity

In the womb the baby has a different experience of space, time and gravity from what it experiences after birth. The baby's experience of physical space changes dramatically throughout pregnancy and birth. At first it floats like an astronaut in inner space, supported by the waters and tied to the mother through the umbilical lifeline. In the uterine space the baby is hidden and safe in the fetal position. As the baby continues to grow it feels the mother surrounding and protecting it and has its first possibility of body awareness through encountering the resistance of the uterine walls. Then space becomes more confining, making movement less free as the months go by. Sometime around the eighth month the baby usually finds that it cannot get out of the head-down position due to gravity and the heaviness of the head, so there it stays until delivery, approximately ten lunar months from the time of conception.

With the birth process, the baby's experience of physical space again changes. It goes through a narrowing process as contractions make its space smaller and propel it through the birth canal. Then suddenly the baby is born into seemingly endless space, where it encounters nothing when it flails its arms or legs. This is why giving a warm bath, holding a baby's arm, or swaddling it can be so consoling for a newborn or young baby. Having been used to the security of surrounding touch, babies need to be reassured by touch after they emerge from the womb.

Turning next to the baby's experience of gravity, we bring to mind Archimedes' discovery that an object floating in water has about 1/50 its usual weight. Thus the baby in the womb is protected from too strong a dose of the earthly influence of gravity, but suddenly becomes about fifty times heavier at birth![4] Imagine yourself floating in a warm swimming pool when someone pulls a huge plug and you suddenly find yourself lying on the concrete bottom, helplessly moving your arms and legs. At birth the baby truly becomes an earthly being, helpless in the face of gravity. Indeed, it must spend the next year gradually overcoming the forces of gravity so that it can hold itself upright in balance between the forces of heaviness and lightness.

Birth brings with it not only an experience of gravity, but also the experience of time. Although a baby seems passive to the course of birth and when it will be born, in fact labor seems to start through an interaction of the fetal and maternal hormones. To the extent that there is a spiritual reality hidden within real astrology (not the horoscopes in the daily paper), it makes a difference when one is born, and the time should not be chosen according to the attendants' convenience. It may be that we choose the planets and stars and those influences that will enable us optimally to take hold of and live out our destiny on earth. I don't know, but I think this possibility is more valid than the practices of inducing labor because the doctor has a golf game, or setting a "convenient" date for a scheduled cesarean.

## Birth as an Experience of Temperature and Breath

We have seen that birth also brings the baby's first experience of temperature change. As warm-blooded creatures, we feel good only within a narrow range of internal body temperature. A low-grade fever makes us feel out of sorts, and a high fever results in our being unable to distinguish reality: we become delirious and unable to move. People who lose their body heat and experience hypothermia also lose their relationship with reality and often die from making decisions based on delusions.

Thus we see that only within a narrow range can our "I" be in right relationship to the outer world. Steiner calls the circulating blood and other elements that maintain our bodily warmth the "warmth organization," which gives our consciousness the possibility of controlling our body and our emotions. The "I" cannot interact properly with the external world when our internal body temperature becomes too high or too low.

The change in temperature from womb to room is a cold shock for the baby. When you are in a shower that suddenly runs out of hot water and turns icy cold, you inhale sharply and then usually voice a loud complaint. The baby does the same thing when thrust from womb to world. It responds by drawing inward and taking in the first breath, so vital to the process of coming into the body and earthly life.

We can see in our own lives how cold tends to be "incarnating," or makes us feel strong and able in our bodies. Think how fresh and ready for work we feel on a crisp autumn day; we feel invigorated and ready to tackle all of the projects we've let slide over the summer. Heat, on the other hand, tends to be "excarnating." We find ourselves driven slightly out of our bodies and into sleep when we're in a room that is too warm, to give a simple example. We need equilibrium to be in right relationship with the world, and the baby especially needs to be helped to maintain a constant temperature, one that is slightly warmer than we adults prefer.

In addition to temperature, stimulation of the baby's skin plays a role in the first breath. The massaging of the baby's body by contractions and its passage through the birth canal help to start the breathing process. Changes in oxygen and carbon-dioxide levels as the placenta ceases to function also help trigger the first breath.

What happens with this first breath, in which the baby exchanges the water sphere for the air sphere? Many things happen physiologically as the lungs expand for the first time, the foramen ovale in the heart closes, and your baby changes from dusky gray to pink right before your eyes. But many things are also happening in terms of the incarnation process during this vital first breath. To understand them, let us first consider the nature of breath itself.

Breath, with its rhythmical in and out quality, is the mediator between a person's inner and outer worlds. It is the medium through which our emotions, or what Steiner calls *soul life*, are expressed. When we are afraid, we hold our breath; being happy is exhaled in laughter; contentment is expressed in a sigh. All emotions are expressed on the breath, which is the physical realm for the unfolding of our soul activity in the life of feeling.

With the first breath, inner emotional life begins, and the breath serves as the connection between the inner and outer worlds. With the first in-breath, the possibility exists for the soul life to enter into a deeper relationship with the body, a relationship it will keep until the last expiration.[5] Although the baby is both spiritually present and physically responsive to stimuli while in the womb, the soul cannot come into the body without the breath. Then the soul gives expression to our emotions through the breath as sound and speech. The breath thus forms the link between body and soul until death, when we breathe out the soul with the last breath. In fact, we incarnate and excarnate a little with each inhalation and exhalation, and many meditation practices focus on that still space between the inspiration and the expiration.

Everyone senses how important the first breath is for the baby. Those present at a birth tend to hold their own breaths until the baby breathes and pinks up. The baby is still receiving oxygen through the placenta, but we need to remember to keep breathing ourselves! The breath marks the true time of birth, for the first breath means that the baby has successfully completed the journey from fetus to newborn and accepted earthly life outside of the womb.

## The Contraction of Consciousness at Birth

Birth involves a narrowing of consciousness for the baby from the dimensionless "space" of eternity, or whatever you want to call it. As spiritual beings we are dimensionless, as "large" as the whole spiritual world. From this limitless, macrocosmic existence we find ourselves bound to a physical body and born into the earthly realm of space, time and gravity. Just as the baby's physical body passes through the narrowness of the pelvis and the birth canal, so the spiritual being experiences a narrowing of consciousness which culminates in the incarnation of the spirit and soul into a physical body.

This contraction of consciousness from the cosmic to the earthly is a dramatic event for the being who experiences it. Usually the cosmic or spiritual world is forgotten, though we feel echoes of it in myths or fairy tales. The Greeks described this threshold as the crossing of the River Lethe (or River of Forgetfulness), when we leave or enter this world. This forgetfulness allows us to have ordinary earthly consciousness and be full citizens of this planet, though at times we may sense a dim memory, feel a yearning for something that can guide us back to God or our original nature.

This passage from one level of existence to another is a very significant and holy time, and anyone who can maintain some awareness of what the baby is going through during this time is a real midwife for the baby. It is similar at the other end of life, which is why some of my friends who work in the hospice movement call themselves midwives for the dying.

The birth process thus involves both physical narrowing through the birth canal and a narrowing of consciousness for the being coming into this life. This densification of consciousness into matter can be a painful experience for the one who is coming into this life, which is so much more limited. Steiner says that the mother, if she consciously experiences the discomfort of labor rather than being anesthetized, is strengthened in her bond with the being of the child and has a much closer understanding and compassion for what the child is experiencing in the process of incarnation; others present can only try to hold it in their awareness.[6]

The process of birth is painful for the new being from only one perspective, for it is also a joyous participation in the pendulum swing between expansion and contraction that permeates all of life. As parents and birth attendants, we rejoice with this first breath, thankful that a new being, so full of promise, has decided to join humanity.

Pondering the tremendous threshold that birth involves can help us to better understand our children and ourselves. For a young child who has only recently crossed this threshold, the door to the spiritual world is not yet closed, as it is for most adults. The fact that young children still have access to the spiritual world helps to explain why they can "see" things we can't and why true fairy tales, which are descriptions of the spiritual world and the incarnation process, are so nourishing to them (more on that in Chapter 8). Understanding this concept—that incarnation into earthly life is a gradual process—can clarify how we perceive our children, how we interact with them, and how we help them to realize their full potential.

Working with the perception that there is a vertical stream of knowing individuality as well as a horizontal stream of hereditary characteristics in each child can help in our parenting. It can help us to realize that, while we are important in our children's lives, they are unique individuals and not extensions of us. It can lend credence to the possibility that our children choose us as parents. The movie *Back to the Future* expressed elements of this idea in its comical portrayal of the main character's need to bring his parents together so that he could be born. If we are having particular difficulties with a child, it can provide the reassurance that we may be together for particular reasons and particular growth.

A view that takes into account the vertical stream can also help to explain certain behaviors, fears, or characteristics that children seem to bring with them rather than acquire from any experiences of which we are aware. For example, Steiner said that one explanation of particularly difficult children is that the "fit" between the spiritual and material elements isn't quite right and is frustrating for the child.[7] One of our tasks as parents and educators then can be to help harmonize these two streams, without one dominating at the expense of the other. Being open to the possibility that there may be more going on than meets the eye helps to keep the spiritual potential open for the growing child.

# THE SENSITIVITY OF THE NEWBORN

The sensitivity of the newborn at birth was dramatically brought to awareness by Leboyer's work in the 1970s. Medical science had fallen into the belief that babies don't see, feel or experience very much in the womb, during birth or as a newborn; Leboyer himself said he had experienced three thousand deliveries before he realized that the newborn's cries were really made in distress.[8] Nowadays it is hard for any thinking and feeling person not to be aware of how vulnerable the senses of a newborn are to sight, sound, temperature and all the other experiences of the world. In fact, studies on the newborn have burgeoned in the past two decades, and films such as *The Amazing Newborn*[9] reflect the wonderment scientists have experienced in rediscovering that babies see, hear and respond to so much more than previously thought. Research even indicates that the fetus in the womb is much more aware than was previously believed.[10]

More than sixty years ago Rudolf Steiner spoke about the completely open senses of a baby and young child. In 1924 Steiner said, "In the first part of his life . . . the child is, so to say, altogether a sense organ. This we have to take very literally. What is the characteristic function of a sense organ? It is receptive to impressions from the environment. If something striking occurs near him—for example, a burst of anger—then the reflection thereof goes right through the child. It will affect even his blood circulation and digestive system."[11]

A baby does not have the ability to filter out unwanted impressions as adults do when, for example, they read while the television is on. A baby is bombarded by everything in the environment, and its only escape is to go to sleep in order to "digest" the constant flow of sensations. Steiner states: "The child needs so much sleep because it is entirely sense-organ. It could not otherwise endure the dazzle and noise of the outer world. Just as the eye must shut itself against the dazzling sunlight, so must this sense-organ, the child—for the child is entirely sense-organ—shut itself off against the world, so must it sleep a great deal. For whenever it is confronted with the world, it has to observe. . . ."[12]

Thus the newborn, coming from the womb to the world, needs special regard for the openness of its senses, not only at birth, but also in the months following. Hospitals are just beginning to question whether it is good for newborn and premature babies to have bright lights and the radio playing in the nursery twenty-four hours a day!

## STIMULATING AND PROTECTING YOUR BABY'S SENSES

Much has been written today about the importance of stimulating your baby's senses, and maternal deprivation studies in the 1940s showed that children in institutions who did not receive adequate stimulation from a primary caregiver failed to thrive, showing developmental lags that could not be made up later. However, American popular psychology has interpreted "infant stimulation" to mean that you *constantly* need to be stimulating your baby with bits of colored plastic and flash cards. Rather than these artificial means, a baby needs the holding, rocking, talking, concern and love of its mother or other primary caregiver in order to develop normally. More sensible child-development experts remind parents that infant stimulation is not something you need to do separately from caregiving.[13] If you

1. touch or hold your baby often,
2. talk to him or her,
3. spend time face-to-face, making eye contact, and
4. generally respond quickly to fussiness or crying,

you are providing most of what your baby needs for healthy development. Stimulation of your baby's senses is important for development, but overstimulation can be detrimental. By understanding the sensitivity and needs of the newborn, you will gain confidence that you are providing your baby with the best possible start in life.

### The Sense of Touch

Your baby is perhaps most sensitive to touch, the skin being our largest sense organ. The entire birth process is like a massage for the baby, stimulating its skin senses and getting it ready to breathe. The cold air hitting its skin at birth gives the baby its first sense of body definition, of inner and outer. This is in contrast to life in the womb, which is like being immersed in a warm bath.

Your baby's sensitive skin, which has only known water, will now be exposed to all of the elements of ordinary life. No wonder babies are so prone to rashes—it's quite an adjustment! One of the best things for your baby is skin-to-skin contact, which is why many mothers like the baby to be put on their bellies immediately after birth, or why fathers sometimes take off their shirts to hold the newborn skin-to-skin. Not only are the tactile sensations reassuring for the newborn, but the smell of your skin and the beating of your heart are also reassuring for your baby. Joseph Chilton Pearce, author of *The Magical Child Matures*, points out that mothers instinctively hold their children more on their left sides, regardless of whether they are right- or left-handed; on the left side, your baby is in touch with your heartbeat, which he or she has heard throughout the pregnancy. Pearce states that it is important to re-establish that "heart connection" after the birth.[14]

The widespread use of baby carriers (soft front packs) is beneficial in that it keeps the baby next to the mother's (or father's) body and frees the parent's hands for other work. However, a word of caution is necessary. The weight of the head and brain and the weakness of the neck place a lot of strain on the central nervous system. In many other cultures, the baby is not held vertically until she can hold her head up by herself. The Central and South American way of wrapping a young baby in a rebozo or shawl is illustrated in *The Incarnating Child*, and several commercial horizontal carriers which can be adapted for older babies are listed at the end of this chapter.

Something else to keep in mind about baby carriers is to be careful *where* you take your baby. Fourteen years ago I was eager to prove that giving birth was normal and babies were hardy, so I took my son to discount department stores when he was about a week old. Such places make me zingy, but I figured the baby would sleep through it. Now I would reconsider, understanding more about the openness of the newborn's senses and the special nature of the first six weeks of life.

Returning to the sense of touch, it is helpful to think about what kinds of materials you want to have touching your baby's skin and to choose fabrics that are soft, warming and pleasurable against the skin. Natural fibers are especially beneficial because they breathe. If some kinds of synthetics make your skin crawl or make you feel like you're in an air-tight container, the effect is magnified for your baby. Not only do cotton, silk and wool allow air to flow through the fibers, but wool wicks moisture away from the skin and keeps your baby drier than other fabrics. Hospitals have found that premature babies gain weight faster when they are placed on wool sheets, but no one knows why.[15] Steiner would say that natural fibers can actually contribute to the body's vital energy, whereas some synthetics rob the body of energy.

Department stores are increasingly carrying baby clothes made of natural fibers, and numerous natural clothing mail-order catalogs exist. Alternatives to paper diapers include "soakers" which are worn over cloth diapers in place of rubber pants. Several brands, such as "Biobottoms" and "Nikky," are available in wool fabric, or it is easy to knit or crochet your own soakers. Cloth diapers admit air to lessen diaper rash; a diaper service is as economical and convenient as paper diapers, and it is ecologically sound.

A special blanket of natural fibers can be used to build associations of sleep and comfort. When your child is a toddler, this blanket is not carried as a "security" blanket but is used at night and nap time to help reinforce the idea of sleep. It can work wonders, because a young child is very connected with surroundings and is comforted when they are the same.

## The Sense of Sight

When babies are first born they seem to have a "quiet alert" phase for the first thirty to sixty minutes after birth. If you request that your baby not be given any eye prophylaxis until after this time (and then request a substitute for silver nitrate that is less burning to the newborn's eyes), you will find your baby beginning to look at you and respond to your voice, especially if you have talked or sung to your baby before the birth. Newborn's eyes focus best on objects that are about ten inches from their faces, about the distance between a nursing baby and its adoring mother's gaze! Researchers have found that babies respond best to patterns of light and dark resembling the human face. They therefore suggest putting a simple black and white drawing of a human face on the side of your baby's crib at eye level. While this may help parents feel that they are "doing something" in terms of "infant stimulation," there is obviously no substitute for carrying and interacting with your infant and providing the soul contact that comes through the eyes when human beings look at one another.

Many mothers tuck their babies into bed with them at night when they are small, and certainly while they are nursing. It's impossible to roll over and smother the baby! The advantage of having a bassinet or hooded basket for the newborn is that it provides a small, enclosed space for her during the day—and it gives you room to stretch out or be with your partner when you want to, without waking the little one. Bassinets may be draped with colored silk to filter the light coming to the baby. A combination of blue, pink, and rose silk provides an especially soft light. A similar effect can be achieved by putting the silk over a lampshade. A resource for inexpensive white silk that can easily be dyed is listed at the end of this chapter.

Is it necessary to take such care with a newborn? Certainly not in the sense of survival. Babies are hardy creatures and can even survive the fluorescent lights and Muzak in the premie nursery. But it is helpful for us to be aware of how completely open to outside influences a baby is. Burton White, in *The First Three Years of Life*, states that the baby in the first six weeks

> is generally unusually sensitive. . . . It is perfectly normal for an infant to startle and cry at any abrupt change in stimulation during her first weeks of life. Such common reactions include a response to sharp nearby noises, or to jolts to the crib or bassinet, or to any rather sudden change in position, particularly when the baby has been inactive. A second, less dramatic indication of sensitivity at this age is the infant's avoidance of bright lights. A Phase I infant [birth to six weeks] will keep his eyes tightly shut in a brightly lit room or when outside in the sun. In fact, he is much more likely to open his eyes and keep them open in a dimly lit room than in one at an ordinary level of illumination.[16]

So while it isn't "necessary" to put silk over the lampshade, it's good to be aware of just how sensitive your newborn is. Keep the room dimly lit and avoid bright lights or sun so your baby will feel free to open up and explore the world at a level she can manage.

## The Sense of Hearing

Just as bright lights cause a baby to "close down," loud noises will cause your baby to throw up her arms and legs in the startle reflex and begin to cry. While you'll want to avoid slamming the door or dropping things near your baby, this doesn't mean that you need to tiptoe around the house all the time. Your baby should become used to the natural sounds of your household and will learn to sleep through most of them.

It *is* good to focus on the quality of the sounds that reach your baby's ears. One measure of quality is loudness; another is harmony and rhythm. One of the most pleasing sounds to your baby is your voice. Not only does she start to recognize your voice and your partner's, but if you hum or sing, she will be especially soothed. Many parents like to make up a little song for their baby that they start singing when pregnant; they have reported that the baby pays attention and is soothed by the song and seems to recognize it, even right after birth. You don't need to be a talented musician to sing to your children—even someone tone deaf can hum! Getting into the habit of singing will help your child's language development and sense for music and rhythm, and it's a delightful way to share together.

The quality of aliveness that comes through the human voice when you sing to your baby is very different from a tape of soothing music for babies, or even a tape of your own singing. There is a nurturing quality in things that come from living sources that disappears when they are transferred to film, record or tape. Children, especially, have come into this life to be alive and to grow. That which comes directly from a living source connects them with life on earth and the forces of growth, while that which is mechanical is further removed from them. Devices now on the market that simulate the noise of a car going fifty-five miles per hour may drive your baby to sleep, but what an affront to a new-born's senses!

It's obvious that your baby's experience is totally different when you or your partner are singing to her (however ineptly) from when a tape recorder is the source of the sounds. Not only is the experience of a real person's presence missing with record-ed music, radio and television, but the *quality* of the sound is different, regardless of the complexity of the sound system. Stein-er said that the quality of the sound from mechanical sources had a detrimental effect on the young child, both on the developing sensitivity of the ear and on the entire organism, because every-thing from each sense affects the entire body.[17] This is not so much the case with a child over the age of seven. Paying atten-tion to the quality of the sounds your baby hears can only be beneficial.

### The Sense of Warmth

The sense of warmth is especially important for your baby, because her ability to regulate body temperature is not fully ma-ture. Also, the newborn's head is so large in proportion to the rest of her body that the potential for heat loss is tremendous. Any outdoor person will tell you, "If your feet are cold, put on your hat," because most of the body's heat is lost through the head. Many hospitals are beginning to put stockinette caps on babies in the nurseries, and it is a good idea to keep your baby's head covered throughout the first year. The baby's brain grows as much in the first year as it does throughout the rest of life, and for this process it is good to keep the head warm and protected.

A baby hat not only prevents heat loss, but keeps the fon-tanelles covered. The fontanelles are the "soft spots" in the baby's skull. The one toward the back of the head is harder to feel, but the one toward the front can take up to eighteen months to close. During this time the brain and central nervous system are just beneath the fontanelle skin instead of being under the bony layer of the skull. The fontanelles should neither be bulging nor sunken when your baby is at rest (they will bulge when she cries). Many mothers have found that putting a hat on their baby has a calming effect when they are out in the world, for it seems to keep the baby more insulated from outside influences. I personally recommend fitted hats over the stretchy stockinette variety, because stockinette caps fit poorly and tend to always be riding up and need pulling down. This can be irritating to a newborn—perhaps too much like the birth process it has just come through!

## WHAT CAN YOU EXPECT FROM YOUR NEWBORN?

While we can be open to the transcendent aspects of birth and of this new being, we are also very much interested in the physical aspects. Is the baby all right? Does she have all her fingers and toes? Look at all that hair, or lack thereof! And who is this "intimate stranger" that you have known for nine months on the inside and now see for the first time?

One of the things you'll notice right away is that your newborn sleeps a lot, which is a blessing for the new mother, who needs to recover her strength and adjust to having a new baby. Researchers have found that in the first few days babies average about three minutes an hour of alertness during the day, and less at night, lengthening over the first month to an average of six or seven minutes an hour.[18] Many babies are placed on their tummies to sleep, for fear they may spit up. However, letting the baby be both awake and asleep on her back opens her to the cosmos and the soft color coming through the silks, and I know of no reports of difficulty. If the baby is wrapped in a blanket, she will still feel secure when sleeping on her back.

When your baby is awake, you may find her distressed one minute and happy the next. Quick changes of mood are characteristic in the first few months. Babies can also differ markedly from one another in their characteristic moods from the first days of life—even babies born into the same family. Over the last decade a fair amount of research has been done on congenital differences in temperament among infants, establishing that some babies are far more difficult to live with from the very outset than others.[19] We will discuss Steiner's insights into temperament in Chapter Six.

The special nature of the first six weeks is recognized by contemporary researchers. In *The First Three Years of Life* White states, "The first four to six weeks of life seem more like a transitional period between very different modes of existence than a time of rapid development."[20] He is referring to the obvious transition between womb and world, with its differences in breathing, eating and so forth. We have also seen how this period is a tremendous transition in levels of consciousness for the child. Your baby and you need for this transition time to be as peaceful and free of demands as possible.

Many cultures intuitively honor the openness of the newborn by setting aside forty days during which the mother and baby are "confined to quarters" and taken care of by relatives or by women in the community who specialize in postpartum care. Recognizing how much in the "other world" the baby still is and how open emotionally the mother is to the creative power of the universe can be honored by giving yourself time to just be together as a family in the special energy that surrounds birth. It will pass soon enough. Practical advice for the postpartum period can be found in my books *Special Delivery* and *Pregnant Feelings*.

### Reflex Responses

When your newborn is awake, you will observe many patterns of reflex behavior that will disappear as your baby gets older. At birth your baby has many more reflexes than he will have later in life. Animals, of course, have complex instinctual patterns of behavior that govern their entire lives. The human being is the most helpless of all mammals, and many of the reflex responses present at birth are later replaced by learned behavior and choice. For example, your newborn has a *placing* and a *stepping reflex* when the soles of the feet come in contact with a surface. But this disappears and must be replaced by learning to walk as a controlled act.

The *grasping reflex* is such that the newborn's hands are usually clenched. However, once you unfold her fingers, she will grasp an object. Whether she quickly drops it or holds onto it for several minutes, she seems oblivious to it and won't bring it to her mouth, touch it with the other hand or look at it.

The *Moro reflex* is also called the *startle reflex* because your baby will bring up her arms and cry when she is moved suddenly through space or experiences a loud noise or jolt. This reflex worries some parents, but it is completely normal and will disappear within the first few months.

The *rooting reflex* assures that your baby will turn toward stimulation and start sucking, thus finding the breast and nourishment. Therefore, to prompt a baby to nurse, you should stroke one cheek rather than touch both cheeks as you guide the baby to the breast.

The *tonic neck reflex* or "fencer's pose" is the characteristic posture of a baby on its back: the same arm and leg will be extended, and the head will look toward the extended arm. If the head is turned the other way, the opposite arm and leg will automatically extend. Both hands will be fisted.

These reflex behaviors will become more efficient and reliable through repeated use and will become coordinated through activities like bringing the fist to the mouth and sucking or gumming it. Such reflexes form the foundation elements of later intelligence and cease to be reflexive as the baby begins to be more "present" and coordinated.

## Control of the Body

Your baby's body is dominated by an inordinately large head and small, weak limbs. This is in marked contrast to the rest of the animal kingdom. I was greatly impressed by the opposite extreme of development with lambs: The lower halves of their legs are so well-developed at birth they have the same feeling of sturdiness as the adult sheep's.

A baby's head is so developed and heavy that, when on her stomach, she will barely be able to clear the mattress with her nose for a moment or two. It takes several months for a baby to gain full head-neck control, and the head should always be supported when the baby is being lifted or held.

If your baby is on her back, she is incapable of rolling over or moving very far. You will still need a soft bumper placed around the inside of the crib or bassinet, because some babies manage to dig their heels in and thrust their legs out, propelling themselves the entire length of the crib.

Your baby's ability to converge and focus her eyes on small, nearby objects is not present at birth and develops gradually over the first two months. Researchers have observed that, as early as the first week, a baby shows a tendency to look toward the eyes of the person holding her. As the windows of the soul, the eyes are perhaps the most "alive" part of us.

The ability to track a moving object develops around six weeks of age. Before that time your baby won't seem to notice her hands when they move into her line of vision. Looking at her hands leads to mastering their use in reaching for objects and the development of problem-solving behavior.

Can your baby smile, and what does it mean? There is great debate about this in the literature. Many parents report that their infants do smile, and this is illustrated by the day-old baby in Leboyer's *Birth Without Violence*.[21] Social smiling, however, takes longer to develop.

When I was a teenager, I heard people say that babies smiled in their sleep because the angels were whispering to them, and I thought, "How quaint." Then a high-school teacher said that babies couldn't really smile and it was just gas pains, and I thought, "How offensive." Now I suspect they really are in the angelic spheres when they sleep, but since I can't prove it I have to ask, which view is more furthering? Have you ever seen your baby stare right over your head or into the corner of the room with absolute intensity or with a smile? Who is she looking at?

## WHAT DOES YOUR BABY NEED?

Since babies are totally unable to take care of themselves, you need to provide everything, twenty-four hours a day. The main ingredients are love, nourishment and comfort.

### *Comfort*

It doesn't take long for parents to distinguish their baby's various cries and to recognize the difference between hunger and a cold diaper, for example. If your baby is full and dry and doesn't have an air bubble that will come up, rocking or walking her is often so comforting or pleasurable that it can at least temporarily override discomfort from many sources. Swaddling a baby by wrapping her tightly in a blanket or holding the arm of a disconsolate infant will often be very calming as well. But sometimes you try everything to no avail, and you just need to be there holding the baby without any noticeable success. Keeping calm yourself is of primary importance, because it is almost impossible for a distraught parent to calm a baby. We are too connected emotionally. To the extent that we can be peaceful ourselves and provide a peaceful environment for the newborn, the baby will benefit.

A baby should not be left to "cry it out" on a regular basis! What this teaches the baby is that the world is an unfriendly place in which he or she doesn't count. Infants in institutions cry less and less during their first year of life, having learned that it usually leads only to exhaustion. Studies have shown that babies whose cries are ordinarily responded to quickly do continue to cry more than institutionally reared infants (thank goodness), but less than babies also raised at home but whose cries are responded to inconsistently.[22] You can't spoil a baby by responding quickly and consistently to its needs!

## Love and Bonding

The love and warmth that surround the baby are vital for its healthy development. The mother is in a unique relationship with the newborn, but the love and caring of both parents are like a wonderful cloak that surrounds the baby and counterbalances our questions and uncertainties about how to take care of this infant. By touching your baby frequently and responding promptly to cries as often as you can, you give your baby a feeling of being loved and cared for that is perhaps the most important thing you can do with your infant. It affects the rest of his or her life!

There is a lot of talk today about "bonding," or "attachment." This has arisen from studies of cases where bonding failed to happen. We hear of "failure to thrive" by infants raised in institutions with no primary caregiver, or a breakdown in bonding due to early separation between the mother and the baby, as with some babies in intensive care nurseries. The studies by Klaus and Kennell have helped to change routine birthing procedures that often kept mother and baby separated for twelve hours or longer.[23] Now there are rooming-in, early dismissal, and so-called bonding rooms in most hospitals.

Immediate and continuous contact between mother and baby is wonderful and should be the norm, not something that is "allowed" for a few minutes or hours. But don't feel that all is lost if circumstances prevent it. Human beings are more complex than other animals, and there is no "critical period" in human bonding, which if missed is detrimental to the whole experience. Your baby will not follow the nurse home like a duck might follow a dog, and your baby will love you without any difficulty, because babies *are* love. (Even children who are physically abused still love the parent.) The real question in bonding is how we, as busy, self-centered adults, are going to make room in our lives twenty-four hours a day for a new and helpless being. Bonding is not something that happens exclusively in the first half-hour after the birth. The baby tends to be alert in the first hour after birth and the mother is wide open emotionally, so uninterrupted contact during that time is wonderful, but bonding starts in pregnancy and continues through the birth experience and through interaction with the baby after it is born. I'm convinced that we are bonded or "in love" any time we recognize that the other person is a being rather than an object. It's not something that happens or fails to happen once and forever.

I bring this up because many mothers feel loss or guilt if they have been separated from their babies immediately after the birth, due to complications. It is natural for the mother to feel loss. She has been totally one with the baby and now they are separated; being together eases that pain of separation and helps to start their relationship on the outside. But the baby isn't suffering irreparable damage if it's being held by dad in the nursery or is sound asleep while mother has stitches.

Love is complex and functions on many levels. Your children will open your hearts, teach you about love and service, and bring to consciousness the blinders which make it possible to do the hurtful things we do to the people we love.

## Nourishment

Nourishment includes food, love and touch. Touch is of primary importance to your baby because the young child experiences everything with its entire body. Ashley Montagu, in *Touching: The Human Significance of the Skin*, describes just how important touch is in development.[24] Holding and lovingly touching your baby provide her with a sense of security and a sense of the nearness of those who love her.

Some parents feel newborns are so tiny that they are nervous about touching them. Babies are not frail creatures, and they *need* your touch and closeness! They are much more responsive to handling than they are to seeing and hearing. Carrying your baby, rocking, skin-to-skin contact and massage all communicate your closeness and love to your baby.

Not only is it important to touch your baby, but *how* you touch is also important. In "Touch is the First Language We Speak," midwife Ina May Gaskin emphasizes the importance of touch:

> After the baby is born, the mother communicates something to him in every way she touches him. This is the way that babies get their information about the Universe that determines to a very large extent what kind of personality they will have as grown-ups. If the mother's touch is tentative and light and ginger (maybe she's afraid that the baby is so soft and new and delicate that she'll bruise him like a ripe peach), she's likely to find herself with an irritable baby who cries a lot.[25]

Holding your baby with a good firm touch tells her that she can relax, you're not going to drop her, and everything is fine. For the very young baby, holding and cuddling is probably better than intentional "baby massage." You may disturb the infant by undressing her for a massage session or taking her out to massage classes.

Breastfeeding is, of course, ideal in providing both the perfect nourishment for babies and the closeness of skin-to-skin contact. Anyone who is pregnant or is having difficulty breastfeeding should contact LaLeche League, whose counselors know how to give practical help and can recommend valuable books on how and why to breastfeed.

Breastfeeding is especially important during the newborn period so that your baby gets colostrum, which stimulates the digestive processes and provides passive immunity to certain diseases. Also, breastmilk is ideally suited to babies and prevents worry about food allergies or illness from poorly sterilized bottles. Breastmilk not only has a different composition from cow's milk and formula products (which keep trying to imitate it), but, by coming from the mother's body, as did the child itself, it has subtle qualities different from milk from soybeans, cows or goats. It also has no chemical additives.

Digestion is an all-consuming event for an infant. When your baby is hungry or has an air bubble, nothing else exists. There is only that sensation. Similarly, when your baby rolls back its eyes in ecstacy while at your breast, you know that the satisfaction goes all the way down to its toes.

Many babies have trouble with "colic" or pain and crying in the first three months. Ina May Gaskin explains that she has cured several babies of colic by pointing out to the mother that the way she was handling the baby while he nursed made his stomach and intestines cramp up. She points out that if a mother rubs her baby's leg while the baby is nursing, or plucks at the baby's toes, marvelling at how soft and well-formed the baby is, it's "the same as tapping on someone's shoulder and trying to get their attention while they're trying to make love."[26] Holding the baby firmly and keeping your attention on the baby rather than talking on the phone while you're breastfeeding can help digestion as well as your own centeredness and sense of calm. Breastfeeding can be a time of sharing more than just physical nourishment with your baby.

About ten percent to twenty percent of all babies have colic, starting in the first few weeks and usually ending by around three months of age. Dealing with a disconsolate baby is very distressing for parents, but the most important thing is to stay calm yourself and not become angry or frustrated. Research on colic is inconclusive, relating it to food allergies, hormonal imbalances, overstimulation, temperament, or immature nervous or gastrointestinal systems. Aletha Solter, in *The Aware Baby*, has found through her own work with a technique called "co-counseling" that crying is one way we have to process hurt and release stored tension and pain. She feels that being there with the baby while it cries can help it to let go of birth and other trauma. When a baby is not crying from physical discomfort, it sometimes just needs to cry out its tensions. Staying calm yourself and being present in a loving and collected way can help the crying to be healing rather than creating more frustration.[27]

## CAN YOU HELP YOUR BABY DEVELOP SPECIFIC SKILLS?

### The Importance of the Environment

During the first six weeks, your baby needs gradually to adjust to earthly life and to get her digestive system functioning smoothly. Because she sleeps so much and her perceptual abilities are so limited, any kind of "enriched environment" will be wasted on the infant. Be skeptical of commercial and media hype regarding the needs of the newborn.

Much of the push to "stimulate your baby's senses" comes out of a misinterpretation of the studies in European orphanages, as discussed earlier. Babies need the love, the holding and the connection with a primary caregiver (mother or mother substitute) if they are to take up life fully. They need to be welcomed and held in a peaceful and supportive environment which feeds body and soul, rather than be affronted by buzzers, brightly colored objects and other stimulation to their senses. Your baby won't even be very interested in the world around her until about two months of age.

If an "enriched environment" is wasted on your baby, an aesthetic one is not. Creating a feeling of calm in the room (and in the mother) communicates to the baby and helps with sleep, digestion and peacefulness. Most of the commercial things for babies are expensive and unnecessary. If you do have the luxury of decorating the nursery, avoid garish wallpaper and cartoon characters. Greens, browns and grays are also much more "earthy" than the infant and young child, who is still closely connected to heaven and doesn't yet walk firmly on the ground. The rose-pink-blue environment created by the silks over the crib is especially soothing for babies, and a color Steiner called "peach blossom" is especially suited to young children. Looking at the space in which your baby sleeps with attention and reverence adds those qualities to the environment. Adding a little table with fresh flowers, some photos or art reproduction, and some objects from nature like a pretty rock or shell, can remind you of your own still center in the midst of all the demands of caring for a new baby.

Steiner suggested that many paintings by Raphael express higher truths, and he especially recommended that pregnant women contemplate Raphael's *Sistine Madonna*, which is also wonderful to have in a young child's room. Meditating on this picture can reveal many things to the mother about the nature of the eternal feminine and the incarnation process. About this particular painting Steiner says, "The painting of the Madonna with the child is the symbol of the eternal spirituality in people which comes certainly to the earth from beyond. Yet, this painting, through parted clouds, has everything that can only arise or proceed from the earthly."[28]

## Skill Development

What skills does your baby develop in the first six weeks? Aside from the digestive system maturing, your baby develops the ability to hold her head off the mattress for longer periods of time and comes to stare and smile at faces (and face patterns) when they are eight inches to twelve inches away. These developmental skills don't require any special action on your part. Burton White, in having observed that newborns' heads are almost always turned to the side whether they are on their backs or stomachs, suggests that if parents want to do anything that they make a "stabile" instead of the traditional "mobile" (which hangs over the crib and is useless during the first two months). A stabile doesn't move and is placed at the baby's eye level on the side of the crib. White recommends drawing a human face, because that is what babies respond to best.[29] I personally wouldn't do that because it seems to me like the first of many substitutions for the human being that parents buy into. (Pacifiers, lullaby bears, stories on tape and television are others.) We can thank White's observations for reminding us that babies don't really look overhead until they are about two months old.

## Language Development

Because your baby is learning to understand language long before he or she can speak, it is good to get into the habit of speaking intelligently to your baby from the start. Unfortunately many parents don't talk much to their children before they become verbal at around eighteen months of age. Although your baby will be about six months of age before she shows understanding of specific words and commands, talking to your baby not only helps her to develop language skills but demonstrates your respect for her as a human being.

Dr. Emmi Pikler, the Hungarian pediatrician whose work with child development and orphanages is noted worldwide, emphasizes the importance of treating the baby as a person, as a partner (rather than an object) in such routine activities as diapering and bathing. This involves interacting with your baby, sharing attention and words while you do things together, rather than being distracted and ignoring her, however small she may be.[30]

Steiner also emphasized the importance of avoiding "baby talk" and of providing a model of language that you would want to have copied, because your baby will be learning to talk by imitating the people around her.

## WHAT IS IT LIKE BEING WITH A NEWBORN?

Being with a newborn is usually shocking, at least the first time around. Having just given birth, the mother is wide open emotionally and physically. Hormones, starting to breastfeed, interrupted sleep and roller-coaster emotions put a woman much more in touch with the beauty, vulnerability and overwhelming aspects of life. Being a new mother or a new father involves a change in *being*, a stretching of who we are. We need to take on the responsibility and the twenty-four-hour-a-day care of another human being, who (for a while at least) is completely dependent on us.

Most people agree that the first six weeks are the hardest. It gets easier after that, and is easier with subsequent children because everything is more familiar. However, a second or third baby can be surprising in the amount of work she adds to a system where parents may already have felt there wasn't enough of them to go around.

Being with a baby involves doing a lot of repetitive things (diapering, nursing, washing clothes) that can look like nothing because they seem to involve maintenance rather than creative development. So when your husband comes home from work and says, "What did you do today, dear?," you think about it and burst into tears. I found I could accomplish *one thing* (one task in the world outside of the baby) each day, if I was lucky, during the first two months. For someone who was used to being active and effective, that was a real shock.

How can this period of transition after the birth be made easier for the parents? Detailed suggestions for things to think about and do can be found in my book *Pregnant Feelings*, but the most important thing is to get adequate help. This may mean having a relative come to stay with you, hiring someone to come in and straighten up the house (postpartum support services are becoming more common, thank goodness), or organizing a circle of friends to drop off a casserole and do a half-hour of what's needed every afternoon during the first week or so.

To the extent you feel that you can just *be* with your baby, you'll be more at peace. This may involve making sure that all other responsibilities are handled and that all deadlines fall before your due date, or it may mean giving up on cleaning the house for a while. When we finally surfaced about five days after the birth of our first child, every plant in the house was withered, and we were sad!

The first six weeks are a very special time to be together as a family, to just "be present" with your new baby, adjust to the changes in your life, and regain your strength and bearings. If you can honor the magnitude of the event, arrange for some help and schedule few or no activities, you may find your adjustment much less rocky. Allow yourself to be nourished by the wonderful energy that surrounds a newborn.

The energy of creation that is present at a birth is very powerful and holy. This is true at every birth, but it is more accessible if the energy is acknowledged and protected. Mothers certainly feel it, unless their baby is whisked away to the nursery and they are completely ignored while the doctor repairs the episiotomy—then the mother may feel let-down and empty rather than filled with excitement and accomplishment. Midwives respect this special time together for the family in the hours immediately following a birth, and I have always been amazed to leave a home where a birth has occurred and find that the world is still the same outside. The energy inside and outside are so different! I sometimes wonder how the mailman can be walking down the sidewalk and the children playing next door. Don't they know what has just happened!

Because babies are so close to the spiritual world, they call forth love and giving from all sorts of people—some of whom you won't have heard from in years. Learn to receive, to let people do things for you, to say thank you. Use the time to practice doing nothing, to just be centered in the heart or in your breath. If you have other children, you will be especially busy after the birth. See if you can find brief moments to just sit and watch the baby sleeping. Such moments nourish you for the constant demands of mothering. Try to take advantage of the connection to the spirit that your baby has and to which you still are open in the postpartum period. Life will return to a new "normal" soon enough.

Earlier in this chapter I talked about how most of us forget the life of the spirit when we take on this earthly life. The prophets and the saints are often people for whom the veil of forgetfulness has never come down or for whom it was not very thick. Similarly, some of the great poets seem to remain slightly more in touch with their origins than most of us. William Wordsworth wrote:

*Our birth is but a sleep and a forgetting;*
*The Soul that rises with us, our life's Star,*

*Hath had elsewhere its setting,*
*And cometh from afar:*
*Not in entire forgetfulness,*
*And not in utter nakedness,*
*But trailing clouds of Glory do we come*
*From God, who is our home:*
*Heaven lies about us in our infancy!*

On a young child's birthday in the Waldorf preschools we often tell a story about a little angel who wanted to come down to earth and got permission from its big angel to come over the rainbow bridge after it had had a dream about its earthly parents. The little angel finally agrees to leave its wings behind when its big angel assures it that they will be safely kept until his or her return. Then the little angel crosses through the many colors of the beautiful rainbow bridge, while on the earth the seasons change three times. Then it becomes very dark, almost like going to sleep, and when the little angel opens its eyes, there is the loving woman and the man with the kind heart who were in the dream. And the little angel knows it has found its earthly home.

Such an image nourishes a young child by affirming that we know there is more to him or her than just the body. A similar knowledge is reflected in the image of a regal white bird bringing a baby, for such a bird is always a symbol of the spirit, and especially the spirit link between heaven and earth (as when the Holy Spirit descends like a dove, or when a white bird guides Hansel and Gretel through the forest). In speaking of the stork bringing babies, our forebears were not ignorant of where babies came from—even children probably had more exposure to birth through farm life than do our own. Rather, they were giving expression to a sense that the spirit came into earthly life with the birth of a child, something which was perhaps easier for them to perceive but which is still accessible to us. Looking at your baby in this way will not only help to open your heart, but can help you to have patience when the house is a mess and you've been walking the floor for two hours with a fussy four-week-old. Babies do complicate your life, but they also offer tremendous opportunities for growth and development.

# RECOMMENDED READING

(Because many of these titles may be difficult to find, the letters in parentheses indicate mail-order book services listed in Appendix A.)

*Babies, Breastfeeding and Bonding* by Ina May Gaskin (IBP). A valuable guide for new mothers from one of the first midwives at The Farm, an intentional community in Tennessee.

*Birth Without Violence* by Frederick Leboyer. Insights into the newborn's experience and ways to receive him or her.

*Born Dancing* by Evelyn B. Thoman and Sue Browder. (B) Parenting as a dance instead of a list of "shoulds." Especially geared toward the first year of a baby's life.

*Conception, Birth and Early Childhood* by Norbert Glas (AP, IBP). Written from the author's experience as a doctor working with the insights of Rudolf Steiner.

*Cradle of Heaven* by Murshida Vera Justin Corda (IBP). Exploration of the psychological and spiritual dimensions of conception, pregnancy and birth (the author is a Sufi; the ideas are universal).

*The Incarnating Child* by Joan Salter (IBP, SG). My favorite book based on the insights of Rudolf Steiner and the author's work at the Gabriel Baby Centre in Australia.

*Pregnant Feelings* by Rahima Baldwin and Terra Palmarini (IBP). A workbook on psychological aspects of pregnancy, birth and parenting.

*Special Delivery* by Rahima Baldwin (IBP). A practical guide to pregnancy, birth and the postpartum period.

*Touching* by Ashley Montagu. (B) An important book on the significance of the skin in human development.

# RESOURCES

Sureway Trading Enterprises, 826 Pine Ave., Suites 5 & 6, Niagara Falls, NY 14301. White silk for only a few dollars a yard (request #1 pongee 5mm).

Weleda Pharmacy, 841 S. Main St., Spring Valley, NY 10977. Natural baby-care soap, powder, oil and cream.

The Natural Baby Company, R.D. 1, Box 160, Titusville, NJ 08560. Offers a free "Natural Diapering Handbook" and sells baby-care products.

## *Natural fiber clothing and bedding are available from:*

After the Stork, 3002 Monte Vista, NE, Albuquerque, NM 87106.

Cotton Dreams, 2962 NW 60th St., Ft. Lauderdale, FL 33309.

Garnet Hill, Franconia, NH 05380.

Hanna Anderson, 1010 NW Flanders, Portland, OR 97209.

Mother Hart, 11293 Wingfoot Dr., Boynton Beach, FL 33427.

## *Horizontal baby carriers are sold by:*

California Diversified Manufacturing, 208 Avenida Pelaya, San Clemente, CA 92672.

Co-op America Order Service, 126 Intervale Rd., Burlington, VT 05401.

Hearth Song, P.O. Box B, Sebastopol, CA 95473.

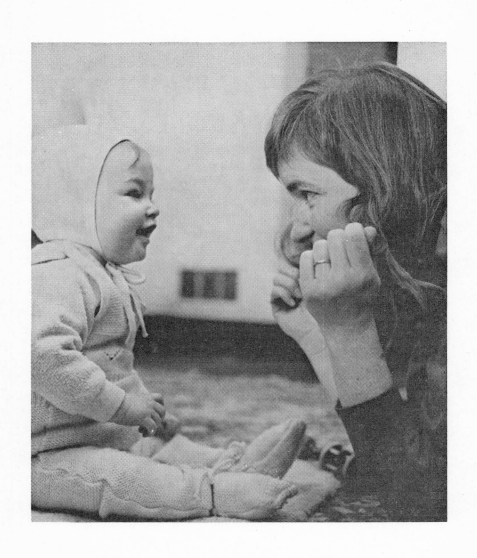

# 3 | *Growing Down & Waking Up*

We think of children as growing up, but we could also say that they "grow down," in the sense that they seem to gain control of the body from the head downward. First they gain control of the eyes and the neck, then the torso in rolling over, and finally the limbs in crawling and walking.

At the same time, they are changing from sleepy newborns to alert and lively toddlers who run circles around their parents. This change in consciousness from infancy to three years involves waking up, in the sense that the participatory consciousness of the newborn gradually becomes replaced by a strong sense of self (just try opposing the will of a two-year-old!). Before this strong sense of *I* can emerge, the child must first develop language, thinking and memory.

Penetration of the body, which culminates in walking, is a fundamental task of the baby's first year. Talking is a key task of the second year. And thinking and memory are areas of tremendous development in the third year. All these fundamental milestones of the first three years occur by themselves, according to their own timetable. We need only provide love and nourishment, and refrain from doing things that hamper the child's basic pattern of unfolding.

This chapter presents a picture of the tremendous developmental changes occurring in the child during the first three years. The next two chapters suggest many practical things you can do as your child's first teacher that are consonant with healthy and balanced development.

# GROWING INTO THE BODY

## Control of the Head

A newborn's head is very large compared to its body, and its limbs are relatively undeveloped appendages, good neither for walking nor eating as they are with other mammals. With such a huge head, control first begins in the eyes, which must start to focus on objects about ten inches away—just the distance between a breastfeeding infant and her mother's face. Next the baby learns to follow something with her eyes when it comes into her range of vision, which extends to about twelve inches at two months of age. She may begin to turn her head toward a sound if it comes in one ear more strongly than the other. She begins to be able to hold her head up off the mattress when on her stomach and to turn her head more toward the midline when on her back. But it will be many more months before sufficient head-neck strength will be present for her to sit unassisted.

At three-and-a-half months she can hold her head more centered and look straight up, and her arms and legs are no longer confined to the "fencer's pose" of the younger infant. She will have the ability to control her head through 180 degrees, but she probably can't turn over before fourteen weeks. When on her stomach, she will be able to hold her head straight up off the mattress for several minutes at a time.

During the time from six to fourteen weeks, the muscles in your baby's legs are strengthening by kicking out and being held slightly flexed, but there is no real leg control.

Control of the head also manifests in visual ability, which increases rapidly and is nearly completely under control by three-and-a-half months. Once your baby can focus clearly on nearby objects and create a single image of them, she will discover her hands and stare at them—sometimes for five or ten minutes at a time. Between six and fourteen weeks her hands will no longer be held in a fist most of the time, and she will start bringing her hands together and clasping them. Eye and hand convergence is something only primates and humans have, and it is an important step in the development of intelligence.

You will see eye-hand coordination developing as your two- or three-month-old swipes at an object and later brings it to her mouth. This coordination increases with practice and maturation, so that by six months a baby usually has complete control of the use of her hands.

Reaching is an important developmental skill, one of the major ways that children begin to explore the world and build the foundations of intelligence. Your baby will almost always reach for anything that is nearby and will either bring it to her mouth or look at it, sometimes moving it about or taking it from hand to hand.

### Control of the Torso

As the months go by, your baby gains increasing control of her body from the head down. Sometime before six months she will probably succeed in turning from her back to stomach, followed a few weeks later by being able to turn back the other way. These accomplishments are usually preceded by many attempts to roll over. The first time is often a surprise, so be careful not to leave your baby unattended on a changing table or bed where she can flip off! Even a much younger baby can sometimes unexpectedly succeed in turning from back to stomach through powerful leg thrusts, especially if she is angry.

Further control of the muscles of the torso will result in your baby's being able to sit up unassisted, usually between six and eight months of age. This first achievement of an upright position marks a significant maturing of the muscles. A vertical posture is a uniquely human attribute; it is perhaps a symbol of our unique position between heaven and earth.

Once your baby is adept at turning over in both directions and can sit alone, she will try to bring herself from a lying to a sitting posture. This new ability is usually accomplished by around eight months of age.

A baby who can sit up is interested in everything. Her eyes are now more inclined to focus on objects several feet away, but she cannot yet move under her own power. If left on a rug in the middle of a room, she is not able to move her body any distance (exceptions are some babies who learn to propel themselves from place to place by rolling over and over). Coordinated use of the limbs for locomotion will be the next major developmental achievement.

## Control of the Legs

All of the movement and kicking your baby does helps to strengthen her legs. Sometime around four months of age she will discover that she has feet, since her eyes had been unable to discern them earlier. But she won't be able to use her legs in a controlled fashion. That changes around eight months of age, when she learns to crawl. Some babies are eager to go and may even be frustrated by their inability to get things they want; others are happy to sit and watch the world go by, and they may first crawl four or five months later than the "early" ones. The normal range is tremendous. Don't compare your baby with the neighbor's! Insights into later character traits can sometimes be gained by observing how your child learns to crawl and walk. Simply observe and encourage your baby and trust that she is developing according to her own timetable. If you have questions about how your child is developing, seek answers to them rather than worry!

Most children try to move about as soon as they are able. This may involve "classic" crawling (getting up on hands and knees and coordinating all four limbs to propel themselves) or it may start with "scooting" (using the elbows to pull themselves about while the legs are fairly inactive). Babies usually love to exercise their new motor skills and are eager to reach the many things they have been able to see from a distance for several months.

Physical therapists now tell us how important crawling is in later development. The rhythmical pattern of *cross crawling* (opposite arm and leg being thrust forward) is significant not only for the development of proper physical coordination, but also affects the development of the brain and how a child learns. Some learning and emotional disabilities are related to a lack of crawling or can be helped by *patterning,* moving an adult's or older child's limbs through hours and hours of the crawling pattern.[1] For this reason, anything that shortens a baby's time spent crawling (baby walkers, leg splints or braces) should be avoided during this critical period.

Crawling is followed by the baby's ability to pull herself up while holding onto a table or sofa. The ability to walk while holding onto things is followed by increased balance and coordination and the wonderful first steps alone.

Once your baby can crawl, you will find everything changes! Because crawling is such a momentous change for parents and walking is such a momentous accomplishment for babies, I want to discuss parenting the baby up to the age of eight months before going on to discuss walking.

## WHAT IS YOUR BABY LIKE BETWEEN SIX WEEKS AND EIGHT MONTHS OF AGE?

We can say that babies "grow down and wake up," for while they are growing and developing physically, they are also becoming more alert and more interested in the world around them. We have seen how they develop physically; let's explore how they behave as they become more "present" with each passing day.

Your baby will sleep less as the weeks go by, and will pay close attention to what is going on around her. Once she discovers her hands, she will use them whenever possible to grasp and explore objects with her eyes and mouth. The tongue and lips are sensitive organs of exploration, and when your baby starts to teethe during this period, counterpressure can sometimes help sore gums. There are many teething rings on the market, some of which can be put in the refrigerator to chill. We especially recommend "Hyland's Homeopathic Teething Pills," which, amazingly, are sold by many major drugstore chains. Being homeopathic, they present no danger of overdose or side effects. It is not unusual for babies to be fussy while they are teething, or even occasionally to have a fever or runny nose.

By three months your baby will probably be smiling regularly at anyone who gets her attention. Three-month-old babies are delightful to be with, and most of our images of babies from television or advertising are of a three-month-old rather than a newborn. We now have much more of a sense that there is a real person present, someone who seems to respond to us. Indeed, a baby does begin to show more special behavior, such as smiling more with her parents or primary caregivers from the fourth month on. But there is still openness and friendliness to all people at this age.

The baby's sense of *self* and *other* is slow to emerge, for the consciousness of a newborn is very diffuse. There is no *inner* and *outer*. As we watch the baby slowly distinguish between parents and others, we have the sense that he is more present in the body. It is interesting that you cannot elicit a tickle response from a baby before about fourteen weeks of age. Burton White postulates that tickling depends on the "ticklee" perceiving that another person is producing the stimulation (you can't tickle yourself). He states, "The child younger than about fourteen weeks of age is probably not well enough developed socially to have reached whatever awareness of another is necessary to make the tickle functional."[2]

This is consonant with Steiner's idea of the gradual incarnation of the *I* and the slowly developing consciousness of the self, which is necessary for any perception of "other." Steiner described babies as "sleeping" in their consciousness, "dreaming" in their emotions and most "awake" in their willing, which manifests in the body. We can see the strength of this willing in the tremendous growth and movement of the body and in the insistence with which a baby demands that its physical needs be met. Try to argue with a crying baby that she's not really hungry, and she ought to be able to wait! The force of will behind the physical functions of a baby does not respond to reason or consolation—only to physical activity such as eating, sucking or rocking.

A next step in the differentiation of "others" is evident in the common phenomenon called *stranger anxiety*. Sometime in the first year, four out of five babies start reacting with hesitation and fear to anyone who is not in the immediate family. This reaction can start as early as six months, and it is not a sign that anything is wrong.

Aside from becoming wary of people who aren't familiar, most babies enjoy themselves most of the time during the first year. They are basically happy, curious and growing throughout this time.

## LEARNING TO WALK

During the period from eight to sixteen months of age, most children master their physical body and learn to walk. Note that there can be as much as eight months' difference between early and late walkers.

Children learn to walk through practice and through imitation. It has been found in the rare cases where human babies have been reared by animals in the jungles of India, that the child never achieves a truly upright posture. There is a strong inner drive in children to stand and to walk, and to be like the people around them. It is something inherent in children and does not require baby gymnastics or other devices to aid its progress. Baby walkers do not lead to early walking; in fact, many physicians now believe infant walkers may adversely affect muscle development and coordination and lead to a delay in walking.[3] Due to the large number of accidents involving walkers, the Canadian Medical Association has asked the government to ban their sale.[4] Time spent in walkers also takes time away from opportunities to creep and crawl.

Infant walkers don't seem to lead to increased social and explorative behaviors, as their proponents say; studies have found no difference in these behaviors for infants in or out of walkers. They may give parents some free time, but not without physical and developmental risks to the baby.[5] There is similar concern about baby bouncers (cloth seats suspended by a spring hung over a door sill) by many pediatricians because of potential damage to the baby's bones or joints if they are used on hard floors.[6]

Watching your child learn to walk on her own can sometimes provide insights into character traits, because walking is something the child achieves through her own efforts. Is there a driving will to move, or a great solidity and contentment in sitting? Are falls taken in stride, or are they discouraging? Keep watching and see what your child "tells" you. All you need to do is be there to encourage and share your child's pride in those first steps.

It is valuable to watch the process of learning to walk for what it can tell us of the child's nature and the incarnation process of the "I." Steiner states, "Walking does not merely mean that the human being ceases to crawl and acquires an upright position. It means that the child attains to the equilibrium of its own organism within the cosmos, learns to control its movements and acquires a free orientation."[7] He continues,

> And for anyone who is able to observe such a matter in the right way, the most remarkable and most important of life's riddles actually find expression in this activity of learning to walk; a whole universe comes to expression in the manner in which the child progresses from creeping to the upright position, to the placing of the feet, but also in addition to holding the head upright and to the use of arms and legs.[8]

To explain this further, once the baby achieves equilibrium in the upright posture, Steiner observes that the hands and arms are freed to serve the inward life, while the legs serve for bodily movement:

> The liberation of the hands and arms affords the possibility for the soul to find its equilibrium. The function of the legs, the treading, the raising and bending, the harmony between right and left, brings about a relation to what is below us. It has the effect of bringing into the life of body and soul the element of rhythm, of measure, the ceasuras of existence. The soul elements which live in the hands and arms become free; this introduces an element of melody, a musical element into the life of the child.[9]

Watching a young child with awareness that more might be going on than meets the eye can make us more open when we are with young children. Even though I can't articulate any great insights I've had, I know that those times of openness and remembrance seem very valuable for me as a spiritual-physical being, for my parenting and for the child.

## THE SECOND YEAR: MASTERING LANGUAGE

A child's first birthday is as much an anniversary for the mother as for the baby. Exactly one year earlier she was going through labor and she remembers vividly what she felt holding her baby for the first time. As dramatic as the changes in the baby were in the first year, they will be equally dramatic in the second. By the time a child is two there is much greater distance from the dreamy dependency of infancy and a much greater sense of who this person is in his own right.

Just as mastering the body and learning to walk were the dominant activities of the first year of your baby's life, so mastering language and learning to talk are the major tasks from age one to two. Language development consists both of comprehension, which develops first, and the ability to speak. Learning to talk, like learning to walk, seems to involve both an innate capacity of the brain and a need to encounter models in the environment. Because language comprehension is so fundamental to all later learning and to good social development, it is valuable to consider it in some detail.

### Language Comprehension

I hope you will have been talking to your baby from birth on as if she were a person worthy of respect. This attention and respect not only increase her sense of self-worth and her loving interaction with you, but by using good language rather than baby talk, you are providing a model worthy of imitation.

Your baby will usually pay attention to you when you talk to her while changing her diaper or bathing her. It may seem that she understands what you are saying (I'm convinced that babies are knowing beings). But the first unmistakable signs of word recognition usually occur around eight months of age. If your husband says, "Where's Mommy?" while several people are in the room, she will turn toward you when she really knows that word. That depends, of course, on your having referred to yourself as "Mommy" or "Mama." If all your child ever hears is your husband referring to you as "Jane," she will also call you by your first name. There is something to be said for having your child refer to the two of you as "Mommy and Daddy," "Mama and Papa," or some such words because the sounds of these words are appropriate and easy to learn, and because it expresses relationship (parent and child, family).

Because so much depends on the development of language, it is important to watch your child for hearing disorders. If your baby is having frequent ear infections, it is advisable to look for allergies or other possible causes of fluid build-up in the ears. Impaired hearing can impede development in many other areas during these critical years of early childhood, so try to find a diagnosis and plan of treatment that you can support.

One of the best things you can do for your child is to sing to her. The melodic quality of language and the emotions present in a lullaby or a nursery game are very valuable for your baby's development. Comprehension is not the only part of language, although it tends to be overemphasized by our intellectual adult nature. Nonsense rhymes and action verses such as "To market, to market" become favorites of the toddler and teach the melodic quality of language. This kind of interaction is valuable not only for the developing child, but can also make parenting tasks go more smoothly. For example, getting into the habit of using songs for activities such as washing her hair or going to bed can melt away the resistance of a willful two-year-old. For more concrete ideas, see the lovely book *Catch Me & Kiss Me & Say it Again*.[10]

As your child comes to understand specific words, she will begin following simple instructions, like waving bye-bye or sitting down. Once your child starts to walk, she will frequently be coming to show you things or ask for assistance. Such times, when her attention is clearly directed toward you, are excellent times to talk about what is at hand, and then to act on it. Many parents underestimate what their child can understand at this age. This does not mean to explain everything to a one-year-old! It does mean to talk intelligibly about what is happening in the present— what the child is seeing and doing. Between the first and third birthdays, language comprehension increases to the point where most children understand most of the words they will use in ordinary conversation for the rest of their lives!

## Being Able to Talk

The ability to produce language proceeds much more slowly than the ability to understand it. While your child will show increasing understanding of words before her first birthday, very few children speak before they are one. The reason for this, according to Steiner, is that language development grows out of movement and the ability to walk. Steiner comments:

> The relation between physical equilibrium (action of the legs) and psychical equilibrium (action of the hands and arms) forms the foundation which enables the child to come into contact with the outer world through the medium of language.
>
> When we observe the formation of sounds and sentences (the rhythm and melody of speech), we can easily see the part played by the upper and lower limbs respectively in their formation. Speech arises from the human being as a whole. The outer, rhythmical element arises from the movement of the legs, the inner thematic element from that of the hands and arms.
>
> When a child walks sturdily and steadily, it has the bodily foundation for a correct syllable-division. This means that in learning to walk the child learns to form its sentences. If it walks unsteadily, we shall find that it does not observe a proper division of sentences; it drowns its thoughts in a sea of words.
>
> If a child does not properly learn to use its hands and arms harmoniously, its speech will disintegrate. Its voice becomes somewhat harsh. If we cannot get it to feel life in its fingers, it will with difficulty develop a true sense for the modulations of speech.
>
> The child should learn to walk before it learns to speak. Speech must have its basis in the equilibrium of the movements of the limbs. If it lacks this foundation in the whole being, it becomes a stammering or bleating.[11]

Modern neurolinguistic work supports the relationship between learning to walk and grasp, and learning to speak. With this in mind, we can watch not only how our children learn to walk and the quality of their movements, but can also observe the quality of their speech as it develops over the years and see if there is any discernable relationship between the two. Certainly both physical and speech therapists, conventional ones and those working out of Steiner's indications for "curative education," can see it. In such curative settings, movement and sound are often used separately and in combination to help overcome developmental difficulties.

## The Development of Speech

Dr. Karl König, working with handicapped children and adults, distinguished three levels in speech development, which he called *saying, naming* and *talking*.[12] *Saying* involves a desire or emotion that comes out as a one-word sentence, like "Here!" or "Cookie!" *Naming* involves learning the names of things and the beginnings of the thought processes that link concepts with perceptions and draw relationships between the general ("dog") and the specific ("Fido"). *Talking* involves dialogue as we are used to it. As the child experiences the world and the way it is expressed in language, with its inherent logic and grammar, he begins to use whole sentences between ages two and three.

## Archetypal Images

While the toddler is learning the names of things, a great deal is happening on the preverbal level in the rapt attention with which the child contemplates each object. For example, while an adult or a school-age child will be most interested in what he or she can *do* with a ball, a toddler will be most interested in the ball itself—its shape, texture, color and the fact that it rolls away when it slips out of her hands. Our adult consciousness has lost the connection with what goes on in the dreamy depths of the child's soul, with what is happening behind his dreaming, wondering or delighted eyes. Daniel Udo de Haes, in his excellent book *The Young Child*, develops a fascinating picture of the unspoken "soul language" by which simple objects speak to the child of qualities in the spiritual world and the nature of the soul's journey on earth. We can get a taste of Udo de Haes's perceptions in his description of the fascination young children (and adults) have with water:

Every human soul is aware, consciously or unconsciously, of a connection with this watery element. Does not each of us long for the clarity which pure water can manifest? Does not every soul feel its own ability to stream and flow in all directions, to wave and to dash, to seethe and toss or to refect calmly? Ultimately its capacity of rising to the heavens and descending again to earth, is brought to expression by water. The little child experiences all this much more directly and intensely than we do, though less consciously, and it is for this reason that he feels his connection with water and plays with it with such abandon.[13]

In a similar way, Udo de Haes explains children's delight in drawing houses or making houses out of the sofa pillows as arising from a reawakening of something within the child's own soul when it encounters "houses" on earth. He states, "Descending to earth, the soul bears within it the task of helping to build the 'house' that it would have to live in during the life that was about to begin; for the task that it was assigned was to help in forming its body. We should therefore not be surprised at the joy with which the child builds a little house, thus symbolically fulfilling the task of building his body."[14]

In *The Young Child* a very enlivening (and not at all sentimental) picture of the inner life of the young child is developed by Udo de Haes, which I have found valuable to hold as a possibility when I watch a toddler contemplating an object. Jesus said, "Unless you change and become like little children, you will never enter the kingdom of heaven." (Matthew 18:3) What is the world like for a little child? This is a question worth holding by anyone who cares for young children. And to the extent that their wonder in the world around them can become real to us as well, the rediscovery of this aspect within ourselves can, without our noticing it, be a help to the young child who is exploring his own world of experiences.

Because of the fascination the young child has with simple objects and the resonance within the soul which such objects awaken, Udo de Haes recommends archetypal toys such as a ball, a bowl and cup (with sand or water to pour), a little wooden house, a box with a hinged lid or a small wagon.

The fact that the objects of nature and the simple objects of human life speak to the inner life of the child, reminding him of truths from the spiritual world, is echoed by the seventeenth-century English poet Thomas Traherne:

> WONDER
> *How like an Angel came I down!*
> *How Bright are all Things here!*
> *When first among his Works I did appear*
> *O how their Glory did me Crown*
> *The World resembled his Eternitie*
> *In which my Soul did Walk;*
> *And every Thing that I did see,*
> *Did with me talk.*

## THE EMERGENCE OF THINKING

Just as walking and talking can be seen as the major tasks of the first and second years of life, so thinking is a major accomplishment of the time from ages two to three. But thinking in its most rudimentary forms can be seen as early as the first year, when the baby pushes an obstacle aside in order to grasp an object. Piaget describes this problem-solving behavior, with its element of intentionality, as one of the first signs of intelligence.

This early, practical or *sensorimotor* intelligence isn't replaced by reflecting on ideas until around the age of two. Prior to that time children tend to use trial-and-error for problem solving. As they turn two, you will increasingly see them pause and think about various alternatives or about the action they are going to do before doing it.

Thinking emerges between ages two and three, *after* the child has learned to speak. Many people will suppose that one has to think in order to speak, but remember that speech develops as a result of *imitation* and of *feelings*. The first words are interjections, and Steiner says, "When the child says 'Mama' or 'Papa,' it expresses *feelings* towards Mama or Papa, not any sort of concept or thought. Thinking is first developed from speech."[15] This is true not only in the formation of concepts associated with individual words, but also in the inherent logic and grammar found in speech, which forms the matrix for the child's thinking. We are often blind to the effects of language on our perceptions and thinking until we study and master a foreign language.

In learning the names of things, a child begins to combine a *concept* or idea with a *percept* (the perception itself, devoid of any conceptual content). Meaning emerges as images and ideas start to form, connecting the outer world with the inner, mental world. However exciting it may be to see your child start to show signs of thinking, this doesn't mean you should start providing lengthy explanations of things or reasoning with her. The young child is still centered in the body and the will, and is not governed by thought and reflection. *Imitation* and *example* are still the keys for working with a child before the age of seven, as we will see in subsequent chapters.

## The Development of the Memory

The development of thinking depends on the process of language formation and the maturing of memory. Steiner points out how the development of the child's memory echoes the historical development of humanity. The first type of memory is *localized or place memory*, which involves recalling something when the child is in the same environment or receives similar sensory cues. For example, she may only visit grandma's house every few months, but she immediately remembers where the toy cupboard and the cookie jar are when she walks in the door. Historically, this kind of early memory is represented by monuments, cairns, monoliths and other "markers" that remind people of the events which occurred at that location. This type of memory is very strong in the young child, who cannot pull up memories at will until the age of six. For example, if you ask preschoolers, "What did you do at school today?" they will typically say, "Nothing." But if they get other cues—you start to sing one of the songs or they see or smell something similar—you can get an amazingly detailed rendition of the morning's activities.

The second type of memory that developed historically can be called *rhythmical memory*, in which history was carried in verse by poets or bards who would recite epic tales to remind people of their heritage. The rhythmical element makes memorization much easier, as with a young child's "ABC song" or "One two, buckle my shoe." With such songs the child can go through the entire sequence, but is unable to start in the middle or remember individual elements without reciting the whole verse from the beginning.

The third kind of memory, *picture memory*, begins to develop in the third year and involves the child's being able to use images and ideas. Lois Cusick, in *The Waldorf Parenting Handbook*,[16] diagrams the progression in the accompanying illustration.

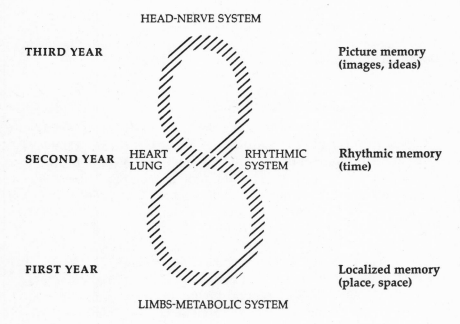

HEAD-NERVE SYSTEM

THIRD YEAR — Picture memory (images, ideas)

SECOND YEAR — HEART LUNG — RHYTHMIC SYSTEM — Rhythmic memory (time)

FIRST YEAR — Localized memory (place, space)

LIMBS-METABOLIC SYSTEM

## THE EMERGING SENSE OF SELF

Your toddler is very different from a baby, not only in her ability to walk and talk, but also in her sense of self. By the time your child is eighteen months old you will have no doubt that you are dealing with another human being of power.

A baby has what can be called *participatory consciousness.* There is no separation between self and other. Certainly the individuality is present and can be sensed in an infant, but it seems to surround the baby as the process of incarnation gradually occurs. The young baby participates in all the sense impressions of life without any distance, only gradually distinguishing various sensations, various adults and the "10,000 things" of the created world.

We have talked about the common occurrence of fear or shyness with strangers that most babies go through around nine months of age, and during the second year you will see other signs of the emerging sense of "I" and "not-I." During the second year, toddlers begin to feel themselves as separate beings, using their own name, starting to be possessive about toys, and starting to resist simple instructions from their parents. What psychologists call *negativism* is a normal stage in the second half of the second year of life. As the concept *no* begins to have meaning for them, children will pit their will against that of their parents.

In *The First Three Years of Life*, White writes, "Why a child has to become ornery and stay that way for a minimum of six or seven months is one of the mysteries that makes the study of early human development so rich and fascinating. . . . The next comparable step seems to occur at puberty and takes the form of adolescent rebellion. We leave it to other researchers to delve further into this fascinating problem."[17]

Steiner's explanation of such behavior is that the child's "I" is being experienced more strongly, making him more awake and more centered in the power of his individuality. These times occur at ages two to three, around age nine, and again around age thirteen. Finally at age twenty-one the individuality is fully incarnated into earthly life.

The toddler's emerging sense of self is strengthened by the development of memory, which results in the first conscious use of the word "I." Indeed, there can be no awareness of oneself without memory. Memory comes from an accumulation of experiences with the "not-I." Things that are painful—a knife that cuts, hard cement steps that cause a bump—interrupt the young child's participatory consciousness and separate the world from the self. Memory arises from these and other encounters, increasing the sense of the *observer* or the *experiencer* and the *thing experienced*. This sense of distance or separation is in contrast to the infant's unfocussed consciousness, which doesn't distinguish between self and other, which participates completely in whatever sensation is at hand.

The emergence of memory, thinking and the self go hand in hand, and sometime in the third year you will notice your child first saying "I" instead of calling herself by her name. Prior to this time she will say "Susy do it" or "Susy book," imitating what she has heard herself called. Saying "I" can only be done by the person herself, and the earlier ways of talking will disappear.

The age between two and three is an exciting time, one in which your child wholeheartedly says to the world, "Here am I!" This wonderful step in development can be accompanied by "self-will" as the child asserts her newfound power of individuality. Having an understanding of the changing consciousness of the child can help us as parents to gain perspective on the forces behind a child's actions, and can help us offer guidance and correction (insisting on "right action") without our own emotional reactions muddying the waters. Examples of creative ways of coping with negative behavior will be given in Chapter 5.


## IN CONCLUSION

Having insights into your child's physical development and the changes in consciousness from birth through age three can help you understand and respond creatively to your child. In the next two chapters we will consider ways in which you can help your child's development during these crucial first three years.

# RECOMMENDED READING

(Letters in parentheses indicate mail-order book services listed in Appendix A.)

*Conception, Birth and Early Childhood* by Norbert Glas (AP, IBP). Deals with development and parenting through the first three years, based on the view of the young child given by Rudolf Steiner and the author's experience as an anthroposophical doctor.

*The First Three Years of Life* by Burton L. White. Valuable for his common-sense approach based on many years of observing parents and young children. Not at all Steiner-oriented, but I found it helpful in its descriptions of behavior based on unbiased observation and his emphasis on balanced development.

*The Incarnating Child* by Joan Salter (IBP, SG). Carries through the second birthday (Steiner-oriented). Highly recommended!

*Waldorf Parenting Handbook* by Lois Cusick (IBP, SG). Valuable section on early childhood, as well as a description of the Waldorf (Steiner School) curriculum through adolescence.

*The Young Child* by Daniel Udo de Haes (AP, IBP). Creative living with two- to four-year-olds, with an emphasis on language development and appropriate stories. The author works out of the inspiration and ideas of Steiner.

# 4 | *Helping Your Baby's Development in the First Year*

Your baby's rapid physical development in the first year forms the basis for the development of intelligence in the years that follow. In addition, your baby is beginning to develop emotionally and socially, and the lessons about love and trust learned as an infant form a foundation for later emotional health. The nurturing discussed in the chapter on the newborn applies throughout the critical first year of life. Remember that babies who do not have a primary caregiver fail to thrive, and if a baby's cries receive no response, she becomes apathetic and unresponsive.

The work of parenting in the first year may seem mundane, in that it involves tending to the baby's physical needs for food, cleanliness, sleep and touch. However, there is tremendous value in the care parents provide, for the infant is being shaped by his relationship with parents and the environment. The parents' feelings and interactions have a subtle impact different from that received in even quality daycare. With more and more women putting the baby in full-time childcare at six weeks to return to their careers, we appeal to mothers and fathers to be with their child as much as possible in at least the first year of life! With the possible exception of your baby's grandmother, in your own home, no one can provide the calm environment and loving attention that the mother or father provides. The idea of "quality time" does not apply to an infant. She needs the constant proximity, the breastfeeding, the carrying, the being in a carrier or on the floor next to you while you do something.

No other mammal is born as helpless as the human being, and no other has such potential for development. In many ways a baby is not "ready" to be born when compared with other mammals, and yet it must be born after nine months' gestation or the head will become too large and calcified to fit through the mother's pelvis. But the baby's needs for being close to the mother's body do not stop at birth; they continue throughout the first year and longer. Most "less developed" cultures practice some form of marsupial mothering, carrying the baby in constant contact with the mother's body up to the age of nine months—almost like a second gestational period. At that time there is a noticeable change, as the baby becomes much more interested in the surrounding world, reaches for table foods, and is able to crawl and then walk on her own.

In addition to the special connection that exists hormonally and psychically between a mother and her baby, the father's ever-expanding relationship with the baby also contributes greatly to the child's growth and development. This relationship can begin during pregnancy, as the father takes time to be in touch with the developing body and being of his child. In experiencing the birth with his wife, he finds his love and connection with this child strengthening dramatically. By sharing in the care of the baby and watching it grow, the father's relationship deepens, so that he finds other times and ways to be with the baby, especially when it is being breastfed. As the baby develops and is increasingly able to respond with smiles and play, the relationship of father and child deepens. In addition to the special love and protection a father can provide for his baby and his wife, there are many ways in which he can interact with his baby during the first year. Fathering is of benefit not only to the baby, but also to the man, who allows the nurturing aspect of his personality to develop. Mothers enjoy seeing their husbands interact with the baby; in fact, studies have shown that marital satisfaction for women with children is connected with seeing their husbands active as a father.[1]

We will present no recipes for producing a "super baby." In fact, what most new parents need is confidence that they themselves are important and can provide the best possible care for their babies. However, based on an increasing knowledge of child development and the gradual nature of the incarnation process, certain priniciples and activities can be especially helpful for you and your baby.

## PHYSICAL DEVELOPMENT

As we have seen, all babies go through a normal sequence of development that involves assuming control of the body. The differences in developmental rates of individual babies have more to do with timing than with the order in which skills develop. Freedom to move the arms and legs assures that muscles will strengthen and that processes such as language and cognitive development, which are related to physical movement, will unfold appropriately. If you are having serious questions about your baby's development, check with your family doctor or a specialist to reassure yourself that your baby is developing normally. This is especially true if you suspect a hearing problem or if your baby has frequent ear infections. So much of learning depends on good hearing!

Your baby does not need baby exercise courses or other fancy stimulation to develop well. Expensive infant stimulation or home exercise kits are a waste of money and make the false assumption that we know better than the baby which muscles she should move. You can have all the benefits of positive interaction with your baby without spending the thirty-five dollars simply by enjoying being with your child and rolling around on the floor together. If you are doing something because it feels good in the moment (massaging your baby or watching him grab at something), then you are interacting positively. But if you are doing it for results (so he'll be serene when he grows up or will walk sooner), then you are out of the present moment and have fallen prey to the media hype that tells us we should help our children to progress faster.

Understanding how your baby develops can help you to have realistic expectations and to provide toys and a physical environment that are developmentally appropriate.

Remember how completely at one with the environment the baby is. During the first six weeks this means providing a very protected atmosphere for the incoming spirit. After around six weeks there is a developmental change, and you will find that your baby has outgrown the silks over the bassinet and is ready for more interaction with the world. Lying outside and experiencing the interplay of light and shadow through the leaves of a tree in the garden will delight a baby if she is warm and not in a draft.

While your baby is still primarily a horizontal being, you can delight her with a mobile in which the objects are horizontal and thus visible to the baby (remember that what is visible to you is seen as a narrow edge by the baby in the crib). Appropriate toys for a baby who cannot yet sit up include a solidly made crib gym, or other objects suspended across the crib that she can grasp while on her back. While babies seem to enjoy batting at objects on crib gyms, some experts suggest that objects that hang on sticks rather than strings are preferable because they are easier for the baby to catch.

Crib toys should not produce loud noises or flashing lights. *It is important for safety to remove hanging crib toys when your baby seems nearly able to pull herself up to a sitting position.*

Something you can make which encourages leg action for the baby between three and six months is a kick toy, a nicely colored stuffed toy attached to the end of the crib that allows your baby to practice leg extensions safely.[2]

Before a baby can sit up, it is fine to have her near you on a blanket on the floor. Babies don't object to being on their backs or on their stomachs instead of sitting. Our culture is visually oriented, and we think that babies always need to be sitting up in molded infant seats when they are awake. Some researchers on developmental learning disabilities feel that babies should not be propped up into a sitting position by infant seats, but should be given the opportunity to achieve the sitting position entirely unaided.[3] It is a question of not jumping ahead of the normal progression of development. You'll also want to carry your baby a lot for closeness and touch. In the last chapter we discussed options for wrapping the baby in a shawl or using a front pack that keeps the baby horizontal until she can sit up by herself. Be sure to care for the head-neck relationship when the baby is in a stroller. In Europe babies are taken out for walks in "prams" or baby buggies in which they lie horizontal until they are able to sit up by themselves. While our folding-umbrella strollers are major conveniences for today's mobile mother, the strollers do allow the young baby to flop about, and the babies are facing the wrong way! A baby or toddler would be much more comfortable facing her mother, whom she knows and with whom she feels secure, rather than being exposed to the crowds, dogs, exhaust fumes, and sensory stimulation of our streets. (A few European and American strollers now have the option to face in either direction; they're worth searching for.)

Once your baby can sit up, you'll find she loves to play with small objects, which are important in the development of physical coordination and intelligence. Especially valuable are toys and small objects that can be banged, thrown or dropped. Think of things you already have that she will find fascinating. (Remember that everything ends up in the mouth, and small pieces that can break off are dangerous. Anything smaller than 1-1/2 inches in any dimension could get stuck in a baby's throat.) A wooden spoon, a beautiful shell, a cloth ball and a small dried gourd can be favorites. Your kitchen is full of wonderful "toys"—measuring spoons, pots and lids, nesting bowls. The rattle, of which the infant was unaware, and which the three-month-old would hold or drop indiscriminately, gradually becomes interesting for its texture and sounds. Several sources for natural toys are listed at the end of this chapter. While there is nothing wrong with chrome and plastic, it seems appropriate to honor the natural connection that young children have with the living world.

The playpen is another invention that doesn't take into account the real developmental needs of the child. Until the baby crawls, playpens are totally useless. A blanket on the floor serves just as well, and a basket for toys can be handy for picking things up when the baby takes a nap. Once the baby starts to crawl, playpens are a real barrier to development.

## When Your Baby Starts to Crawl

Development from a parent's point of view seems to go in phases where first everything is all right, then it's fairly difficult, then all is well again, and so on. Joseph Chilton Pearce, in *The Magical Child*, speaks about each developmental step being preceded by a return to the *matrix* (structure, safety, mother) and then followed by a voyage out into the world to find new experiences and new abilities.[4] This expansion and contraction is like breathing, and it is important for development that times of *regression* (inwardness, clinging behavior) be understood not as backsliding, but as preparation for the next surge forward toward independence.

This "regression" often happens just before a baby starts to crawl. You might find yourself carrying around this heavy child much of the time and wondering, "When will it ever change?" And then suddenly it does, and your baby is off, having mastered the first means of getting around on his own. Parenting changes at this time, because your baby is suddenly *into everything*. Planning ahead can save you a lot of grief and make this an exciting time in your lives.

Sometime before your baby starts to crawl, you will need to "babyproof" your home, making it safe *for* and *from* the baby. Starting with the kitchen, where your baby will probably spend the most time, make sure that all poisonous and dangerous items are out of reach and put simple toddler locks on cupboards that you don't want the baby to get into. You should also check for unstable objects, such as an ironing board or a potted plant. Breakable items should be put on high shelves or put away for the duration. Putting hooks on the bathroom door and on screen doors is a must. If you have older children, make sure they keep small items out of the baby's reach.

Stairs pose a special risk of falling, but babies love stairs. An invaluable suggestion from White is to place the child guard gate about three steps up instead of at the bottom of your staircase. This gives your baby a place to practice climbing without risk of getting hurt.

Making your home a safe place for the baby is one of the best things you can do to aid your child's development. The objects in your home provide wonderful stimulation for her, and you won't have to say no all the time. It is much better to let your baby roam than to keep her in a playpen, because babies need to crawl, need changing stimulation, and need to be around you. In his observations of families where children developed beautifully, White found that parents had made their homes safe and open to children rather than keeping them caged in playpens, where they rapidly become bored. He states, "It is my view that to bore a child on a daily basis by the regular use of a playpen for extended periods is a very poor childrearing practice. The same principle applies to the use of cribs, jump seats, high chairs and other restrictive devices" when they are used to limit a child's movement for long periods every day.[5]

## THE DEVELOPMENT OF INTELLIGENCE

Your baby is learning constantly through her physical activities. As movements become more coordinated and are repeated hundreds of times each day, your baby learns eye-hand coordination and how to grasp something she sees. According to both Piaget and Steiner, these things that seem like the foundation of physical development are also the foundation for later intellectual development.

Between the ages of six and eight months a baby's interests usually change from her own motor skills to the world around her. Interest in dropping, banging and throwing small objects starts to teach the baby about cause-and-effect and temporal sequence, important foundations for later thinking. For example, the seven-month-old will repeatedly drop a spoon or toy from the high chair and watch where it goes. Toys that involve doing one thing and causing another part to move are also favorites for a child of this age.

Understanding the gradual development of memory is also important when considering the growth of intelligence. When a young baby drops something, it is completely gone—there is no memory of it. Piaget and others created several experiments to determine when short-term memory develops in the child. In one such experiment, a toy was repeatedly hidden under a scarf in full view of a baby, on the baby's right side. The baby would easily remove the scarf and find the toy. Then the same toy was hidden under a scarf on the left side while the baby watched (the first scarf remained on the right side). Babies would typically reach for the object on the right, where they had previously found it, rather than on the left side, where they had just seen it placed. Piaget explains that at first the existence of a small object is tied to the activities that the child has been involved in with that object, rather than to concept of object permanence.[6] This supports Steiner's contention that the baby experiences the world primarily through movement and its body. Short-term memory gradually increases from seven or eight months of age, so that by the time a toddler is eighteen months old, a desirable object hidden in front of the child one day will immediately be found the next day.

Because babies live very much in the present moment without the same kind of memory as an adult, it is effective simply to remove an object (or remove the baby) when she has some precious object. This is better than saying no, which should be almost unnecessary if you have babyproofed your house.

It is pointless to address a baby's learning ability in an abstract fashion from birth until eight months of age, because all babies go through the normal pattern of development unless they are abused or otherwise disabled. Most parents' concerns are more with the physical care of their young baby, but today's emphasis on early learning takes it even into the crib, so that some parents are using flash cards with nine-month-olds! Directly cognitive activity is wasted on babies! Instead, play with your baby through movement and enjoy one another.

We've talked about your baby's desire to hold, study and taste the things she sees. Now she will also become interested in dropping and throwing objects. A baby sitting in her high chair and dropping her spoon for the tenth time is not doing it to annoy you. Rather, she is observing the wonderful phenomenon we call gravity, and playing with the idea of appearance and disappearance (which makes peek-a-boo such a favorite game). In this play we can see a metaphor for the coming in and out of existence or manifestation which the baby is exploring by its very being. There is as yet no memory to give an object permanence; mother disappears and reappears as suddenly as the baby itself appeared in the physical world.

Babies around six to eight months of age also love to bang things and explore sounds. Having a cupboard in the kitchen that is the baby's (and putting guard locks on the others) can be a real blessing. While you're busy, your baby can be occupied swinging the door, banging the pot with the wooden spoon, stacking the unbreakable bowls or rattling the taped container with rice inside.

At this stage it is impossible to separate physical development and the development of intelligence, but one is not predictive of the other. In other words, a child who crawls at six months and walks at eight is not more intelligent or highly developed than a child who crawls at ten months and walks at fourteen. What is important for the development of intelligence is that the motions are gone through; the internal timetable is usually just a question of individual differences within the wide range of normal. Researchers have been unable to find dramatic evidence of poor development in the first year with children who will do poorly later, probably because they have not yet developed the deficit.[7] In other words, most parents manage to provide all that is needed for their baby's development in the first year. So relax, enjoy and put your attention in the spheres that are more open to parental input during the first eight months.


## EMOTIONAL DEVELOPMENT

A baby's sense of well-being depends on having its needs met for love, warmth and food. Emotional development is based on the love, trust and touch found in the baby's first relationship within the family.

When you respond promptly to your baby's cries, she learns that the world is a friendly place to live in and that your love and protection surround her. Mothers who follow their instincts know this, and it's nice to find psychologists now stating that you can't spoil a young baby. Unfortunately, however, mothers are still likely to hear grandparents or perhaps even their husbands comment that they are spoiling the baby—or even that it's good for babies to cry. Surrounding your baby with love, warmth and touch provides a secure foundation for later life that is almost impossible to make up if it has been lacking.

Researchers have observed that babies usually cry only in response to discomfort until around four or five months of age. Then a new kind of intentional behavior can be seen for the first time: crying to bring an adult to pick up and cuddle them. In other words, she has learned, through successfully having her physical needs met, that she can also cry for attention. It is important that she have confidence that an adult, and a pleasant experience, will come when she calls. (Remember that babies in institutions learn that their cries won't bring a response, and so they do not exhibit this new way of getting the attention of adults.) Most professionals would rather see a baby between three and six months cry too much for attention than cry too little and risk inadequate attention during the first few months of life. Beginning to distinguish between the two types of cries is a valuable skill to start developing. Because babies have neither reason nor a sense of time, you can't tell the child to wait or to stop it. You probably will spend a great deal of your time carrying or holding your baby before he learns to crawl.

During the months before your baby learns to crawl (perhaps between six and eight months) your baby may become demanding in the sense that she can see everything, wants to experience it, but can't get to it. This driving force for crawling and walking is positive, but it can result in a baby who requires frequent changes of scenery, adult input or carrying to avoid boredom. White, in his quest to find what creates a pleasant, unspoiled three-year-old, as well as a bright one, has traced the origins of "spoiling" back to those parents who fall into a pattern of constantly responding to their six- or seven-month-old's cries for attention. "If you find that you are picking up your child and playing with her seven or eight times an hour for six or seven hours a day, you are probably moving into a pattern that will cause you some grief fairly soon," White states.[8] I found this statement interesting because White is a sensible observer, and he must have observed some sort of correlation, but I don't see how he could mean that you should ignore your baby's calls for attention (a nearly impossible task, anyway!). It seems that the potential problem must lie in developing the pattern of a whiny baby who is picked up six or eight times an hour. One of the ways to avoid the pattern is to involve your baby in your life. For example, mothers with one or two other young children don't have this problem as often—they haven't the time! Also, the siblings provide interaction for the baby, so attention needn't always come from the mother.

Another way to avoid the baby's learning to whine louder and louder to get mother's attention is to have other adults about. Our culture, with its lack of extended family, puts a real strain on the mother. A friend of mine who spent many years in Mexico wanted to practice "total mothering," by always carrying her baby in a *rebozo* or shawl as most of the Mexican village babies are carried. By the time her son was nine months old, she felt burned out and was beginning to resent never being able to put him down without his fussing. Then she realized she had made a mistake only a foreigner could make. Yes, the babies she had seen were almost always held, carried and receiving attention, but *not always by the mother*. Sometimes the aunt had him in the sling, sometimes a cousin or older sibling, other times it was grandma who was tending him while mother sewed or sorted beans nearby. How much you hold and carry your baby can have an effect on him, but it also needs to be balanced with your own needs and emotional well-being.

If it is possible to have the baby nearby while you do things, he or she may be more satisfied. Backpacks can be handy for letting your baby see what is happening while leaving your hands free, but getting down on the floor while your baby sits or lies on her stomach is also a good practice. You can knit or read and be nearby while your baby spends valuable time in the horizontal position, getting ready for crawling. While baby walkers provide a great deal of non-mother-directed time for the baby, they have definite drawbacks, as discussed previously.

## LANGUAGE DEVELOPMENT

Nothing can substitute for the love and attention you give your baby when you talk to her. She will turn toward the sound of your voice, and she is always interested in your face! By talking to your baby when you change her, for example, you are providing loving stimulation and a model for language development. At around four months your baby will turn and smile when you say her name. This is a stage called *pre-language comprehension*, because any name will work equally well—but it is an exciting time. By eight months she will probably be responding to a few specific words, which usually include some variation of *Mother*, *Daddy*, *baby* and *bye-bye* if English is your primary language in the home.

Babies prefer sounds that are high pitched, and respond especially well to the voice when it is rhythmical and melodic—hence the use of lullabies with babies throughout all cultures. But nursery rhymes and songs are also enjoyable to do with your baby when she is awake and alert. In *The Laughing Baby: Remembering Nursery Rhymes and Reasons*,[9] Anne Scott not only shares songs and rhymes from around the world, but combines the traditions of age-old cultures with current research regarding infant development, showing that such instinctive behavior has its justification in scientific fact. If you can't remember songs or rhymes from your own childhood, perhaps books such as this one can help us to regain the intuition that spawned these ancient pastimes.

Any time you hum or sing to your baby, you are doing her a wonderful service. Some parents worry that they "aren't musical," but everyone can hum, and songs can be extremely simple, involving only a few words and one or two notes. I spontaneously made up a little song for each of my children that became "their song." My son's went, "Sweet, sweet, sweet little baby-o. Sweet, sweet little baby-o. Sweet, sweet, sweet little baby-o. Sweet little baby-o." While no great work of composition, it had a wonderfully calming effect on him, and on me. I realized the extent to which I had fallen into singing it when he was fussy or things were stressful one time when I had left him home with his dad so I could get to a store before it closed. Traffic was awful, I couldn't find what I wanted, and I was becoming more frustrated and hurried as they announced the store's closing. I found myself singing "Sweet little baby-o" and was surprised to find that I didn't have the baby in my arms—I had started singing it for *myself,* as an automatic calming reaction I had built up for stressful situations!

A simple musical instrument called a children's harp is very soothing at nap or bed time and can help parents bring the musical element to their young children. The harp is tuned in a special way that is called *pentatonic,* so that anything you play sounds angelic—there are no wrong notes. Sources for the children's harp are listed at the end of this chapter.

Another area of language development is a baby's ability to make sounds. Often during the fourth month babies begin to play with sounds they can make, especially when they have saliva in their mouths. This enjoyment in playing with sounds continues throughout the following months, and it is delightful to stand out of sight and listen to your baby when she is talking to herself. Babies are equally fluent in all languages, having the ability to make all the sounds of which the human being is capable. Through model and imitation, your baby will begin to focus on those sounds that are part of the language that surrounds her.

## TOYS FOR THE FIRST YEAR

At the Center for Parent Education in Newton, Massachusetts, Burton White and Michael Meyerhoff have done extensive observations and reviews of toys on the market to see which ones children play with, whether they are developmentally appropriate, and whether they are labelled for the proper age group. They found that even products of good quality are often labelled for the wrong age child, and they warn parents about the hard sell and the oversell, which pressure you to believe that terribly expensive items are necessary. If you are going to buy toys from your local toy store, White and Meyerhoff's findings are invaluable.[10]

In this chapter I have already discussed some toys you can make or buy for the baby, including a mobile, crib gym, kick toy and rattle. Items from nature and from your kitchen are also favorites. Toys that show simple mechanisms through moveable parts are especially good for the child discovering cause and effect (around seven months). For example, toys that involve turning a crank to make a windmill go around or pulling a stick to make the woodsmen chop their wood are fun for children to manipulate. Similarly, anything with hinges is a welcome toy: boxes with hinged lids, cupboard doors or books with stiff pages (don't expect much interest in pictures or stories until after eighteen months).

Balls of all sizes and varieties are favorites of toddlers. Felted wool balls are ideal for inside play because of their softness. Ping pong balls can be chased all over the room and a large beach ball can be carried, chased, thrown and kicked.

Even very young children love water play, and objects for floating or pouring can also make bath time more enjoyable.

What your baby needs is a balance of playing with objects, exercising to practice physical skills and interacting with people. Interaction can come through the daily care you give your baby— through breastfeeding and later spoon feedings, changing and bathing. Just make sure that you are attentive and aware of your baby as a human being during these times, rather than treating her like an object or a chore that has to be accomplished. Talking and singing to your baby can lead into playing games as she becomes a little older. Babies love to play peek-a-boo after they are about six months old, delighting in the appearance and disappearance of themselves and the world. Simple movement games like pat-a-cake or so big also delight a one-year-old.

RECOMMENDED TOYS AND EQUIPMENT

- A rocking chair

- A children's harp

- An infant carseat (birth to nine months); a child carseat (nine months on)

- A cloth baby carrier for front-carrying babies (but remember about head support) and a back-pack for older babies

- A baby buggy and later a stroller for outdoor walks

- A stainless steel mirror (especially around four months of age)

- A crib gym (from six weeks until the baby is sitting)

- A kick toy for the crib

- A stair gate placed on the third stair to allow for safe climbing practice, or you can construct three steps and a platform

- A baby food grinder to fix foods from your table (no need to give solid food before six months—and *your* food is fresh and salt- and sugar-free, unlike processed baby foods)

- A large box or basket to keep toys in (when he's asleep and you want the house to look tidy)

- Several balls of various sizes, including a cloth or felt ball for the younger child; avoid foam balls, which can easily be pulled apart and eaten.

- Pots and pans (six to twelve months)

- Containers with lids; hinged boxes (seven to fifteen months)

- A box or basket with about a dozen safe objects (large wooden thread spools, a large shell, pieces of driftwood, a pretty rock)

- Books with stiff pages

- Low four-wheeled toys that can be straddled (seven to fifteen months)

- Water toys

## OF QUESTIONABLE VALUE

- **Pacifiers**   Perhaps nursing, or your finger, would work as well? Some babies do need to suck more than they need to eat, and a pacifier can be soothing during the first year of life, but its danger is that it replaces human interaction. Toddlers and older children who have a pacifier pinned to their clothing often have it stuck in their mouths just to keep them quiet.

- **Props for Bottles**   Propping a bottle means that your baby is losing the love and attention that accompanies breastfeeding or bottle feeding. Letting a baby fall asleep with a bottle in his mouth can result in serious tooth decay, because the juice or milk sits in the mouth and the sugars encourage bacterial growth and "bottle mouth syndrome."

- **Baby Bouncer** This gets the baby vertical before he can stand, and the force of jumping can have a negative impact on the leg bones.

- **Baby Walker** Although babies love the mobility, it makes them vertical before they can stand and takes time away from crawling; it is also implicated in many accidents in the home.

- **Playpen** This is not worth the expense for the rare moments you need your baby to be confined. Better to baby-proof your home!

- **Swimming Classes** Although these were formerly in vogue, many mothers reported negative experiences and no real gains.

- **Baby Gymnastics** Your baby knows best how to move to develop! Gymnastics can be all right as an excuse to meet other mothers if it's non-directed, but it tends to be too stimulating and can place your baby or toddler at risk.

SOME THINGS TO DO

- Value touching, carrying, skin-to-skin contact.

- Talk to your baby; focus on her as a person when you're caring for her.

- Hum and sing to your baby.

- Value contact with nature: your baby will love to see the interplay of light and shadow when under a tree; toddlers love sand and water play, indoors or out; avoid overexposure to bright sun.

- Nursery rhymes and movement games, including peek-a-boo, pat-a-cake, this little pig, hickory, dickory dock and where's baby?

Here are some other simple games you might find your child likes (make up actions to match the words):

*Clap your hands, 1, 2, 3.*
*Clap your hands, just like me.*
*Roll your hands, 1, 2, 3.*
*Roll your hands just like me.*

*Mix a pancake,*
*Stir a pancake,*
*Pop it in the pan;*
*Fry the pancake,*
*Toss the pancake,*
*Catch it if you can.*

## RECOMMENDED READING

*Catch Me & Kiss Me & Say It Again* by Clyde Watson. A lovely book with delightful rhymes to amuse young children and help harmonize activities of daily life.

*Fingerplays* from Mercury Press (IBP). An inexpensive little volume of childhood favorites.

*The Laughing Baby* by Anne Scott. Nursery rhymes from around the world.

*Your Child at Play: Birth to One Year* by Marilyn Segal. A practical book with numerous photos.

## SOURCES FOR TOYS

For valuable reviews of conventional toys on the market, see *The First Three Years of Life* by Burton L. White or inquire about the review of toys he has prepared for the Center for Parent Education, 55 Chapel Street, Newton, MA 02160.

*For toys for babies made from wood, wool, cotton and other natural materials, write:*

The Ark, 4245 Crestline Avenue, Fair Oaks, CA 95628.

Hearth Song, P.O. Box B, Sebastopol, CA 95473.

(See a complete list at the end of Chapter 7.)

## *For children's harps, write:*

Choroi, Karen Klaveness, 4600 Minnesota Ave., Fair Oaks, CA 95628.

Harps of Lorien, 610 North Star Route, Questa, NM 87556.

Hearth Song, P.O. Box B, Sebastopol, CA 95473.

Song of the Sea, 47 West Street, Bar Harbor, ME 04609.

# 5 | *Helping Your Toddler's Development*

## ENCOURAGING BALANCED DEVELOPMENT

Between the ages of one and two, your toddler is improving physical mastery of her body and also developing facility with language. With the development of language, you will start to see your child use ideas and images in her mind rather than physical actions to solve problems. This growth of thinking and memory interact with her behavior, so that a two-year-old is a highly complex social being. This aspect of development is marked by the emergence of individuality and personal power, the growing sense of "I."

The main tasks of parents as first teachers during the time from twelve to twenty-four months is to encourage a balanced development. Physical development involves practicing new motor skills; emotional development centers around her relationship with her mother, father or other primary caretakers; intellectual development comes primarily through exploring the world around her.

Your toddler's natural inquisitiveness is best met by letting it unfold naturally in a babyproofed home, free from restraints.

Much of her time will be spent exploring objects and mastering skills (such as taking things apart, stacking them up and knocking them down). Hinged doors, stairs, climbing up on a chair to look out the window are favorite activities. The toilet bowl is a favorite source of play, so be sure to keep the bathroom inaccessible. Outdoor play is encouraged since there are so many things to explore. Children in this age range love to swing and to play in the sandbox.

Because everything she explores still goes into her mouth and will be swallowed if possible, make sure that toxic items are stored out of reach in *locked* cupboards (toddlers love to climb). We wonder how children can swallow gasoline or cleaning fluid, but their curiosity is stronger than bad tastes or smells and children may swallow just about anything. Take time to recheck your home for safety when your child is between one and two years of age!

In terms of social development, a child in the second year will be focussed primarily on her parents, not going very long without checking back in with them for nurturing, advice, assistance or just making sure they are there. By being available when your child wants you and letting him explore without you, you are teaching your child both independence and security. And your encouragement and interaction when she brings you something to look at fosters her natural curiosity, showing that you value both inquisitiveness and learning.

Positive social interaction among two-year-olds is not very common—they usually lack the social skills to play together. The only advantage of a play group at this age is the social interaction it provides the mothers. The children, in fact, will need to be closely supervised to make sure they remain harmonious. Play will be more side-by-side than interactive.

In terms of interest in practicing motor skills, you will find your baby from the age of fourteen months able not only to walk, but also to climb. Running will also start to develop. Your eighteen-month-old will also probably like toys that she can straddle and "walk" along. The ability to operate a tricycle usually isn't present until after the age of two, and such toys are best delayed until the child is older.

The best way to keep a balance in these areas of exploration, movement and social interaction is to provide an environment where the child can explore by herself (with adult awareness of safety but not always with adult interaction). This will usually be your home, made safe and provided with a few simple toys in addition to common household items.

## "Aids to Learning"

Because of the natural impulse to want to provide the best opportunities for their children, many parents are turning to classes to help their eighteen-month-old learn to swim, read, become a gymnast or whatever. Programs to teach infants to swim were very popular several years ago and have since drawn a great deal of criticism. Most mothers' experiences were that early gains were lost, and their children's experiences were often heart-wrenching. Trust yourself, and don't do anything you don't feel good about. Putting your child into a frightening situation is not worthwhile. *No* classes are necessary for optimal or even enhanced development. If you do go to any kind of group, make sure that you stay with your child, that the activity is appropriate for his age, and that the environment is not overwhelming on a sensory level. As mentioned before, a baby gymnastics class can be fun as a social experience for mothers with cabin fever, but such classes can push children beyond their developmental stage. The toddler knows best which muscles to exercise to develop optimally. An excellent summary of reasons parents want their children to be in classes and why it is better to avoid them is contained in *Miseducation: Preschoolers at Risk* by David Elkind.[1] Even a play group is probably not very appropriate for a child of this age, but a mother's support group, in which one or two mothers take turns watching the children while the others meet together to talk can be a tremendous support. (They can also meet at night while dad watches the children!)

Similarly, any kind of emphasis on intellectual development that takes time away from physical movement can lead to imbalance. There's a saying, "Don't push the river." Your baby is developing according to his or her own inner clock. Tampering with the mechanism by trying to speed up one area can lead to problems in other areas.

Parents wonder if their child will be missing out if she doesn't watch "Sesame Street" or other programs designed to promote early language skills. However, children learn how to use "before" and "after" in their speech perfectly well from hearing you speak—they don't need Grover to give a lesson on it! Burton White corroborates this by saying, "Rest assured that if he never sees a single television program he can still learn language through *you* in an absolutely magnificent manner."[2] Before the age of two, children who are exposed to television don't really watch the screen for more than a few seconds at a time. The medium is totally inappropriate for the toddler, who needs to be moving and actively exploring. Fortunately young children are unable to sit and watch the screen; if they do so with older siblings, it is more in an imitative and social way than through paying attention to what is on. Keeping the television off prevents noise and extraneous visual stimulation, especially when there is no one there to comprehend the meaning of the images.

As your child's first teacher, you have primary responsibility for him in the first years of life. One of the most important things you can do is to pay attention to all that surrounds your child. This includes the food, clothing, images, toys, sunshine, sand and water. It also includes the less tangible "nourishment" that comes from your warmth and love and the emotions that surround your child. To help your toddler develop, work on yourself, which means cultivating patience and firmness and getting rid of blame and guilt when you are not the ideal parent. No one is, but it is the striving and the effort to grow inwardly that speaks most strongly to children, who are so involved with physical and emotional growth. Our children come to see our faults and forgive us; our orientation toward inner growth through parenting fosters change within ourselves and is a great gift to our children.

Understanding your child's development, you will be less likely to do things that impede it (such as boring him by restraining him in a carseat, playpen or high chair for hours every day). You will also avoid unrealistic expectations of your child, such as expecting her to remember that certain things aren't allowed or trying to reason with her. Remember the principles of imitation and movement in correcting her actions! This will make you better able to provide the correction and guidance that are needed, and to avoid the emotional annoyance that can lead to telling your child she is "bad" for exploring things you want her to stay out of.

## DEALING WITH NEGATIVE BEHAVIOR

One of the challenges of living with the child from eighteen to thirty-six months is dealing with the "negativism" which he manifests. If you can recognize your child's emerging sense of self and power as something positive, you won't fall into the trap of thinking that you have done something wrong ("If only we hadn't moved . . ." or "He must be selfish because I have a short temper"). You can take the adult and parental viewpoint of enjoying your child's development *while providing the guidance he needs.*

Most first children are over-indulged, whether from love, insecurity or mistaken ideals. With a second or third child, there just isn't the time to indulge her every whim, and life has to become more rhythmical and orderly or mother won't survive. With my first child, I fell into the philosophical pit of not wanting to be authoritarian, and chaos reigned until I realized that I could (and should) insist on right behavior. This needs to be done with calmness rather than anger, but with absolute certainty that the child can and will learn what is expected. It is appropriate that parents be guardians and guides (less charged words than *authorities*) and help children in the process of becoming pleasant as well as bright three-year-olds! Your children unconsciously trust you to know more about becoming adults than they do. Because their ego is not yet fully incarnated, you must provide the ego for them (that is, the source of wisdom and responsibility that holds them and keeps them from getting "out of themselves"), just as an effective teacher does this for an entire class in school.

In observing families where parents had already produced "outstanding children," White found that *"the effective parents we have studied have always been loving but firm with their children from early infancy on.* The principal problem that average families run into in this area is allowing the child to infringe on their own rights too much."[3] This means, for example, that you set up your house so that the child has maximum freedom and requires a minimum of no's and then you are firm about what is not allowed. It is wonderful for your child to be curious, but he doesn't have to play in your makeup, which can be met with a stern no, removing the child from the scene, and then putting the makeup in a less accessible place. There is no need to punish the child, because a toddler is unable to understand what he has done or to remember the next time.

Preventing your child from running your home becomes more of an issue when he starts to assert himself by saying no to you. Sometimes you can get around the almost reflexive negativism of a two-year-old by starting to do the very thing that just evoked a verbal no. Because children are so imitative, their bodies often can't resist moving with you. Young children tend to be very verbal, and parents often fall into the trap of relating to them on a rational level. Asking your two-year-old, "Do you want to . . ." invites a negative answer from a child of this age. Instead, positive and neutral statements such as, "It's time to brush teeth for bed" can be very effective when combined with the absolute certainty that there is no other choice and it is impossible to argue with time. Adding a bit of fantasy, movement or song while going upstairs can also engage the child and circumvent negativity.

Keeping things the same as much as possible can also avoid problems with this child. Many two-year-olds hate change and fall apart during transitions between activities. Everything has to be a certain way or pandemonium breaks loose. This doesn't mean you need to give in each time or put up with whiny behavior, but understanding this child's attachment to order can help you avoid problems. It is a phase that will ease off in intensity as your child matures. You'll no doubt find he's not attached to order as an adolescent!

One mother I know lights a candle while she sings a song, and then lets the child blow out the match, which is an exciting incentive to get the child to go into the bedroom. Then they go into the bathroom to put on pajamas and brush teeth. The mother has turned off the bedroom light, so when they return, they have to tiptoe and be very quiet as they enter the softly lighted room and lie down together for songs and playing the children's harp.

However, sometimes your child will just be negative, and she may astonish you with the force of her refusal. When this happens, you can still physically move the child to the required place, leaving her there a few moments, or sitting and holding her if that seems appropriate. You may wonder if there is anything going on—is she overtired, possibly coming down with a cold—or there may be no apparent explanation. Sometimes one or two minutes of your leaving the room will calm a child right down (what's the point when no one's watching?); other times singing a song or starting a favorite fingerplay can bring the child into a better mood. Regardless of what works, you then need to lovingly and firmly follow through by insisting on the action that caused the problem. What *doesn't* work is becoming angry, hitting or belittling the child, or giving in and letting her have her way.

One of the most effective ways of handling negative behavior is removing the child from the area of activity. With a young child, this requires going with her and staying with her until she is ready to return. For example, fussiness and throwing food at dinner can be quickly handled by taking her down the hall, telling her that when she is a happy clown the two of you can go back and standing there like a stone until she comes around. It usually takes about one to three minutes, because it's very boring being out of the action with a deadpan mother or father who won't interact until you're ready to do what is expected. This is infinitely more effective than the usual scenario of ignoring the child (trying to talk around her), objecting, threatening and finally losing one's temper, which results in tears and a big scene. If it is absolutely clear that inappropriate behavior can't be present at mealtime, the learning curve is very short.

If temper tantrums occur, removing the child is probably the best technique. Parents are always physically stronger than a child under two, and the child first trying a tantrum is almost always asking for limits to be set. Calmly but firmly carry the child out with the absolute conviction that such behavior is not allowed. Tell the child simply that he must stop screaming, banging his head or whatever he was doing. After the child has settled down (five to ten minutes?), then bring him back to the situation. If the tantrum recurs, you need to repeat the procedure. Perseverance furthers! Don't hold it against the child, feeling that he ought to be better or is just doing it to annoy you; but don't ignore it or give in either. You are the adult, and you can insist on right behavior while keeping your own temper.

Knowing that you can correct behavior helps you to maintain your patience and keeps you from allowing a child to walk all over you and then resenting it. Correction always occurs in the present moment, where the child lives. You can't expect your two-year-old to "remember" not to do that again, which is why punishment will not work. If you have an especially willful child, you may need to set the limits again and again during this period, but persistence pays off. Setting firm and consistent limits throughout the second year will usually prevent temper tantrums after the child turns two. Temper tantrums and the Terrible Twos are common, but not inevitable. In *The First Three Years of Life*, White encourages parents to teach the child that he is terribly important, that his needs and interests are special, *but that he is no more important than any other person in the world, especially his parents*.[4] If a child moves into the third year without it having been made clear who runs the home and whether you really mean it when you forbid something, you are in for trouble. More detailed discussion of discipline and the importance of rhythm in home life can be found in Chapter 11.

## ENCOURAGING THE DEVELOPMENT OF LANGUAGE AND UNDERSTANDING

Because we cannot really be certain what the child experiences when she contemplates an object, it is best to leave the toddler in peace until there is a natural break in her activities, or she comes to you with something. Because of our lack of awareness, and our desire to take advantage of teaching situations, we are constantly interrupting children to tell them the names of things when they are happily engrossed in an object. Instead, we should observe them and let them explore the world. Daniel Udo de Haes, in *The Young Child*,[5] makes the valuable suggestion that you do your teaching when you *give* the child an object, not when he or she is playing with it. For example, you might say, "Water . . . water," when you give your daughter a bowl full of water and some measuring cups to play with, perhaps even picking up some of the water in your hand while you say the words. Then let her play by herself. Similarly, if she has discovered something fascinating in the yard, don't rush over to teach her about it. Wait until she wants you and then be there to comment on what she has found ("Bug. What a big bug!").

If we are conscious of the "silent language" of objects, then we can let our human language interact with it harmoniously. For example, after the child hears the wind rustling in the trees we might say *rustling*, letting the child hear in these sounds something of what the rustling tree has first spoken to him. In this way it is possible for the child to experience through our words an inner connection between the language of things and the human language.[6]

With the toddler it is best not to speak *about* things, but to let the things speak for themselves whenever possible. In other words, there is nothing harmful, and even something beneficial, in letting the doll say, "Good morning!" to the child or in personifying or animating objects and letting them speak for themselves. For the young child, all the world *is* alive, everything *does* speak; the time to be able to distinguish reality from imagination lies in the future and will come naturally. As adults we tend to offer far too many intellectual explanations to our young children, having forgotten how to experience the world in movement and in pictures. If the personification of objects is done in a natural and responsible manner, it can strengthen an inward listening in the child.[7]

Around the second half of the second year, your child will become more interested in the pictures in books, than with turning the pages. Several sources of good books for young children are listed at the end of Chapter 7. There is a value in bringing before the young child a picture of what he has experienced in nature. Just as an artist can help us to see something, so a picture book can help the child to recognize that others share his visions and experiences. With this in mind, pictures of everyday objects, far from being trivial, have great value in bringing before the child the most fundamental aspects of life on earth, and have the recognition value of mirroring the child's own experience. In this sense, a picture of baby's cup might be more valuable than an elephant, which the child won't yet have experienced! Thus pictures of the simplest objects, with no story thread, are best for the child before the age of three.

Because the child is trying to experience the world and gain a picture of life as it is, it is helpful to put before her appropriate and true pictures of life, rather than caricatures of a rabbit wearing clothes or cartoon depictions of characters. The young child does not have the sophistication to laugh at cartoon renditions of absurd events, which imply that the observer, like the artist, is placing himself over and against it in judgment and laughter. A picture book has value for the toddler when he finds in it a portrayal, created by adults with dedication and respect, of everything that has resonated in his inner being.[8]

Very few good books for toddlers exist, but if we understand the value of sharing the same book over and over (even several times in the same day), then very few are needed! It is beneficial to read only one book at a sitting because each book has its own atmosphere, and mixing them can clutter the child's soul, especially at bedtime. Similarly, too many pictures give the child no time to digest them, and destroy the quiet intimacy that belongs with each picture. Children may bring another book and always want more, but being clear that one story is enough will not only help your child to live fully with those images, but will help convey the value of the individual experience in contrast to always having more of something.

It is also very valuable for your child if you draw your own picture book for her, preferably with her watching. Most adults think they can't draw, usually as a result of their own experiences in childhood. But the child is not concerned with our artistic ability. Rather, the magical quality appears when our attempts, which she invests with her own imagination, call forth her own inner recognition-experiences. By so doing, we show the child that her quest for the earthly world is understood.[9]

Another source of books for toddlers is to use a story book whose pictures meet this criteria, but omit the story content. Simply comment in simple language something like, "There is Mother

Hen with all of her little chicks. Peep. Peep. Peep." Then when we turn the page (or the child does) we can let him look at the picture for a while before adding our simple words. At first the child may turn pages at random. Later he will want you to read or tell the story with the same words each time, and will be nourished by their familiarity. As the years go by, stories can gradually be made more complicated, or you can begin conversations about a story, so that a good picture book can last from toddlerhood throughout the preschool years.

## THE BEGINNINGS OF IMAGINATIVE PLAY

A young child's earliest play involves movement for the pure joy of it. Running, jumping, whirling and standing on tiptoe are enjoyable in themselves. The imaginative element will start to enter in when your son or daughter hops like a bunny or rides a stick horse. In the second year you may have glimpses of imaginative play as your child begins to pretend she is eating or drinking or talking on the phone. Through imagination, the child is able to unite herself with the world at the same time that memory and thinking are separating her from it. Fantasy and play are like complementary opposites to memory and thinking. The creative power of imaginative play continues to develop throughout early childhood, blossoming between ages three and six.

For the young toddler, pretending first begins as imitation and is carried out as actions rather than words, like pretending to drink something from a real or imaginary cup. As children approach the age of two, their growing facility with language enables their pretending to be more conversational and interactive. Simple toys further your child's imagination. For example, having a toy plate leads to talking about what is on it. This soon develops into preparing food, which can be easily done as a chair is turned into a stovetop with an oven underneath.

A toy telephone also leads to conversational play, but your hand can do just as well. Many times, messages delivered this way can make the next set of activities into a game:

*Mother* (with hand to ear): Ring. Ring. Heather, your phone is ringing.

*Heather:* Hello.

*Mother:* This is Mommy. I need to buy some eggs. Get your shoes on and you can come to the store with me.

*Heather:* Okay!

*Mother:* Bye.

A bit of fantasy goes a long way in circumventing your child's negative reactions. For example, holding a washcloth like a puppet who talks to the child may soon convince him to rub noses with this talking wash cloth. Or suggesting that all the little mice pick up the crumbs (scraps of paper) will immediately result in a "little mouse" helping you to clean up the mess.

## PROVIDING A RICH ENVIRONMENT FOR YOUR TODDLER

You don't have to spend a lot of money on fancy toys to provide a rich environment for your toddler. Making accessible the items in your home, plus a few free or inexpensive items, such as a beach ball and a cardboard box, will provide your child with hours of valuable exploration. Your toddler will want to touch and explore everything in your home, seeing what it feels like, if she can carry, empty or fill it and whether it comes apart. The toddler age requires constant supervision, because your daughter can hurt herself or other things the minute you turn your back. It's a time when you'll need to start teaching discrimination: it's all right to play with her toy telephone, but not the real one; she can play with the large necklace in her drawer, but not go into your jewelry box. It's understandable that it takes time for toddlers to learn the difference!

One valuable suggestion is to provide lots of things that your child can touch and explore—for example a cupboard in the kitchen with a pot, wooden spoon, flour sifter, and metal coffee percolator; a drawer in the family room that is hers—filled with old envelopes, a magazine and other things which you change periodically as the child loses interest in them. Remembering how much your child likes to imitate, you will find that adult objects are probably more fascinating than many toys designed for children. By providing alternatives to the items you wish to protect, you can give your child areas where he can explore without having to be told no all the time.

One valuable thing you will be teaching your child during this time is how to touch and how to care for things. Because your child is such an imitator, always demonstrate the behavior you want and make positive statements such as, "Touch the kitty gently," rather than "Don't hurt the kitty." Or "Here, sniff the pretty flower," rather than "Don't crush the flower!" You will also need to start teaching the lessons of "Sharp!" and "Hot!" by modelling the behavior of taking your hand or your child's away from the object in question.

Toddlers are delightful if you can view their being into everything as their way of exploring the world, of experiencing new sights and touch, of emptying, filling, exploring gravity, using their muscles. They have no sense of adult order or goal-directed behavior. If you want Joey to clean up, start putting the toys in the basket with him. He's glad to help, but he's equally glad to dump them all out again if you walk away from him. When you find yourself being annoyed, take a minute to enter into a toddler's world, and you will realize that he isn't doing it to annoy you. Quite the contrary, he's probably doing it out of pure "doingness" and is quite oblivious to you. You *can* (and must) correct and teach him what is and is not acceptable, but you needn't be annoyed when you do it. If you want to get your toddler to do a specific action, the key is to model the behavior you want, while he or she watches and/or does it with you.

Even though it is necessary to know where toddlers are at all times, it's good to provide them with time and space to explore the world while you appear not to be looking. Independence is fostered by not always interrupting them, but being accessible when they come to you for assistance or to share a discovery.

Besides loving to explore, your toddler loves simply to move for the joy of movement. She will delight in running, jumping, climbing, pushing, carrying. All of these activities help in the development of the large muscles and express the young child's nature: to be in movement. Aside from deciding which furniture it's all right to climb on and jump off, you can provide your child with a low balance beam made from placing a wide board over a couple of low concrete blocks. If the bridge you have made is too challenging for your one-year-old, place it next to a wall; raise it as she becomes more skillful.

Toys that help with the development of large muscles include the very popular indoor wooden slide and ladder with crawling space underneath. Four-wheeled straddle toys that are low to the ground are also favorites of toddlers. A push cart or doll carriage is also a good toy. Make sure it is sturdy enough to take the child's weight.

Toddlers love to be outside, and a sandbox (covered to keep cats away) and wading pool provide long periods of enjoyment. Again, make sure that you have inspected your yard and have a locked gate or other means to keep the child away from the street. Most children love to swing, so a sturdy swing is good from age one on. Toys for sand and water play are also valuable inside when the weather is bad.

Many of the toys listed in the preceding chapter will still interest a toddler. As a guide for buying toys, always take into consideration safety and durability—a toddler will still pull things apart and put them in her mouth. As she becomes more adroit at manipulating objects, stacking boxes or nesting dolls are very popular (Hearth Song has had a set of Russian nesting dolls at a reasonable price). Wooden toys with moving parts are especially recommended for young children by Rudolf Steiner, who stated, "What a healthy toy it is, for example, which represents, by moveable wooden figures, two smiths facing each other and hammering on an anvil. Such things can still be bought in country districts. Excellent also are the picture-books where the figures can be set in motion by pulling threads from below, so that the child himself can transform the dead picture into a representation of living action."[10] The ability to have an effect on something and to tranform it through movement suits the young child's nature.

Your child will love to stack things, so we suggest making a set of blocks by cutting the trunk and large branches of a tree into blocks of various sizes and shapes. (See photo with Chapter 7.) Unlike the geometrically perfect blocks you buy in stores, these irregularly shaped blocks will be used throughout the preschool years for much more than stacking. Their unfinished quality lets the child use his imagination with them; they can easily become people, cans of cat food or baby bottles; flat pieces from a trunk can be used as plates or cakes. Your child's imagination will be endless. But your toddler will be most interested in stacking them up and knocking them down.

When purchasing toys, consider not only their safety, but also their aesthetic qualities. Are they beautiful? How do they feel to the touch? What kind of picture of the world do they put before the child? Darth Vader figures or chartreuse ponies with platinum hair are caricatures of reality that simply are not beautiful or true representations of the human being or the world. Everything the young child takes in makes a profound impression on him. The effect of toys and the power of imitation was strikingly illustrated by a photo which appeared in *American Baby* a number of years back. This prize-winning photo showed a six-month-old baby next to a Cabbage Patch doll; the baby was copying *exactly* the inane expression on the doll's face. Such imitation is completely unconscious and would have been missed if the photographer hadn't been there. Such a photo captures in black and white how deeply sense impressions penetrate the child and are manifested through the physical organs.

In another remarkable case described by Professor of Child Therapy Alfred Nitschke, a ten-month-old baby girl was admitted to the hospital with extreme lethargy. She was unable to sit up, being doubled over in a jack-knife position; she had a listless expression and a blank gaze. No one had been able to diagnose the problem. Finally one doctor was inspired to notice that the child looked exactly like her constant companion, a floppy stuffed rabbit that was long-limbed and droopy with large, fixed eyes. The doctor brought a new toy which was friendly looking and had a well-defined shape. The child soon became attached to the new toy, and within a few days had begun to improve in her posture, appetite and mood without any other treatment![11] In contemplating stuffed toys or dolls for your children, you might remember these examples.

Especially for the young child, the simpler and more archetypal a thing is, the more possibilities it holds for the child. Steiner states:

> As the muscles of the hand grow firm and strong in performing the work for which they are fitted, so the brain and other organs of the physical body of man are guided into the right lines of development if they receive the right impressions from their environment. An example will best illustrate this point.
>
> You can make a doll for a child by folding up an old napkin, making two corners into legs, the other two corners into arms, a knot for the head, and painting eyes, nose and mouth with blots of ink. Or else you can buy the child what they call a "pretty" doll, with real hair and painted cheeks . . . . If the child has before him the folded napkin, he has to fill in from his own imagination all that is needed to make it real and human. This work of the imagination moulds and builds the forms of the brain. The brain unfolds as the muscles of the hand unfold, when they do the work for which they are fitted. Give the child the so-called pretty doll, and the brain has nothing to do.[12]

Because the young child is not fully conscious of its own body, what it is most aware of in itself and others is the head. Thus a knot doll with a large head is quite recognizable and satisfactory for the young child. For a very young child, you can change the basic doll into a "baby" by stuffing the bottom like a blanket or pillow instead of making a body and legs from the two bottom corners.[13]

## TOYS AND EQUIPMENT

Check the list at the end of the last chapter. Many of the toys will still be enjoyed by your toddler.

- Low four-wheeled toy that can be straddled

- Push cart or doll carriage (sturdy enough to lean on)

- Wooden slide and climbing toy

- Wooden blocks cut from various diameters of a tree

- Wading pool, low container for water play outdoors, water and bath toys

- Sandbox and sand toys

- Outdoor swing

- Toy telephone

- *Simple* first doll of natural materials

- Balls of various sizes, especially an inflatable beach ball

- Wooden toys that have moving parts (pecking chickens, two men with hammers)

- Wooden nesting dolls

- Simple picture books with stiff pages

- Books with parts that move

- Large empty cardboard boxes to play in

- Crayons (age two on); especially good are block crayons, as described in Chapter 9

SOME THINGS TO DO

- Let your toddler start "helping" with things you do (loading the dishwasher, stirring the cake, putting things in the trash, sweeping, folding clothes, watering the plants); it will take you longer, but it is true quality time.

- Help your child experience nature through walks, parks, feeding the ducks.

- Set up a "nature table" at home with things you find on your walks (a pretty shell, a plant). Change the colors of the cloth and the themes to match the seasons.

- Your toddler loves to be lifted up to the ceiling or be like an airplane on your extended legs while you lie on your back; a friend said she liked the ocean so much because it was the only thing big enough to toss her around the way her father did when she was little.

- Simple hiding games are fun: you and your child can take turns hiding under a blanket (we always played "lump in the bed" while trying to make it); hiding objects in your pocket is also fun for toddlers, who love to find them. Chase, catch and hug is a favorite game, too.

• Use a song or bit of fantasy for daily activities like brushing teeth or getting dressed. Several excellent verses can be found in *Catch Me & Kiss Me & Say It Again*.[14] I made up a little tune for when I wanted my daughter to lie down in the bathtub and get her hair wet: "Mermaid, mermaid, swimming in the water. Mermaid, mermaid, see my little mermaid."

• Continue singing to your child!

• Here are some action rhymes you and your child can do together:

*Teddy Bear, Teddy Bear, turn around,*
*Teddy Bear, Teddy Bear, touch the ground.*
*Teddy Bear, Teddy Bear, touch your shoe,*
*Teddy Bear, Teddy Bear, that will do.*
*Teddy Bear, Teddy Bear, go upstairs,*
*Teddy Bear, Teddy Bear, say your prayers.*
*Teddy Bear, Teddy Bear, switch off the light,*
*Teddy Bear, Teddy Bear, say good night.*

*I'm a little tea pot, short and stout,*
*Here is my handle* (hand on hip)
*Here is my spout* (arm bent like spout)
*When I get all steamed up, then I shout,*
*Tip me over, pour me out!* (bend sideways at waist)

(Child sits facing you on your foot with your legs crossed and rides the horse)
*Ride a cock horse to Banbury Cross*
*To see a fine lady on a white horse.*
*With rings on her fingers and bells on her toes*
*She shall have music wherever she goes.*

# RECOMMENDED READING

## Playing with Toddlers

- *Catch Me & Kiss Me & Say It Again* by Clyde Watson. Delightful rhymes and verses.

- *Children at Play: Preparation for Life* by Heidi Britz-Crecelius (IBP, SG). Will help you understand how the child experiences the world through play. Draws from Steiner's insights.

- *Fingerplays* by Mercury Press (IBP). A delight for children and adults alike.

- *The Laughing Baby* by Anne Scott. Nursery rhymes and songs for children.

- *Making Soft Toys* by Freya Jaffke (IBP, SG). Directions for making knot dolls and other toys for young children.

- *The Young Child: Creative Living with Two to Four Year Olds* by Daniel Udo de Haes (AP, IBP). Provides many insights into the world of the young child, with numerous suggestions on things to do; Steiner-oriented.

- *Your Child at Play: One to Two Years* by Marilyn Segel and Don Adcock. A practical book with many photos.

## Sources for Creative Toys

- See the list at the end of Chapter 7.

# 6 | *Parenting Issues of the First Three Years*

## WHY DOES PARENTING TAKE SO MUCH ENERGY?

It takes a tremendous amount of energy to mother a baby or young child. Even preschool and kindergarten teachers find that they must get enough sleep to replenish the kind of energy young children seem to demand. Your best intentions about parenting will be ineffectual when you are too tired or irritable. The first thing to do to assure a happy and healthy baby is for the mother to be happy and healthy. This means to be sure you are eating well and taking vitamin supplements for at least as long as you are breastfeeding. Interrupted sleep, especially in the first few months, can compound fatigue and the adjustment to new parenting. Babies are nourished by your love and care just as they are nourished by physical food. The reason that parenting young children takes so much energy is that the life forces of the mother and baby are interconnected throughout the first three years. Young children are surrounded by and consume what Steiner calls *etheric* or *life energy* from their parents, caregivers and teachers. (We might call it vitality or life force.) Mothering is deceptive, because sometimes it seems as if you're accomplishing so little—why should you be so tired? However, caring for young children draws on your vital energy, and you need to replenish your *own* vital forces in order to continue to feel good in your mothering.

Three things that can really help to replenish this energy are: sleep, artistic activity and meditation. Try to make sure that you get enough sleep—schedule a nap when the baby naps. Maintain a quiet time every afternoon for your child when he or she stops napping—as much for yourself as for the child. I know that, when I taught preschool, being in bed by ten was an essential part of my preparation. Otherwise I couldn't stand the noise and couldn't keep my emotions on an even keel.

Artistic activity involves the same vital or creative forces that your baby is using, but it replenishes rather than depletes them. Playing a musical instrument, drawing, sculpting, painting, all can help mothers to have more energy. Writing down your thoughts, experiences and insights can also be helpful. The regularity of doing something like taking a walk each day can also be of great help in keeping you balanced and replenishing your energy. Contact with nature can help us feel refreshed.

Meditation can be as simple as setting aside five minutes before you go to bed to center yourself in your breathing or concentrate on a single thought. Returning to your own center not only helps to replenish your energy but can also help you maintain equanimity in the midst of all the stresses of parenting. If you don't have any regular practices, Rudolf Steiner suggested many simple but powerful exercises in his book *Knowledge of Higher Worlds*.[1]

In addition to setting aside time for meditation, set aside time for yourself alone, out of the house when needed. Even an hour or two can help you in your mothering. Most women in nuclear families live isolated from other adults. You can really get cabin fever with only a toddler to talk to day after day!

The father can play a very important role in helping the mother to maintain her vitality. With a child under the age of three, this involves actively supporting her mothering emotionally and financially so that she is encouraged and strengthened in being with the children. I hate to risk sounding traditional by speaking of men as "providers and protectors," but there is some validity to that image when both partners are applying it with consciousness. This does not preclude men's developing their own nurturing side so they can assume co-responsibility for the children, rather than depending on the mother to rise to the occasion (a crying baby, a diaper that needs changing, a squabble between siblings). Single parenting, with or without a husband in the home, is not an easy task.


## THE IMPORTANCE OF RHYTHM

Most of us were brought up on a bottle every four hours (and not a half-hour sooner), no matter how hard we protested. In reaction to this sacrifice of the individual to the clock or the book, many women breastfeeding today nurse their babies whenever they are hungry or fussy. Demand feeding takes as its model primitive cultures where the baby is carried in a sling next to the mother's body and can nurse any time it wants, which usually involves nursing frequently for short periods. Many mothers who take their babies to bed with them find this same pattern of frequent nursing continuing throughout the night as well.

Most everyone today agrees that a young baby's needs should be met as they arise, and mothers feel confident in trusting their instincts to respond with love and the breast to their babies. But when does this change? At six weeks, six months, two years, or later?

I would like to propose an alternative to the polarity of feeding on demand versus feeding according to a schedule: working toward establishing rhythm, which will change as the baby grows. This idea of rhythm fits in very well with Thoman's metaphor of parenting as dancing in her book *Born Dancing*.[2]

One of the tasks of the growing child and one of the functions of parenting is to bring the child into rhythm. Consider how arhythmical a newborn's breathing is. Sometimes she takes short gasps, other times she holds her breath—it's quite startling if you really listen to your newborn breathe. Babies' heart rates are also much faster than adults'. As the child matures, the breathing and the heart rate gradually become coordinated and then assume the adult ratio of one breath for each four beats of the heart.

Part of what makes the first six weeks of caring for a new baby so hard is that the baby seems to have no pattern to its eating and sleeping—at least nothing you can depend on. Rhythm gradually does emerge from the chaos, and life becomes easier as rhythm provides a framework that can support you in your other activities. This lack of framework can be very disorienting, as when a person retires or a career woman quits work when pregnant and finds she can barely get out of bed in the morning because life has become so unstructured. However, even when rhythm emerges, it will be different for a breastfed baby than for a bottle-fed baby, because of the difference in the type of protein and the amount of liquid the baby takes in at any given feeding.

Working toward rhythm does *not* mean slavishly "going by the clock" or letting your baby "cry it out." It does mean being aware of rhythms as they emerge and change, honoring and encouraging them. This is especially valuable in dealing with naps and sleep and avoiding sleep problems. At first your baby requires sustenance during the night; it's a physiological fact. But after the baby's stomach and digestive system can get enough nourishment to last for an extended period, waking and feeding is for other purposes: simply from habit, to be comforted by your presence, or to play.

If you were to get up, turn on the lights, feed and talk to your baby, he or she might start wanting to be awake and playing at that time every night. Some babies can even get day and night reversed, sleeping most of the day and wanting to be active at night. Nursing mothers are usually able to avoid these pitfalls by somnolently tucking the baby into bed with them and barely waking up while nursing.

You need to decide your style of mothering and what is right for you and your family. As long as you are happy nursing your baby at night, there is no need to change. But when you grow tired of being awakened at night—and your older baby could be sleeping longer—it is possible to change his habit pattern. You need to gather your intention to stop nursing the baby when he awakes at night. When he cries, you go in and say, "I love you, but this is time to sleep." You might hold and rock him, or just pat his back and then go out. It may wrench your insides to hear him cry, but you go back in after three or five minutes and pat him, saying, "I'm sorry you're upset, but it is time to sleep," keeping your voice and actions very drowsy. You go out for a longer time and repeat as necessary. The child soon learns that food will not be forthcoming, but also doesn't feel abandoned, because of your love and concern. With no possibility of food or play, he will soon start sleeping longer without waking up. My own experience is that it generally takes three days or nights to change a pattern, but it can also take a week or longer.

There are so many schools of thought on what babies need and how to parent. I encourage you to trust your own heart and to be as aware as possible of your baby's needs and of what you are really feeling. If you're content nursing your baby all night, it's wonderful. But if you feel as though you'd appreciate uninterrupted sleep at night, and are starting to resent the cry in the night or the constant nuzzling against your body, you should realize that it's all right and easy to change your child's behavior if it's done with love and awareness. Bringing the child into rhythm when the time is right is part of life in all cultures. Only you can decide when that time is for your baby, for you and your family.

## WHERE SHOULD BABIES SLEEP?

I hope you have realized by now that I don't put much store in "shoulds." In previous times and in other cultures, the questions that are issues for us wouldn't have been raised. Whether the entire family slept in one room or the baby was off in the nursery with a nanny would have been a given by the culture in which you lived, and you would have felt fine about it. But we live in a time in which the customs and dictates of our culture no longer hold in the same way. We have gone past the stage where our minds can accept the givens of our culture without questioning them. We have to bring issues of childbirth or parenting into consciousness so we can reintegrate our minds, feelings and actions. Steiner describes this time in history as being the time of the "consciousness soul," a time when we must integrate our consciousness and our actions through the mediation of the heart. We are products of and contributors to our time, just as all people in history have been.

In *The Family Bed*,[3] Tine Thevinin develops arguments for children of all ages sleeping with their parents. The closeness, warmth and comfort are so wonderful that most adults don't want to sleep alone, so why should a child? In the early months the closeness of the mother and baby and the ease of nursing make tucking the baby into bed seem natural. It is virtually impossible to smother your baby or to roll over on top of it. The mother is still so strongly connected to the baby that she could not sleep that soundly. In fact, she'll probably wake up the same second her baby does, just as she can hear him three rooms away when she is asleep. The connectedness between mother and baby is so strong that researchers are now investigating whether being close to the mother and her breathing pattern can prevent Sudden Infant Death Syndrome (SIDS), in which babies seem to "forget" to breathe.

However, there may come a time when it doesn't feel good to have the baby in the same bed, or even in the same room, with you all night. While it is valuable for your child to establish a nest in which she feels comfortable being apart from you, there are no right or wrong answers as to when that should be. You need to consult your awareness, emotions and intuition in the present moment to see what is needed. There is nothing wrong with your feeling that more distance is needed, and taking it. Mothers *can* have some space without feeling that they are causing psychological damage to the baby, and couples can have the space to make love and nurture their marriage without having to worry about waking the baby.

Styles of parenting are very different, and will certainly have different effects on the children. But those effects aren't predictable or even scientifically measurable. For example, without the cultural or religious support for having a son circumcised, I would not do it because I know that the baby feels the pain, and that it would be an awful thing for me to do to my baby for social or pseudo-medical reasons. But in terms of future effects, researchers cannot distinguish circumcised from uncircumcised men by any kinds of personality or psychological tests that have been devised. I would have to do what felt like the most aware and loving thing in that first week after birth, without thinking that I was doing it to get some kind of future benefits. The same is true about where your baby sleeps. Feel your freedom and do what is most aware and most loving, taking everything into account that you can. Don't sacrifice either yourself or the baby to some idea of how it *should* be.

## WHAT ABOUT WEANING?

This same criterion applies to weaning. Breastfeeding is a couple relationship. Once the baby is able to eat table foods (around nine months) the nature of breastfeeding changes to fulfilling a need that is more emotional than nutritive. La Leche League speaks of *baby-led weaning,* pointing out that some babies really do wean themselves and others don't (they might be three or four years old). The League and *The Continuum Concept* by Jean Leidloff point out how common it is in less technologically developed cultures for children to be nursed two or three years or longer. However, we are not members of other cultures, and their awareness or group consciousness is not necessarily appropriate for us in the world in which we live.

The development of individual consciousness, which is so advanced in the West, is a fundamental question. On the one hand, our extreme individuality has brought us to alienation, anxiety, competition and denial of the spirit. On the other, we can't escape it just because we can read about other cultures. However, something new clearly *is* needed, or we're going to destroy ourselves. Steiner's answer is that our individuality is appropriate, but we must now go on to include a reintegration of spirit and matter from our modern vantage point. *We have to start where we are.*

In considering nursing, I have seen many mothers "suffering through" nursing after the first year, waiting for their baby to wean herself. I cannot believe that an older baby's sucking need is well served by a resentful mother. Babies and older siblings take in emotions just as deeply as actions. Breastfeeding is like making love—nothing is gained in suffering through it!

Having said that, I need to repeat that I feel breastfeeding is the best start you can possibly give your baby, and you should continue as long as it feels good to both mother and baby. Any amount of nursing is better than no nursing at all. If you are considering weaning in the first month, chances are that you are having difficulties; it should be pleasurable for both you and your baby. Call La Leche League or a lactation consultant and get the help you need. Often doctors give the wrong advice, which is less likely to happen with women who are knowledgeable and trained to help nursing mothers. If you encounter special situations, such as going back to work or illness, the League or lactation consultants also can provide the support you need to successfully breastfeed in these circumstances.

In our culture, pediatricians used to want you to introduce solid foods at three months (or earlier), either because your baby was not growing enough or (in my case) because he was too fat! The trend now is more toward waiting until six months. La Leche League has good advice about how and when to introduce foods, and if there is a history of allergy in your family, giving nothing but breastmilk for the first year can help to prevent sensitization to food and other allergies. There is no need to supplement iron for breastfed babies; they don't become anemic in the first year from a breastmilk diet.

Steiner observed that if a baby continued to nurse after it was eating solid foods, the child might remain too connected with the maternal forces of inheritance. As the child achieves uprightness, it is freeing itself from the forces of inheritance; achieving such freedom in the area of nutrition is appropriate at this same time, according to Steiner.[4]

Steiner gave many indications about nutrition that vary quite a bit from information commonly available today. Interested readers can refer to *When a Child is Born* by W. Zur Linden[5] and *Foodways* by Wendy Cook.[6] One interesting thing I have gleaned is that what children eat before the age of three is what they acquire a taste for, and I have seen this to be true many times. For example, we gave our youngest daughter almost no red meat before the age of three, following Steiner's indications that red meat is very dense and inappropriate for young children. Even though we aren't vegetarians, she still won't eat most meat and prefers tofu. A friend brought up her child without any sugar or sweets before the age of three. Then she allowed sweets when the child entered preschool. It was interesting to observe that the girl really had little taste for the cupcakes or other treats at birthday parties. This seemed to go beyond a desire to please her mother's wish that she partake moderately of these foods.

## CRYING BABIES

Since babies can't verbalize what is happening with them, they cry for a wide variety of reasons. We are taught to see if they are wet or hungry. If not, we as a culture try to hush them up or ignore them. There's nothing like a crying baby to bring up emotions in nearby adults and new mothers.

The next time you hear a baby cry, see what feelings and associations it brings up in you. And take some time to think about how you respond to your baby's cues; are you more concerned with your own or the child's discomfort? Many valuable exercises to help parents understand their own feelings about crying, sleep, food and so forth can be found in *Exercises in Self-Awareness for New Parents* by Aletha Jauch Solter.[7] Her book *The Aware Baby* also offers much good advice about crying babies.[8]

Having a "colicky" or high-need infant can be a real strain on parents. Many things can be tried—looking for food allergies, burping the baby frequently, limiting stimulation, putting warmth or pressure on the tummy, giving weak camomile tea—but there doesn't seem to be any statistical correlation between causes and cures for colic. Above all, try to remain calm yourself, and remember that you are not responsible for your child's personality or temperament. Sometimes the best you can do is just be there for the infant, lovingly holding her and letting her cry. Crying can be a great release if done in the arms of someone who loves you.

Vimala Schneider, author and founder of the International Association of Infant Massage Instructors, writes:

> Forcing babies to "cry it out," hushing babies' cries by stopping up their mouths, and letting babies cry "cathartically" can all be excuses for not taking the time to listen to what they have to say. There is no quick fix. A good parent—a good *culture*—must go through the sometimes difficult process of responding to babies' cues individually, with compassion and with common sense.[9]

One father describes his trying to become more intuitively aware of what his daughter's cries mean:

> In the evening, after we put Tara to bed, she sometimes wakes up after about an hour or so. At this point, she starts to cry, and we do not respond immediately, because we want her to learn to go back to sleep without Wendy going to breastfeed her. The decision whether to get up or not is a function of the nature of the crying. There's a kind of crying that is whimpering, where it's clear she is still asleep, and a kind of cry that is screeching, and it's obvious she is awake and distressed. However, there are some in-between cries, where it's hard to tell how she's feeling.
>
> I found myself trying the following technique. Rather than listening with my ear or with my mind, I have started to try and listen first with my heart. I try and let the crying go to my heart and then, with my mind, examine how my heart is feeling and responding. Is she in distress? Does she need comforting? Or is she just complaining, feeling uncomfortable? The distinction is important, in that Wendy and I want her to feel completely trusting of our presence, but we also want her to experience, in small increments, taking care of herself. I do not believe in having her cry herself to sleep, as some parents recommend at this point, where she really screams for long periods of time and exhausts herself. Rather, I suspect the process can be much more incremental and evolutionary, like the changing of the tides. Each night there are small changes that over time build up into a major shift. In any case, the learning for me here is in trying to respond first at an intuitive, feeling level and then consulting that feeling. This is a process I have been exploring for a while, but this feels like a new dimension of it.[10]

Once again, there are no simple definitions for the right or wrong way to parent your child. You need to feel your own way through the easy and difficult times.

# WHAT ABOUT GOING BACK TO WORK?

Today's society dictates that many women must go back to work because they are single mothers or because their income is vital to their family. The percentage of mothers in the work force with children under the age of one year is skyrocketing, so *I am clearly out of step in saying that, if you can possibly stay home with your baby for the first year, please do so.* In fact, it is better to stay home for the first three years! T. Berry Brazelton, America's favorite pediatrician, has written a popular handbook for working mothers called *Working and Caring.*[11] He discusses what mothers need to consider in looking for daycare for a baby or young child, the emotions involved in going back to work, the concern about the primary caretaker replacing you in the child's affection, the increased number of illnesses and need for antibiotics, and so forth. If that list sounds negative, my bias may be showing through. White, on the other hand, became very unpopular several years ago when he said that it makes a difference in development if mothers stay home with their children younger than three. But he decided to stick by his guns and to say it again in the revised edition of *The First Three Years of Life* (1986):

> I stated then (1979), and I will state again now, that full-time substitute care for babies under three years of age, and especially for those only a few months of age, does *not* seem to be in the best interest of babies.[12]

Based on his years of observation and research, White concludes,

> Simply stated, I firmly believe that most children get a better start in life when, during the majority of their waking hours of their first three years, they are cared for by their parents or other nuclear family members, not by any form of substitute care.[13]

The reasons for this are many, including the uniqueness of the parent-child bond that is forming in the first two years. No caregiver can match the enthusiasm and excitement of parents over a baby's accomplishments such as sitting up and walking. Such reactions reinforce the parents' commitment and love and contribute to the child's developing sense of self-worth and security. In addition, the parents are best able to be there to satisfy a toddler's curiosity with all the things she discovers. While studies have shown that *ideal* substitute care situations do no *measurable* harm to children, all situations are not ideal, and no studies show substitute care as being better than any but the most abusive family.

Steiner explains the uniqueness of the mother-child relationship, which White observed in the first three years. Steiner observed that the etheric or vital energy of the baby is connected with and protected by the mother's vital energy, which surrounds it like a sheath, just as the physical body was protected before birth by the physical body of the mother that surrounded it. Just as the child's physical body is freed at birth, the child's etheric body is gradually "born" over the first seven years, with an important freeing from the mother occurring around the age of three. This change is quite dramatic if you are alert for it—suddenly your child is much more independent, much more able to be away from you comfortably and more able to participate in group activities. This is why Waldorf preschools don't like to accept children until around three-and-a-half, after they have gone through this freeing from the mother.

According to Steiner, the baby in the first year is still totally connected to the mother's vital (etheric) energy and nurtured by it. This seems to explain the psychic connection or heightened awareness that exists between mothers and their babies. We experienced a dramatic example of this connection when we lived with a woman and her nine-month-old daughter. The mother had weaned her baby to go into the hospital and have a benign but growing lump removed from her breast. During the surgery it was discovered that she actually had advanced breast cancer. Within twenty-four hours the baby came down with pneumonia, and we were dealing with recovery from surgery, the shock of cancer and a seriously ill infant. It was as if the supports for the child had been pulled out from under her while her mother was in shock. Full-time daycare is not as great a separation as that for an infant, but it is still a shock for the baby and can cause what Steiner calls a "tearing of the etheric sheath" surrounding the baby. As a Waldorf preschool teacher in a community where most of the mothers stayed home with their children or only worked part time (Ann Arbor, Michigan), I can say that the children who had been in daycare since the age of six months stood out quite noticeably. They tended to be sick more often and more used to antibiotics, because their parents couldn't stay home for recuperation time; they were less childlike, having dealt with the stress of other adults and groups for many years. David Elkind in his books *The Hurried Child* and *Miseducation*, speaks of the high level of anxiety with which our children live, and how we push them to grow up and cope with things that should be beyond their years.[14]

If there is any way you can stay home *at least* during the first year, it is of tremendous value for your baby and can be rewarding for you as well. Your baby only begins life once and will grow up so quickly! But there is not a lot of support for mothers to stay home. Leaves of absence are usually too short, careers won't wait for many women who are in their late thirties when they decide to have children, and today's lifestyles often demand two incomes. But if it is your heart's desire, work something out and find the support you need. *Mothering* magazine is a real support for women who value what they do with their children. And *Family Alternatives* is a magazine dedicated to helping parents find alternatives in combining jobs and family life. *Of Cradles and Careers* by Kaye Lowman (from La Leche League) is a valuable book. (See other resources listed at the end of Chapter 1.) Find supportive friends, or find ways of working at home or parttime. Through his work with young children, White found that the best type of substitute care is individual care in your own home; fortunately, the number of agencies handling nannies and *au pair* programs is increasing rapidly. Second best is individual care in another person's home. Next is family daycare, followed by nonprofit center-based care. Last is profit-oriented center-based care, which is often done as a franchise and pays little over minimum wage.[15]

## IS THERE A DIFFERENCE BETWEEN FATHERING AND MOTHERING?

If the mother is going to return to work, having the father or grandmother take care of the baby at home is probably the first choice, because they can be excellent mother substitutes. But is there a difference between the mother's connection with the baby and the father's? In *Pregnant Feelings* I wrote something about "the obvious statement that mothering is different from fathering." My co-author objected vehemently, despite my assurances that I didn't mean men couldn't change diapers or *father* their babies instead of babysitting while mother was out. I finally had to change it to "the controversial statement that mothering is different from fathering."

Fathers, adoptive parents, and other relatives can all learn the art of mothering if they want to or if they must take on the responsibility. (Otherwise they will tend to sleep through the night or not maintain awareness of the child at each moment because "mother" is somehow still doing it.) But there is a difference that the mother experiences physically through breastfeeding and hormonal changes, which is that intangible connection Steiner explains as the interweaving of their life forces in the first three years. Especially during the first year, one of the most valuable things a father can do, in my opinion, is to support the mother in her mothering—financially, emotionally, and by sharing in the increased workload in the home. He may also be fathering older children as his relationship with this new baby unfolds. It's a busy time!

Ideals and values in parenting need to be discussed ahead of time and reevaluated as the realities of a new baby make themselves known. If a father-to-be thinks he's being wonderfully supportive by working overtime to meet the increased financial demands and she's feeling emotionally abandoned by never seeing him, everyone's best intentions won't lead to harmony. *Pregnant Feelings* contains many exercises to help couples communicate about parenting issues, clarify values, and work together.[16]


## WHAT ABOUT IMMUNIZATIONS?

If you are seeing a pediatrician or visiting a well-baby clinic, immunizations will become an issue during the first year of your child's life, since most clinics and pediatricians want to start them at three months of age. There is much controversy today about immunization; the drug companies have halted production of some vaccines because of the number of lawsuits from parents who claim their children have been damaged.

In Europe, doctors who work with the indications of Rudolf Steiner in addition to being fully licensed and recognized medical doctors compromise and do immunize against the more severe illnesses, such as polio and tetanus. But they refuse to immunize children before the age of one because of the shock to the child's physical and vital energy which introducing those illnesses into the body entails. They feel that a child who is not yet walking is unlikely to injure himself outdoors where tetanus germs grow on rusty nails or in manure. However, some unimmunized children under the age of one do get whooping cough, so you need to decide whether you can make the commitment of spending one month or longer at home nursing a very sick child. The issue of immunization will be discussed again in greater detail in Chapter 14.

## DO THE TODDLER'S SENSES STILL NEED PROTECTING?

Obviously you're not going to be taking the same care to put silks over the lamp with a ten-month-old that you might with a one-week-old! The baby is much more "here" and is quickly adapting to earthly life. But is it still beneficial to maintain an awareness of the quality of the baby's sensory experiences? The answer is yes, not just in infancy, but throughout the early childhood years. Continue to pay attention to the quality of the sights and sounds your child experiences. Clothing and toys from living sources feel good to the touch and help introduce your child to the world of nature. Synthetics, those wonderful creations of the human mind, can be introduced when the child is older.

It is especially important to continue to keep the baby warmly dressed (but not overheated!) and protected from the sun. The explanations given in the chapter on the newborn still apply to the baby throughout the first year. It is also important to keep toddlers and preschoolers warmly dressed, especially remembering to keep little girls' legs warm when they are wearing dresses.

The environment continues to be tremendously important to the young child. This includes the emotional as well as the physical surroundings. The best way to help a baby develop in the first three years is to provide warmth and love to meet her physical and emotional needs, and then *to work on oneself*. Is it possible to work toward always treating your child with respect, talking to your baby, not blaming him for being fussy or accusing your toddler of dumping the wastebasket just to annoy you? You'll find yourself having inner emotional reactions that you know aren't appropriate to your child's intentions or level of control. It's all right for you to feel the things you feel (all mothers get frustrated, get cabin fever, even hate their children on occasion), but it's important not to express it around the child. Find other ways of releasing the energy and regaining your perspective. Can you see and dismantle your reactions, or take your frustrations out in chopping wood or jumping up and down in the bathroom rather than in front of the baby? No one is perfect, and the path of parenting is one of growth.

Remember the keys of sleep, artistic activity and meditation. Arrange for time by yourself, when you can center, read or write, or do nothing. Once the baby has established certain rhythms, use one nap time for yourself instead of for the housecleaning (you can always clean with the baby in a carrier or sitting and watching you). Don't make impossible demands on yourself, realizing that you are doing a tremendous amount in providing the best possible beginning for your baby. Raising a young child demands a tremendous amount of just "being there." This seems also to be true of adolescence, for a friend who had four teenage sons reported that being with teenagers was very much like being with toddlers: they need to know you are there, and want you to "hang out" with them or talk about things in which you really have no adult interest. My friend found that she had to cut back her midwifery practice and be home more when her sons became teenagers, just as she had done when they were little.

# SIBLING RIVALRY

Should you have your children spaced closely together in age, or with many years in between? Some parents don't have the option of choosing, and it is necessary to adapt to the changing dynamics of having another child, whether it is after nine months or nine years. Most children are excited with the idea of having a baby brother or sister, but young children are often disappointed when the baby sleeps so much and isn't an equal playmate for them. All of the attention that goes to the baby can also be a cause of anxiety or annoyance, especially when she begins to crawl. Many children who exhibited no sibling rivalry with the new baby will suddenly be very negative when the crawling and walking baby starts to demand mother's constant attention and gets into all their toys. Spending time alone with an older child, figuring out ways to keep the baby out of your other child's prize bug collection or newly built city, can help prevent negative behavior, but it's always difficult to deal with it when it arises. One needs to keep correcting and modeling positive behavior toward both children without feeling guilty or angry that harmony has disappeared.

During the second year the balance shifts with brothers and sisters who are less than three years apart. The baby, who has possibly been the recipient of various expressions of jealousy by an older sibling, has learned to protect herself by crying out. She can now tip the scales by becoming aggressive toward the older brother or sister, who is sometimes innocent in the moment, and who becomes increasingly resentful. This situation creates a tremendous stress for parents, and a sense of impotence or not knowing what to do is common. (You also may experience no such problems, depending as much on your children's temperaments as on your wise or faulty parenting.)

Studies have shown that life is much easier for parents when the children are three years or more apart, but if you're already in the thick of it, the best thing you can do is try to find the moments and the things that will help to keep you from losing your temper and remember to try to model "right action" for the children, stating and acting out the positive behavior that you are trying to achieve (such as sharing) rather than focussing on the negative.

If your older child is still less than three years of age, remember that he is still extremely young and immature. Continue to be firm but loving, and reassure him of your love by spending some time each day alone with him. Also encourage his out-of-home interests. It is interesting that White concluded from his observations, "In my judgment, if the older child is under roughly two-and-a-half years the best preparation for the arrival of a younger sibling is to teach the older child during his first few years to respect the rights of his parents."[17]


## WHAT MAKES CHILDREN SO DIFFERENT FROM ONE ANOTHER?

Parents who have an "easy" child are often silently critical of other parents and think, "If they only would do what I did." Then when their next one comes along and is totally different and a real handful, they are amazed by how different children can be with the same parents. There's nothing like children to keep us humble! Similarly, a mother with a "difficult" child may feel like a failure until she has another child who is sweetness and light.

What we need is perspective on how different children can be, and why. For one thing, *they are unique individuals even if they share the same genetic pool.* In addition, each person has a characteristic way of being and interacting with the world. T. Berry Brazelton, pediatrician and author of *Infants and Toddlers: Differences in Development,* states, "Just as adults have different personalities, so do babies, and these personalities are distinctive almost from birth." He develops the idea of three basic personalities in infants—quiet, average and active—and each is quite normal.[18]

Rudolf Steiner recognized four basic "temperaments" or groups of traits. While everyone is a mixture of several of the temperaments, one tends to dominate. By gaining insight into your child's and your own temperament, you can understand how people can be so different, and will be able to try different ways of parenting and teaching children with different temperaments.

The first type of person Steiner described is one who has an abundance of energy and likes to do things. As adults they are quick to see the future and want to manifest things. Such children are very powerful, with tremendous force of will and action. They tend to dominate in play, using images of power such as eagles, tornadoes or bears. Their emotions tend to be hard to control (especially anger, aggression and annoyance) and they become frustrated if not given enough opportunity to engage their abilities. They can be overbearing, but they also have positive leadership abilities and can be characterized as the "movers and shakers" who make things happen. They tend to be compactly and powerfully built, and walk with their heels dug into the ground. Well-known examples of this *choleric* or fiery temperament would be Napoleon or Teddy Roosevelt.

Contrast that child with one who is very dreamy and likes to sit. Sometimes movement seems like too much effort for this type of child. These children are very concerned with the comfort of their bodies, and their favorite part of the day is often snack time. When they interact with other children, they usually have a harmonizing effect; often they are content to just sit and watch. These children are very comforted by routine and rhythm; they are hard to get started, but they are equally hard to change. Transitions and any kind of changes are hard for these children, and they can have as many temper tantrums as the choleric child. Such a child will become engrossed in anything he starts and will keep at something like a painting until the paper has a hole in it! Such a *phlegmatic* temperament is related to the element of water, with its rhythmical wave action that goes on and on without tiring.

A third type of temperament appears in the child who is almost always bright and happy. He or she is usually very cheerful, with tears changing to laughter as quickly as they appear. This child seems to barely touch the ground, and in fact can be observed to walk on the toes much of the time. These children can be very easy to parent; the difficulty in the elementary grades is in getting them to finish their work. Their interest is so ephemeral that they're like butterflies flitting from one thing to the next.

They are quick and observant and enthusiastically rush into things, but tend to lack follow-through. They are so aware of sense impressions that they are easily distracted by each new thing. This *sanguine* temperament is related to the quality of air, which is light and always changing.

To round out our description of the temperaments, picture a child who is often very inward, more involved in his or her own emotional world than in external action. This kind of child is not so easy to spot in early childhood, because most young children seem to be happy much of the time. But as they grow older, such children seem to take everything personally, carrying a great deal of personal suffering (because someone doesn't like him, or because one child didn't give her a valentine). Crying at his or her birthday party is often typical of this child. The positive side of this temperament is a very compassionate and caring nature, but the negative side is extreme sensitivity, being more caught up in their own reactions than what is actually happening. They tend to live in the past, to contemplate their thoughts, memories and emotional reactions. This *melancholic* temperament is related to the element of the earth, offering resistance to what is happening; but like geode stones with shining crystals inside, such people have a rich inner life of thoughts and feelings.

Knowledge of the temperaments can help us find ways of teaching and disciplining that meet the child's real needs. For example, recognizing that the choleric is centered in the ego (while the phlegmatic is centered in the body) will help you to realize that the choleric can't help being *egocentric*, oblivious to the effects of his actions on others when characteristically behaving like a little king or queen. The task of bringing balance can then replace one's first reaction of anger or frustration in dealing with such a child. Similarly, understanding the melancholic can help lessen one's annoyance or despair when dealing with a child who whines and complains all the time.

Knowledge of the temperaments is an invaluable tool for parents and teachers because it can increase our understanding and compassion for someone who is different from ourselves. A person's temperament changes from childhood to adulthood in characteristic ways, and anyone interested in this fascinating area is encouraged to read *The Four Temperaments* by Rudolf Steiner.[19]

# TOILET TRAINING

Teaching a child to use the toilet is like teaching her to read: when the child is ready, she will learn it. No person with normal faculties gets to age twenty-one without being able to read or be toilet trained. The major cause of "failure" is starting too young. Expecting a child before the age of two to have bladder control is unfair. Sitting him on the potty at the same time each day doesn't encourage him to know when he has to go.

Second children usually toilet train themselves much more easily than first children because they have a sibling to imitate, and because parents are more relaxed about it. Remembering how imitative children are, let toddlers see how it's done, and provide a little potty around the age of two. Many children feel insecure sitting on the big toilet, so a potty chair is very helpful. Making it a special present and praising children each time they use it will reinforce their new behavior. Patience and a cheerful, "Too bad, maybe next time you can run faster," will soon lead to effective training.

# SEPARATION ANXIETY

There has been a lot written in recent years on mother-child attachment, or bonding, and what can happen when this breaks down through prolonged separation, as in the cases of premature or ill newborns. However, we also need to realize that under normal circumstances the mother and child are going through a separation process. They start out as one, contained within one body, united physically and psychically. Instead of trying to create a bond at birth, the question arises, "How can the separation of birth not be so painful or prolonged that the mother disconnects from the child?" The obvious answer is through mother and child remaining together. Increased contact helps to bridge the separation, to establish a new relationship rather than leaving the mother feeling let down and isolated by the passing of the old one.

This separation process of mother and child goes on throughout life as the individuality of the child asserts itself more and more. The mother must constantly let go of her image of the child and their relationship as it has been so the child can more fully be itself and a new relationship can be born.

We have talked about the nine-month-old's common anxiety about people outside the family, and the child's pattern of going away from and coming back to the matrix or source of security. However, separation is also painful for the mother, as anyone knows who has left her baby for the first time. The full breasts, the psychic connection, the concern with how the baby is taking it, the worry that no one can possibly care for this child as well as she does, all pull at a mother's heart strings. The same is true the first time the child goes to school, has her first date, drives the car alone.

We want to protect our children, but we need to realize that they are not extensions of ourselves. Your child is in fact a unique individual who has chosen you to be his or her parents. The individuation process needs to be allowed to occur in order for the child to grow up in a healthy way. In fact, a failure of individuation can cause as great a problem as neglect.

We need to recognize a child as a unique individual from the beginning and do everything we can to avoid putting hindrances in the way of her realizing her full potential and destiny in life. How does this translate into action? For one thing, it means being watchful, but not overly protective. (What if the mother of Sir Edmund Hillary, who first successfully climbed Mt. Everest, hadn't let him climb the stairs as a toddler?) Perhaps it means letting it be all right for your child to climb a tree or climb to the top of the swing set at the park; maybe in another culture she would have become a high-wire artist in the circus! After three trips to the emergency room, you might suggest another activity, but chances are your child will do fine if she undertakes it at all (children are fairly self-regulating if allowed to be so).

Another way of putting it is, "How can we be as relaxed about our first child as we would be about our fourth?" Naturally, we can't be, because everything is new. But the benign neglect and the interaction with siblings that a younger child receives are beneficial compared to the overindulgence and propulsion into adult activity which first and only children tend to receive. As parents, we need always to keep our toddlers in our psychic awareness, but we don't always need to be interacting with them. Raising a child who can play alone, who is self-motivating and not always needing adult input is a real blessing. We need to hold our children in our love and awareness, provide a rich and safe environment for them to explore by themselves, and be there when they come back to "touch base." This may happen every five minutes at first, or every few hours as they become older.

One of the reasons raising children used to be simpler was that parents were doing work that involved movement—washing the clothes by hand, making butter, working in the fields. Toddlers played nearby or were watched by an older sibling or relative, and began to imitate and help as soon as they were able. The idea of a thirty-seven-year-old professional being home all day with nothing but a baby to put her energy into is a uniquely modern situation. Our children do need us for the heart connection, but they don't need constant adult input and intellectual stimulation. Allowing children to be children today means recognizing their need to be in movement, their need to imitate actions and their need for creative play, which is the work of childhood. These topics will be discussed in greater detail in the next chapter.

## CABIN FEVER

Raising a child is a full-time task. *Someone* has to be attending to your child all the time. You as parents have a unique relationship with this person and should value both the time and effort necessary to take care of a toddler. But one person doesn't have to do it all the time: you can trade off, engage grandma, have a babysitter or mother's helper, work out trades with a friend who has a young child. Do whatever you need to maintain your own composure and ability to mother. But don't undervalue mothering, or accept the comfortable illusion that "quality time" makes up for the constant demands of the toddler to be in relationship with you as he or she goes out to explore the world. If you must return to work full time, try to choose an environment for your child that is as much like a home as possible. Having someone come into your home or having your child be part of another mother's "family" by choosing a woman with similar values who is caring for one or two other children in her own home are perhaps the best solutions. Large groups and institutional care (despite the fact that the ratio of adults to children is usually 1:2 or 1:3) is more stressful to a toddler than situations that provide less stimulation and are less likely to overwhelm the child.

Because of the lack of value placed on mothering and the isolation and frustration which first-time mothers often feel, many would rather work to pay childcare than stay home with their children. If you find yourself dying to get away from your children, try exploring some of the reasons and possible solutions. Here are some things to consider:

### 1. Is your child especially clingy?

Could you change the environment and make more interesting things accessible to your child, encouraging his exploration of the world? Can you change your expectations of your child, relaxing and recognizing that "This too shall pass"? Decide to spend three days devoted to nothing but "being there" and observing, without resentment and without trying to get twenty-five other things done. Perhaps your child will start to branch out as he feels the solid base of your calm support. As your child approaches three, having more children around is often easier than having only one. Can you trade days of childcare with a friend, thus making your time with the children more intentional and giving you time away?

### 2. Do you find yourself involved in constant conflict with your child?

List the times of day and the activities that lead to conflict. What could you do to change each situation (lay out clothes the night before, get up fifteen minutes earlier, have more ritual and rhythm at bed time, change your reactions)? What attitudes and expectations do you have? What does your partner feel? Is he supporting you and correcting the child, or ignoring the situation? Do you get louder to try to get a reaction from him?

### 3. Do you miss intellectual stimulation or adult companionship?

Can you find a mother's support group or join a play group? Can you go to the park once a week with a friend who also has a toddler? Satisfied mothers of young children seem to be much more social than someone like me who types all day and tries to meet deadlines. They are often going to visit a friend with children or having them over. Sitting in the park or visiting are not luxuries we have at every stage of life. Can you appreciate them?

Are you in good relationship with your husband? Do you have evenings free? If taking care of the children goes on until 11:00 PM, see Chapter 11 on rhythm and discipline in home life. What is happening sexually between you?

Would learning more about early childhood help make your task seem more worthwhile and help engage your mind? Would a new activity, such as getting out to an art class, satisfy your need? Taking some time away can often improve your state of mind and your mothering. A friend who was a mother of five young children and lived by the airport got her pilot's license after the birth of her sixth child because within five minutes she could be hundreds of feet above all the dirty diapers and toys on the floor. In a similar vein, I took a course to become a travel agent when my children were two and a half and six months. I see it now as one of the main things that kept me sane during a very difficult time. It provided intellectual stimulation two afternoons a week and was pure fantasy fulfillment. (I never became a travel agent!)

### 4. Do you feel at a loss for things to do with your child?

One friend expressed her frustration by saying, "But I find doing puzzles so *boring!*" In general, we need to enjoy our children rather than be concerned about playing with them. By this I mean that we need to have a positive attitude and provide them with things to do, not always do the things they are doing. Think of ways to involve your toddler in the things *you* do, rather than trying to get them done more quickly without him. Children love to "help" do the things adults are doing. Provide things for your child to do and be happy keeping a watchful eye. In the next chapter we will talk more about toys and creative play. Invite children over once your child is older than two and a half and let them play with each other. (It requires supervision and judicious adult input, but lets the child be in his element rather than constantly requiring adult input to play.)

If you are still feeling dissatisfied, see if you can discern why and discuss it with your partner or a friend. You don't have to settle for "getting through it" rather than enjoying parenting and being with your children. New knowledge and perspective, establishing rhythm and discipline, understanding how children learn and play can all help you to enjoy the adventure of parenting. It isn't always easy, but it's always worthwhile and rewarding.

## RECOMMENDED READING ON PARENTING ISSUES

*The Aware Baby* by Aletha Jauch Solter, Ph.D. Insights into parenting from birth through age two.

*Born Dancing* by Evelyn Thoman and Sue Browder. Attitudinal approach to being with a baby and reclaiming intuitive trust in ourselves rather than the experts.

*Exercises in Self-Awareness for New Parents* by Aletha Jauch Solter, Ph.D. Exercises for parents to use in exploring how they were parented and how they feel about parenting issues such as crying babies, sleep and so forth.

*The First Three Years of Life* by Burton White. White's common-sense approach is based on the observations of hundreds of families in their own homes.

*The Four Temperaments* by Rudolf Steiner (AP, IBP). An introduction to the study of the temperaments, which is a great help in parenting.

*The Incarnating Child* by Joan Salter (IBP, SG). Addresses parenting in the first two years from the standpoint of Steiner's indications and the author's wide experience at the Gabriel Baby Centre in Australia.

*Lifeways* by Gudrun Davy and Bons Voors (IBP, SG). Issues of family life growing out of discussions by a women's group working with Steiner's insights.

*Miseducation: Preschoolers at Risk* by David Elkind. Discusses the various styles of parenting and provides support for letting children be children.

*Mothering,* quarterly journal, P.O. Box 1690, Santa Fe, NM 87504. A great support for women concerned with issues of mothering.

*Pregnant Feelings* by Rahima Baldwin and Terra Palmarini. The last three chapters help couples explore their attitudes toward parenting.

# 7 | *The Development of Fantasy & Creative Play*

## THREE STAGES OF PLAY

### *Play Arising from the Body*

While your child is first mastering new body skills, most play consists in pure movement without the element of fantasy. A young child loves to run, jump, walk on tiptoe, climb, turn around or roll on the ground. Like a lamb in springtime, or a young colt, your child delights in movement for the sheer joy of it. And such movement is an important part of muscle growth and the acquiring of motor skills. If left unhindered, your child knows best what movements she needs to develop in a healthy way—there is no need for special baby gymnastics.

Anyone who has ever followed a toddler around knows that she is constantly in movement and expends a tremendous amount of energy! Where does this driving force for movement come from? The energy comes from the process of metabolism, manifested through the movement of the limbs. The *metabolic/will/limb system* is one of three major systems in Steiner's way of looking at the human being; the other two are the *nerve/sense/head system* and the *heart/lung/middle rhythmic system*. These three systems all interpenetrate, and all are active and growing throughout childhood. But Steiner recognized that at different ages one or another system may be dominant. Not only is one system growing most actively, but it also has a major influence on how the child experiences the world and on how she learns. The metabolic/will/limb system predominates in the child under the age of seven; the middle system dominates during the elementary school years; and the head/nerve system is predominant beginning in adolescence.

0–7 years    Metabolic/limb system          Willing/Movement/Imitation
7–14 years   Heart/lung/rhythmic system   Feeling/Imagination
14–21 years  Nerve/sense/head system      Thinking/Analysis

Understanding this shift in emphasis as the child grows can help parents and educators meet the real needs of the developing child.

The metabolic/limb system can be called the *vital pole* because it is the center of vitality—the center for the anabolic processes of assimilating food and turning it into new physical substance. The growth processes are enormously powerful in a young child, whose life and growth forces are so strong that wounds heal almost immediately. Contrast this with elderly people, whose life forces are declining and whose wounds and broken bones mend only with great difficulty.

The movements of a baby and toddler can be seen as an expression of the movement of the energy that is active within the growth and inner processes of her body. The baby kicks her feet in the air and watches the movement; she moves her hands and follows the movement with her eyes. At first her movements lack intentionality and control. Then she loves to drop things, and to fling everything out of her crib, taking joy in the development of her own power. For the infant, the mere moving of her limbs is play enough at first, and a manifestation of the happy unfolding of her powers.

In *Childhood: A Study of the Growing Soul*, Caroline von Heydebrand discusses how the first games of childhood are bound up with the body and have a hidden interplay with organic activities, with the swing of the breath, the rhythmic flow of the circulating fluids, and the forming and excreting of substances. "The small child piles up his blocks so as to be able to tumble them down again. This is more important to him at first than to build a house or a tower. He feels the same satisfaction in construction and destruction when playing with blocks as he does in anabolic and catabolic processes of his organism when they are healthy."[1]

Similarly, when a two-year-old scribbles with a large crayon on a piece of paper, you will see spiral, circular movements punctuated by up-and-down movements. The child is expressing the dynamic of his inner being, not trying to make a representational drawing. This aspect of children's art will be discussed more in Chapter 9.

## Play Arising from Imagination and Imitation

The time when a little child first begins to feel her movements no longer as expressions of energy but as intentional activities within the sphere of her imaginative games varies with every child, but usually first becomes apparent to the observer between the ages of two and three. The first kinds of play you are likely to see are your child's pretending to eat and drink or talk on the telephone. This type of pretend play comes through the imitation of things the child has done or seen the people around her do. Thus if your child sees you picking up potatoes or balls of yarn and putting them in a basket, she will be happy to copy and put pine cones or spools in her own basket. Then she will dump them out again, for a child's play has no utilitarian purpose; there is nothing she is trying to accomplish. Your three-year-old may imitate your sweeping by using her own little broom, but she will be completely involved in the gestures of sweeping and unconcerned about picking up any dust.

Without discriminating, a young child takes in everything in her physical and emotional environment. These impressions, which are taken in by the child without filtering or screening, find their expression in play. A child will imitate not only the activity, but also the "soul mood" or emotions present when an action was performed. Thus if your daughter observes a worker hammering a nail with great anger, she will copy the movement and the anger; or, if you straighten up the room with annoyance, you will see your annoyance in the way she handles her toys. We must pay attention both to the quality of our emotions when we are around young children and to the quality of our movements. Once I was throwing together a cake in a great hurry. I told my four-year-old she could help, but I was going so fast I wasn't paying much attention to her. Suddenly I noticed something was wrong. "What's the matter?" I asked. "You're stirring it too fast!" she said through her tears. And she was right—my movements were an affront to her. I apologized and slowed down!

The progression of play from movement to imaginative play can be seen in a young child's relationship to a rocking horse. At first there is no concept of *horse*, there is just the joy of rhythmical movement. The ideas of being a fast rider and "going somewhere" might come next; later the horse will be incorporated into a five-year-old's elaborate scenarios of being a cowboy or taking care of horses or using one to get away from wolves that are chasing him.

The age between three and five years has been called the *age of fantasy* because all of the intensity that went into learning to stand, walk, speak and begin to think now finds its expression in imaginative play, which becomes a story without end. Beginning with the sheer joy of movement, your daughter becomes a bunny hopping or a kitty wanting some milk as the imaginative element is added. Then she begins to transform objects from one thing to another in a stream-of-consciousness flow of associations suggested by the objects themselves and her interactions with them. For example, a piece of wood may serve as an iron if your child has seen you ironing, then it can become a rolling pin and the clothes, dough for cookies. The rolling pin now changes to a carton of milk to go with the cookies, and a tea party is under way. If you're lucky, you'll be invited.

This kind of play is similar to dreams in the way one object and situation can flow into another, but it represents a high-level use of the child's creative fantasy. Play is the work of the child from age three on, the way by which she unites herself with the world and tries on all of the activities and roles she sees.

## Intentional Pretending

When your child is around four-and-a-half or five, you will see a new element enter and begin to dominate her play. This new element is *intentionality*, and manifests as "let's pretend." Play now tends to be much more socially oriented—a group phenomenon in which as much time can be spent in planning "you be the mother and I'll be the sister and you be the dog" as in playing out the actual scene. Now play begins to arise more from within the child herself, and she is beginning to make a picture or mental image of what she wants to do.

The child now not only manipulates objects and concepts by having one thing turn into another, she also has the self-awareness to plan ahead in pretending to be someone else. By being the mother, the knight, the carpenter or the baker, she is assimilating the world as she experiences it and "living into" the adult world. This is the age when children love bits of cloth and simple costumes to enact little stories. Or they will use dolls and table puppets to put on plays that they make up. Their powers of fantasy and intentionality are also clearly revealed when they model with colored beeswax or clay, paint with watercolors or color with crayons.

# EXPERIENCING THE WORLD THROUGH PLAY

Creative play is the way in which children get to know the world, and it has been called the work of early childhood. "There is nothing that human beings do, know, think, hope and fear that has not been attempted, experienced, practised or at least anticipated in children's play." This opening sentence from *Children at Play* by Heidi Britz-Crecelius[2] is developed further as she explains the various "worlds" the child experiences through play.

## The World of Space, Time and the Cosmos

The tiny baby plays unconsciously with his hands and feet. Von Heydebrand states, "He stretches out to the moon or to the sunlight dancing on the ceiling, not only because he cannot yet estimate distances but because in the dim dawning of consciousness he has a closer relation to distant spaces than the fully conscious, grown-up person."[3] But he soon learns that, while the wooden ring can be caught hold of, the brightly shining moon cannot. His first attempts at grasping objects thus become an adventure of learning about near and far, attainable and unattainable. The infant's first movements in learning to grasp objects put him in relationship to space and time and all the laws of nature. Gravity is delightful when it causes the spoon to disappear over the edge of the high chair, but not so when the baby rolls off the edge of the bed!

The child learns much more about space as he learns to move through it, delighting in the play of running, jumping, climbing and flinging himself onto a pillow or beanbag chair.

The young child is still closely related to the cosmos and delights in play that involves the sun, moon and stars and their rhythmical movements in the cosmos. Such play includes the image of the circle in all its forms favored by young children: balls, bubbles, balloons, circle games. The ball, a perfect sphere, is a likeness of the earth, the sun and the "heavenly sphere" that seems to surround the earth. Soap bubbles are delicate balls that float away on the child's own breath. And watching a balloon floating up to heaven can fill a child with delight or great sadness, depending on his temperament. The form of the circle game also echoes the unified world represented by the sphere; some circle games even involve the planets, such as "Sally Go Round the Sun":

*Sally go round the sun,*
*Sally go round the moon,*
*Sally go round the chimney tops*
*On a Saturday afternoon.*

## The World of Nature

It is through play that children come to know the natural world of animals and plants, and the ancient elements of earth, air, fire and water. With what delight young children play in all types of water, from the bathtub to a mud puddle, as well as water in its winter forms of ice and snow. The element of earth is often first contacted in the form of sand, but clay and stones are also wonderful to play with. And the experience of soil in indoor or outdoor gardening conveys so much more than the commonly used American word *dirt*. Earth and water mix to form mud, marshes and stream beds—how lucky are children who live by a small stream or creek!

Air can be played in with kites, flags, pinwheels, windmills, tissue-paper parachutes and leaves or any light thing tied to a string. Fire is more difficult for children to experience in our age of central heating and trash pickup. But the joys of a campfire are well known, and Britz-Crecelius states that when a fire is built often enough *with* adults, the prohibition of lighting fires without an adult will be easier to enforce.[4]

Getting out of the sandbox and actually digging in the earth puts a child immediately into contact with a myriad of life forms; many worms, centipedes, pill bugs and tiny spiders can be discovered. Similarly, teeming life is discovered when the child turns over a stone by the river or sinks down into tall grass. In a country setting, intimate encounters between children and animals and plants occur without our help; in the cities we may have to help arrange such encounters so our children do not remain strangers to nature for the whole of their lives. Climbing trees, picking fruit and flowers, sowing seeds and watching them sprout, are all important experiences for a child.

Nature is all around us, even in the city. If you can't exercise your powers of observation on a Sunday walk in the local park, you won't experience anything by the sea or in the mountains. "One who cannot see a woodpecker or a squirrel here, need not think he will see a starfish or a marmot there."[5] Contact with nature is renewing for adults, but its importance for children cannot be underestimated. Children are especially nourished by contact with the world of living things because their own life forces are so strong. Child psychologist Bruno Bettelheim reminds us, ". . . the child's thinking remains animistic until the age of puberty. His parents and teachers tell him that things cannot feel and act; and as much as he may pretend to believe this to please these adults, or not to be ridiculed, deep down the child knows better."[6]

Young children feel a natural kinship with baby animals, taking them into their hearts as comrades and companions. Visiting a farm in springtime can be a lovely experience, and even "petting barns" at the zoo can give children a bit of an opportunity to touch animals. If a family does not have any pets, Britz-Crecelius suggests that you could at least find a caterpillar or cocoon and share with your child in its amazing transformation.

It is also important to think about what kinds of animal toys the child has. Realistic stuffed toys are not as beneficial as quite primitive ones that merely *suggest* the form and movement of the animal. A young child does not see the animal as the grownup sees it, and von Heydebrand states, "It is not good for the tiny creature who is striving to become 'man' in the best sense of the word to have to live with animals made in 'realistic imitation' of Nature, looking at them as though they were prototypes of his own supple, yielding being."[7] This is perhaps most visible with stuffed monkeys, which are almost like caricatures of human beings, but the effect can be very strong with other characters such as the floppy stuffed bunny that the lethargic child seemed to be imitating (described in Chapter 5).

This idea may sound quite strange, since we live in a culture in which stuffed animals, plush toys and cartoon characters are an integral part of childhood. It certainly doesn't mean that a healthy child will be ruined by having a stuffed dog or bear! But it is helpful to realize that the young child is trying to get to know the world as it is and lacks the sophistication and humor which most characterizations involve. When animals are taken out of their normal postures, dressed up in clothes and made to imitate people, the image of the human being is also being brought down to a lower level. Respect for our unique position in relation to the rest of the animal kingdom is worth fostering in a culture which tends to reduce the human being to animal or mechanistic levels.

### The Human World

Through play the child interacts first with his parents and those in his immediate family. He can very soon start to help the adults in their work, washing the car or putting away the silverware. Because much of the interesting housework and handiwork that children used to grow into through play is now done by machines, it is all the more important to let children participate in what you are doing whenever possible.

Through observing and helping in the home, the child will start to reflect what he knows in his play. If he is given toys that allow imaginative play, you will see everything your child takes in reflected in his play. Through the taking on of different roles, your child not only tries on what he sees of the adult world, but he can also work through certain difficulties and emotions in the present (as in playing "baby" when a new sibling is expected or has recently been born).

Children don't usually play *with* each other until the imaginative element starts to dominate. Prior to that time they play *next to* each other, each two-year-old engrossed in her own activity or immediately wanting whatever she sees the other child pick up. This characteristic of two-year-olds is a result of the power of imitation. Naturally she is interested in whatever she sees the other child have, and wants to do the same things.

However, once children start to play imaginatively, their pretend situations can easily involve other children, and they will begin to want someone to play with when only adults are around. This is the age where two compatible children are infinitely easier to take care of than one! As they grow, play continues to be an area in which children learn social skills and are able to experience their own influence within the context of their peers.

## The Special Role of Dolls

Through play the child familiarizes himself with the world and assimilates it, making it his own. His senses become sharpened, he is better able to control the instrument of his body and he becomes better able to relate to nature and his fellow human beings. Play with dolls is of special importance because it is one of the ways through which the child can externalize his own inner being. "Through the doll the child finds its own self," Britz-Crecelius states, offering in *Children At Play* many examples of how involved children can become with a favorite doll, so that adults have to be very careful not to commit a faux pas by denying the reality of such a doll.[8] Parents must treat these attachments with respect and stay alert to which dolls are "living" for the child, for it can change with time and circumstances. The favorite doll can become like an alter ego for the child, invested with a bit of the child's own emerging sense of self.

Because a doll plays many varied and complex roles, according to the circumstances, it is easy to understand that the more indistinct and undefined a doll's expression, the less trouble it will cause the imagination of the child. If a doll has a fixed character, it will most often be assigned a specific role in play; it is less useful as a second *I* than a soft doll with eyes but no mouth, which can easily be happy, sad or angry.

Constant invisible companions are used in much the same way, and Britz-Crecelius states, "The disappearance of an invisible companion, the discarding of a doll, are important steps on the path of the child to itself. Being able to do without these supports, it becomes independent. If however, one removes them forcibly and before the child is ready, then one makes it unsure of itself."[9]

Dolls also give children an opportunity to imitate and work out the ways in which parents treat them. For girls, play with dolls is mainly a mother-and-child game, while boys' play with dolls is rarely that. Boys are also less likely to dress and undress their dolls, so they don't need removable clothes and wardrobes as girl's dolls do. However, boys between two and six have a need as great as girls do for a doll that can represent a second *I*, a being the child clasps in his arms when he is beyond himself in order to come to himself again. Many people in our culture are shy of giving dolls to boys, or want to make sure they are "macho images" such as He-Man or GI Joe. However, our sons need both to be allowed to be children and to exhibit nurturing behavior just as much as our daughters!

Most psychologists also support boys being encouraged to play with dolls. Bruno Bettelheim states, "If parents feel relaxed about their son's playing with dolls, they will provide him with valuable opportunities for enriching his play life. For them to do so, it is not sufficient that they simply refrain from disparaging such play. Because of the still prevalent attitude that doll play is only for girls, both parents need to have a positive feeling about a boy's doll play if he is to be able to take full advantage of it."[10]

We need to put our attention into the quality of the dolls our children have. Not only their expression is important, but the quality of the material as well. Is the doll cold and hard, or soft and huggable? Is the hair platinum, and grotesquely matted after a week's play? A soft cloth doll with yarn hair and a neutral expression provides the child with a companion who can change as she does. "Walk, talk, cry, laugh, eat, drink, wet itself, blush, get a temperature, get brown in the sun—*any rag doll, any nice, simple doll can do that in the hands of a child.* The mechanical creatures on the toy market can do it much less well, and provoke every older or younger brother into opening them up to have a look—and rightly so! Because these are not dolls, but machines, whose mechanics leave no room for the little bit of the child's soul that seeks to enclose itself there."[11] Even eyes that close are very mechanical, as evidenced by a little girl who said of her doll with its wooden head: "My Tommy doesn't always need to go to sleep straight away, he can also lie awake sometimes."[12]

The beautiful doll and the anatomically correct doll are a hindrance to the inner development of the child. Not only do they leave nothing for the child's imagination to supply, but they provide more than the young child can hold in awareness. Young children are mostly aware of the head, as evidenced in their drawings. (This will be discussed more in the next chapter.) Giving a child a doll with breasts is projecting her out of childhood into the teenage world. Barbie is a multi-million dollar enterprise, and encouraging our young children to indulge in her designer jeans and convertibles supports values that impoverish the world of the young child.

## THE IMPORTANCE OF PLAY

Noted psychologist Bruno Bettelheim defines a young child's play as activities characterized by freedom from all but personally imposed rules (which are changed at will), by free-wheeling fantasy involvement and by the absence of any goals outside of the activity itself.[13] Not only is play important for the healthy creative and emotional growth of a child, but it also forms the best foundation for later intellectual growth. Bettelheim states:

> Play teaches the child, without his being aware of it, the habits most needed for intellectual growth, such as stick-to-itiveness, which is so important in all learning. Perseverance is easily acquired around enjoyable activities such as chosen play. But if it has not become a habit through what is enjoyable, it is not likely to become one through an endeavor like schoolwork.[14]

Kindergarten, as first conceived by Friedrich Froebel in the nineteenth century, was a place where children would play, as if in a garden. However, during most of the period in which kindergartens have existed, they have been pre-schools.[15] This unfortunate trend toward replacing creative play with academic work has accelerated since the late 1950s. Instead of being allowed to play, children are made to fill in workbooks or are given computers to "play with," which overlooks the fact that play needs to involve movement and "the absence of any goals outside of the activity itself." Similarly, objects that can be played with in only one "right" way are useful only for teaching concepts, rather than allowing the child's fantasy to roam freely. The imaginative play of the young child, in which objects transform from one thing into another, is an ideal foundation for the symbol manipulation involved in later reading. We shouldn't skip the stage of concrete, although fanciful, manipulation of objects in free play by going directly into reading, writing and math. The years from three to six provide a lifelong foundation for creativity that should not be undervalued or foreshortened.

Just as it is important not to skip steps like crawling in physical development, so the age of fantasy should be honored as a valuable part of normal development. Play allows for the development of a wide range of experience, so that what is first grasped through action can later be learned anew through thought. Thus when the adolescent studies the laws of levers and mechanics, he will have had the experience of shifting further forward or back on the seesaw, depending on the size of his friend; or the study of trajectories will have had its foundation in throwing balls or skipping stones.

The imaginative play of early childhood changes as the child matures to reflect the child's growing interests. She may form a detectives' club around fifth grade, when *Nancy Drew* or *The Hardy Boys* adventures are often read. Physical development and imitation will continue to inform the changing content of children's play as they become older. Children from time immemorial have reached the world of adults by a staircase of games. Each step is made up of the games of a particular age group, and each step is important. Children will advance from their natural levels of play only when they are ready. For example, a girl who, although younger than her classmates, is tops in her third grade academically, may still prefer to play with the second graders at recess.

Many factors work against free play today: the emphasis on early academics, the passive quality of watching television and movies, the difficulty in connecting with nature, and the need for constant supervision in urban environments. The fact that adults are so busy and most mothers work at least part-time outside the home leaves adults with little creative energy to put into children's play, or leaves the child in structured daycare from 8:00 AM until 5:30 PM. The abundance of toys based on television and movie characters (and therefore with fixed personalities) also leaves little room for creative imagination in play.

Before I became involved in Waldorf education, my own children were constantly asking what they should do or wanting me to entertain them or take them somewhere. When our friends came to visit from Mexico, their bilingual daughter—who had been raised in a small village with no television—would suddenly bring everything to life. She would organize everyone into a circus or put on a show for the adults; suddenly all the children were playing and having a great time with no adult input. I looked back on my own childhood and could remember doing similar things with my best friend: pretending we owned ranches, with bikes for horses and huge ponderosa pine cones for dogs; or making forts in the rocks down at the creek; or playing "office" with a dozen little characters who lived around our desks; or making pipe-cleaner dolls in second grade and spending the next two months at home making orange-crate houses and furniture for them.

Clearly my children had somehow lost the ability to play. While I was able to diagnose the problem, I was at a loss to know what to do about it. Then I discovered the Waldorf schools and ways in which parents can help their children to play creatively, which I want to share with you. The improvement in their children's play at home was an often-heard observation at the first parents' meeting when I taught kindergarten at the Rudolf Steiner School. If we understand the elements of creative play, we can help our children not miss out on this important part of early childhood.


## WAYS TO ENCOURAGE YOUR CHILD'S CREATIVE PLAY

### Creating an Inviting Environment

The way in which you display a child's toys determines to a large extent whether or not they will be played with. When toys are piled together in a toy box or basket, they aren't inviting to a child. Remember that much of play is suggested by the objects as they spark associations in the child's imagination. While it may seem like extra work to clean up with your child at the end of each day, arranging toys invitingly on shelves will encourage your child to be self-motivating in his play. Arranging little scenes on tables or shelves will also invite the child to "live into" the scene and start to play with it.

Another aid to your child's play is having activity areas, if your home or apartment is large enough. For example, a play kitchen area with a child-sized table and chairs and some kind of toy stove and dishes will provide hours of imitative play. Community Playthings makes wonderful wooden kitchen appliances and other toys for children. You can write for their catalog using the address at the end of the chapter. But it is also possible to make a simple stove-sink combination by finding or building a wooden box, then cutting a hole into which you put a metal bowl for a sink, and painting burners beside it. Hinged doors and shelves inside for cupboard and oven are all the better, but not necessary.

Most of the play dishes, pots and pans sold in toy stores last a few weeks or months before they are broken or dented beyond recognition. Adult items are sturdier and can usually be picked up inexpensively at second-hand stores—wooden bowls, small pots, silverware, saucers and pitchers, for instance. Wooden fruit can be found at many variety stores, and a jigsaw can be used to cut pieces of bread from a scrap of plywood.

Another area of great enjoyment is a workbench with a real vise, small hammer, saw and nails. Children enjoy the activities of hammering and sawing, and they can also make toys such as boats or cars. An old tree stump that can be kept indoors for pounding nails is a great way to engage children's excess energy.

A doll corner is a special place where the dolls can be put to bed each night and greeted in the morning. Cradles, baskets lined with cloth, a small high chair and drawers for dolls' clothes all add to the play in this area. The kitchen or dining room table can serve as an area for painting, coloring and crafts; these activities will be discussed more in Chapter 9.

When you set up activity areas, remember that your child will most often want to play fairly close to where you spend most of your time. A play area in a dining room or family room is often used more frequently than a bedroom that is upstairs and far away from the main activities of the family.

An invaluable aid to play are trestles or blanket stands. These wooden structures can be made in a variety of ways, as long as they are both sturdy and light enough for the child to move himself. They are about three feet high and can have sheets and other lengths of cloth draped over them to form houses, caves and other enclosed play spaces. Simple sawhorses made from lumber and metal braces work quite well, or trestles requiring more carpentry skill can be seen in the catalog from Hearth Song or the book *Making Soft Toys* (both listed at the end of this chapter).

Along with sheets and long lengths of cloth, you will want to keep a box of colored pieces of cloth in various sizes from one to two yards. These will be used for table cloths, baby blankets, rivers and to define a space when a child wants to create an action scene for a doll or puppet play.

## Costumes

A few simple costumes can greatly enhance your child's play. Children love to play "dress up" for the sheer joy of putting on and taking off fancy clothes; they also love to transform themselves into characters who can then act out roles in imaginative play—especially if several siblings or friends play together.

Having a few special hooks for capes and a shelf for hats can make costumes easily accessible and suggestive of creative play. Again, don't make a lot of things at once—give your child a chance to play with and relish each new thing. Try making something as it fits in with your child's play, or engage in a little imaginative play with your child the first time he puts on something new that you have provided. Your interacting with the characters suggested by the costumes will go a long way toward their being used in the future. Here are some suggestions for things you can easily make.

HATS

- Make a crown out of stiff paper; cover with aluminum foil.

- Make a crown by sewing the ends of some fancy braid to a few inches of one-inch-wide elastic to make a circle that will fit your child's head.

- Make a couple of squares of thin material, like chiffon, that can be worn as veils held on by the braid crowns.

- Cut two kitty ears out of colored felt; sew onto bias tape or ribbon; they'll stick up when worn; also works for dogs, bunnies (with paper between two layers to stiffen the ears).

- Collect hats from second-hand stores: dress-up, sailor, farmer, train engineer.

CAPES

- Take a length of material, turn under one-inch casing, put elastic through and sew the ends together for the neck; hem; add braid or other decoration if desired.

- Make a cape with a hood by closing one end and putting casing for the elastic down about ten inches. Sew the ends of the elastic to the edges of the cape and add ties.

CLOTHES

- Capes with elastic around the top are also worn as skirts; or make a simple skirt with elastic to match a cape. Add braid and a crown to delight any princess!

- Make a tunic by cutting a head hole in a piece of cloth about eighteen inches wide; sew a tie to the center back. A must for knights, bears, cowboys, anything your child wants to be.

- Save and collect dress-up clothes: velvets, blouses, jackets, etc.

ACCESSORIES

- Go through your own home, grandma's attic, or rummage sales for aprons, gloves, silver shoes and so forth.

## Toys for Imaginative Play

The less formed and more archetypal a toy is, the more possibilities it leaves for the child's imagination. In *Love of Seven Dolls* by Paul Gallico, the little girl is taking leave of the seven dolls she loves so much. The doll "Monsieur Nicholas," who repairs and makes toys, gives her the following present: ". . . and Monsieur Nicholas gave her an oddly turned piece of wood that was not one but many shapes.

'For your first-born,' he said. 'It is a toy I have made for him that is not any, yet is still all toys, for in his imagination, when he plays with it, it will be whatever he sees in it, or wishes it to be.'"[16]

Shapes and forms from nature have that possibility: gnarled knots from trees, pieces of bark, small pieces of branches or one-inch rounds from a tree trunk. This is where a large box or basket filled with "blocks" made from a tree trunk and branches will be used for much more than stacking and knocking down.

Baskets of natural objects can also be used in many ways by children. Rocks, shells, pine cones, chestnuts or walnuts, if made available in small baskets or other containers, will appear as part of the scenery, pieces of food, small animals or whatever is needed in the moment's play.

It is easy to make several stand-up dolls with which your child can act out various scenes in play. These simple dolls/puppets have cylindrical bodies and no arms or legs. Instructions are available in *Making Soft Toys* and *The Children's Year*. Try making a mother, father, old man, old woman, king, queen, baker or boy and girl. The list is as long as your imagination.

In addition to the stand-up dolls or puppets just described, you will want to have dolls of various kinds. Instructions for making more complex soft or knitted dolls can be found in the books just mentioned. *The Doll Book* by Karen Neuschütz[17] gives detailed instructions for making a large soft doll, or you can buy a kit or one ready-made from Hearth Song. Pick up baskets for cribs at discount or second-hand stores and line them with material, which you can also use to make a matching pillow and blanket. The toys themselves are wonderful, and the fact that you have put your own imagination and creative energy into them makes them even more so!

If you like to play with shapes, you can make animals by sculpting colored wool fleece with a needle and thread. For example, a simple bird can be made by tying a knot in a length of colored wool for the head and inserting another piece crosswise for wings. Attach a string to it and hang it in a window or tie it on a stick for a very successful bird.

Another possibility for sculpting animals is to make them from knitted squares of various colors. Instructions for knitting animals and dwarves are available in the books listed at the end of this chapter.

The magical art of creating forms through folds and knots is made easy to follow through the book *Hanky Panky*, which even comes complete with a large white handkerchief for making into a bunny or mouse.

## Outdoor Play

In addition to a sandbox, swing and slide, one of the best outdoor toys for three- and four-year-olds is a climbing dome. Such a dome is just the right height for these children and will be used for climbing, hanging, sitting on and playing rocket ship.

Another well-used toy will be a balancing board (not yet as narrow as a balance beam). By attaching cross pieces to the underside of both ends, the board can be laid securely across horizontal bars of the climbing frame, be secured across two chairs of equal height and be used in many other ways.

If you can make a small "hill" in your yard, it will be a constant delight for a young child to climb, run down, march up, sit on and sled down if you have snow. Also, make use of any natural landscape you have to encourage little secret spots behind the hedge, construct simple tree houses together and otherwise make your yard accessible to your children.

Trips to the park will be enjoyable for the large climbing and play equipment that is there, but also try to schedule walks with your child down country roads or through a wooded area. And be sure to walk at the child's pace, allowing ample time for exploration and discovery. I was always amazed at what an eye my daughter had for teeny tiny little things: flowers, bugs, bits of colored paper.

Don't be afraid of the elements. While most people with children buy appropriate clothing for outdoor play in the snow, few people let their children play in the rain. Waterproof rubber boots and a good rain coat can give your child lots of pleasure stomping through the puddles. Similarly, be sure to go out when it's windy, letting your child be blown by the wind and fly kites or a large maple leaf attached to a string.

When I've done workshops on early childhood, I've asked participants to introduce themselves and then share an early childhood memory. The overwhelming majority of people remember something having to do with nature. Often it's just lying in a field and watching the clouds. Try to let your child experience nature and the seasons of the year. You'll probably find it refreshing and energizing yourself!

# RECOMMENDED READING

*Children at Play: Preparation for Life* by Heidi Britz-Crecelius (IBP, SG). Describes how the child comes to know the world through play. Excellent!

*The Children's Year* by Stephanie Cooper, et al. (IBP, SG). Directions for soft dolls, knitted animals and many other toys to make with children.

*The Doll Book* (IBP) by Karon Neuschütz. Information on play and detailed instructions for making the large, soft Waldorf doll.

*Echoes of a Dream* by Susan Smith (available from the Waldorf School Association of London, 838 Wellington St. North, London, Ontario, Canada, N6A 3S7). Has many suggestions for crafts and other things to do with children.

*Hanky Panky* by Elizabeth Burns (IBP). A delightful little book (complete with white handkerchief) on the playful art of making magical characters with knots and folds.

*Making Soft Toys* by Freya Jaffke (IBP, SG). Instructions for making dolls, knitted animals, wooden trestles and many more soft and hard toys found in the Waldorf kindergartens.

*The Young Child* by Daniel Udo de Haes (AP, IBP). Contains many insights into creative living with two- to four-year-olds.


# TOYS AND SUPPLIES

The Ark, 4245 Crestline Avenue, Fair Oaks, CA 95628. Many toys and books in the Waldorf tradition.

Child's Play, Box 79, West Somerville, MA 02144. Wool felt and cotton knit for dolls and puppets.

Community Playthings, Rifton, NY 12471. Famous for their large, sturdy wooden toys, kitchen sets, etc.

Hans Schumm Woodworks, R.D. 2 Box 233, Ghent, NY 12075. Delightful wooden animal scenes for creative play.

Heart Wood Arts, Rt. 44/55, Box 126, Modena, NY 12548. Charming wooden castles, gnome houses, etc.

Hearth Song, P.O. Box B, Sebastopol, CA 95473. Dolls, doll kits and many other toys and instruction books.

Sureway Trading Enterprises, 826 Pine Ave., Suites 5 & 6, Niagara Falls, NY 14301. Silk at very low prices.

West Earl Woolen Mill, R.D. 2, Ephrata, PA 17522. Wool batting for stuffing dolls and toys: $10 buys a whole box full.

Wilde and Wooly, 3705 Main St., Philadelphia, PA 19127. Colored wool fleece for hair or animals costs about $4 for a half-pound of any color.

# 8 | *Nourishing Your Child's Imagination*

## THE IMPORTANCE AND DEVELOPMENT OF IMAGINATION

Creativity in the young child manifests in imagination or fantasy, which we see most clearly in a child's free play. The child can easily transform herself from a carpenter to a mother to a firetruck driver, all within the course of an hour's play; similarly, we have seen how the child's active imagination can transform objects from one thing to another and create scenes and dramas with small toys and characters. Play enlivens fantasy and fantasy kindles and diversifies play. As the child becomes older, this creative imagination develops into the formation of images. This same ability later transforms into creative thinking. Developmental psychologists have stated, "The development of imagery in the thinking processes of children is an important part of child development, related to play patterns, to creativity, and to adult achievements."[1]

According to Rudolf Steiner, the life forces that aid in the growth of the physical body "spill over," or are freed for imagination when they are not needed for physical growth and transformation. We see this for the first time between ages two and three, when the body has developed enough for the child to start using imagination in creative free play. Once the physical work of the first seven years is over (as manifested by the eruption of the second teeth) this energy is freed further and transforms into "poetic, artistic fantasy."[2] Thus between the ages of seven and fourteen, subjects are taught in the Waldorf schools in ways that appeal to this artistic, imaginative sphere in which children live. The final transformation of this growth energy is into intellect. At around age fourteen the child's forces are still further freed for abstract intellectual analysis. Steiner explains, "Although it is highly necessary, in view of the nature of our modern civilization, that a person should be fully awake in later life, the child must be allowed to remain as long as possible in the peaceful, dreamlike condition of pictorial imagination in which his early years are passed. For if we allow his organism to grow strong in this way, he will in later life develop the intellectuality needed in the world today."[3]

The role of imagination or the ability to think in images is recognized as an important component in creative thinking. Albert Einstein said he discovered the theory of relativity by picturing himself riding on a ray of light. He said that words did not play a role in his thought.[4] In the well-known story of Elias Howe, inventor of the sewing machine, his dream of being attacked by natives holding spears with holes near the tips enabled him to complete his invention by putting the hole near the point of the sewing machine needle. Along with inventors, artists and musicians often work by trying to give expression to what they have seen or heard in their minds.

The importance of imagination in some other areas of adult life is summarized by Margret Meyerkort, who heads the Waldorf early-childhood teacher training program in Great Britain. She writes:

> The adult needs imagination for a number of reasons. No *initiative* is possible without imagination, without seeing the potential for growth and development in a situation which others experience as static—and therefore hopeless. No *compassion* is possible without our imaginative realisation of our friend's or neighbour's predica-

ment. Nor can *love* flourish without it. If we look at a person in a biological, scientific manner we cannot love him or her. We need to experience a person's potential, the possibilities of his or her growth, the potential for transformation. To fall in love is easy. We are driven to it. To continue to love needs imagination. This imagination is ·no phantasising. It helps us to uncover his or her full stature, profundity and deepest intentions.[5]

The faculty of imagination develops simultaneously as memory develops. In the third year, the child begins to develop memory and ideas through the separation of himself from the world in consciousness. As the "I" comes to experience itself as separate from the world, there is someone present to remember things. At the same time, the child is able to unite his increasingly conscious self with the world through his will in play, and fantasy soon follows. The two simultaneous developmental processes can be diagrammed as follows:

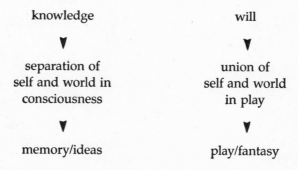

| knowledge | will |
|:---:|:---:|
| ▼ | ▼ |
| separation of self and world in consciousness | union of self and world in play |
| ▼ | ▼ |
| memory/ideas | play/fantasy |

Researcher Dr. Karen Olness asks, "If, indeed, spontaneous play leads to images which are valuable from a creative and coping point of view, how can the quality of spontaneous play be cultivated and retained?"[6]

From the preceding chapter we have seen some of the things that encourage imaginative play:

- Understanding play and how it develops in the first six years.

- Allowing time for free play. Do not interrupt your child all the time. Observe more, intervene less.

- Provide areas of activities, with things arranged in a way that invites the child's involvement.

- Provide simple toys that require the child to complete them with his or her imagination.

- Provide plenty of contact with the world of nature and opportunities for play with sand, soil, water, air, etc.

- Provide examples of real work for imitation; as children see and help adults transform things through work, this will become transformed into their play.

To this list we can add three more things:

- Provide artistic activities that allow the child to express freely what lives within him (these will be discussed in the next chapter).

- Provide nourishing images from stories the child hears.

- Limit the images the child receives from television, video cassettes and movies.

## The Difference Between Auditory and Visual Images

Images a child *hears* actively engage his own imaginative or picture-making processes. A good storyteller knows that she is weaving a cloak of magic around the listeners as she describes the characters and the unfolding action. Just two days ago I overheard my eleven-year-old say to her friend, "I like to read books without pictures best, because then I can picture them any way I want to." Perhaps this is one of the reasons why movie renditions of books we have read are never quite as satisfying as the originals.

Images we make of things we have read or heard are easy to transform in our imaginations or daydreams because we have already given them life by creating them with our mind's eye. Images we see, however, have a tremendous sticking power and are very difficult to change because they come to us already completed. Who can think of the Seven Dwarves without seeing Happy, Sleepy, Doc and the entire retinue as Disney portrayed them?

I was surprised when my two older children talked to each other about cartoons they had seen five years earlier, before we had gotten rid of the television set. But then I realized that *I* could still call up images from television programs seen when I was a child. Television and movies don't have as strong an effect on adults as they do on children. For me, seeing *E.T.* was sort of like eating cotton candy—it didn't make too deep an impression on me. So I was amazed when a year later my children still remembered Elliot's *brother's* name! Not only do images from television and the movies make a deep impression on the young child, who is all sense organ, but their power means that these images will be repeated in play as the child tries to digest and assimilate what he has taken in. Even an older child (and many an adult!) will continually talk about a movie right after having seen it as he attempts to digest it.

Because the images from television and the movies are so powerful and change so quickly, children often do not understand the story line, and are left imitating the rapid movements and the elements that make the strongest impressions: chasing, shooting, crashing and so on. Also, because children are kept passive while watching television, they have all the more need to race about when they are finished. Young children's natural state is movement.

Images from television always reminded me of those automatic reflex responses that bypass the brain, like pulling back your finger from a hot stove before realizing what has happened. In a similar way, images from television and the movies seem to bypass the child himself and come out again in frenzied movement, without the child having transformed them into his own unfolding story. As a preschool and kindergarten teacher, I observed a dramatic difference in the quality of the play of children who did not watch television. Their inside play was much more imaginative and more likely to have a story line, compared to the running around and catching one another that was dominant with the other children. When a child arrived at preschool with a Batman T-shirt, the play immediately turned into chasing one another. I then asked the parents not to send their children in clothing with insignias so their imaginative play could find a little space in which to grow and flower.

Sometimes parents are afraid that if they don't let their children watch television they will be seen as social misfits. On the contrary, they are often welcomed (as I enjoyed my Mexican friend's daughter who brought such a creative element into my children's play). After being involved with Waldorf education for a couple of years, a neighbor said to me, "We love to have Faith come over. She's so creative. Last time she came over. . . ." Needless to say, I was pleased.

Children who do not watch television will still play games with their friends involving TV or movie characters, whose nature they can easily pick up from the plastic figures. But when everyone was playing characters from *Star Wars*, for example, the internal process of play was very different in the child who had not seen the film. The imagination was more active and original in the child who was not relating to the fixed visual images from the screen.

## THE VALUE OF TELLING STORIES

Parents are always encouraged to read to their children, so the children will be exposed to books and to reading. Having parents who read and older siblings who have successfully learned to read increase a child's eagerness to do the same. However, there is also a great deal of value in *telling* stories to your children. Not only do the children gain listening skills, they also appreciate the fact that you are doing something creative with them. When you tell a story, you weave a magic web in which the listeners become engrossed, and there is nothing between you and the children to distract your attention or theirs. By telling a story rather than reading it, you are also free to note the effect the story might be having on the child.

With two- and barely three-year-olds, your stories can be simple descriptions of the world that your child knows. For example, if your child likes to feed the ducks in the park, you might make up something like:

Mrs. Duck called her five baby ducklings to follow her into the water. Across the river they swam, because they saw Jimmy and his mother had come with a bag of bread crumbs. Jimmy threw some of the bread into the water, and "splash" went all the ducks as they snapped up the bread. Jimmy laughed to see how hungry they were. When all the bread was gone, Mrs. Duck and her ducklings swam away and Jimmy and his mother went over to play on the swings.

Everyday events are great adventures for a toddler, and he loves to live through them again and again in his imagination. It is important to describe things in a natural way, letting your words bring to mind what the child has experienced. Introducing ideas from fairy tales, such as an "enchanted stream" or a "poison well," would only confuse a young child who is still taking in the direct experience of water itself. Telling simple stories from everyday life in a slow, deliberate way with a musical tone of voice will delight a two-year-old.[7]

A lot of what your two-year-old appreciates is the special time with you and the soothing quality of your voice, which can bring up images or create a mood of security or fun with its rhythms and rhymes.

Lullabies and nursery rhymes are valuable for the rhythmical qualities of language in which they bathe the child. Many nursery rhymes are a series of interesting but fantastic pictures which have the quality of images we might encounter in dreams. Take, for example, "Sing a Song of Sixpence." Eileen Hutchins, in "The Value of Fairy Tales and Nursery Rhymes," gives indications of some of the possible inner meanings behind such a verse:

> In many rhymes and tales the soul powers of thinking, feeling and willing appear as beings. Thinking has an active and masculine quality and so is represented as the father or the king. Feeling is more inward and womanly in character, while willing, the power which is the least developed and controlled, resembles the child. Birds can represent the flight of time. Thus in this rhyme we find the four and twenty hours of the night and day hidden from sight within the round of time until the moment when they become the present and reveal their secrets. With our thinking we ponder over the accumulated wisdom of the past like the king in his counting house. With our feeling we enjoy the gifts of the present, which like the honey appear before us without any special labour on our part. With our willing, like the maid, we are active in the outer

world. But as our deeds are never really complete and our will during earthly life cannot entirely fulfil itself, something has to be carried over into the future. This is expressed in the picture of the bird who flies away with the nose. Nursery rhymes cast their strange spell because children feel in their hearts that they are true.[8]

Three-year-olds also like the rhythmical quality of nursery rhymes and stories which are built on repeating phrases such as "This is the House that Jack Built" or "Little Tuppens," with its story of what the mother hen must ask of each animal so that the oak tree will give her an acorn cup for some water for Little Tuppens, who is coughing. A help in memorizing such stories is to visualize the sequence of events (i.e., see all the characters in a chain) and to repeat it over and over—rhythm and repetition make memorization simpler! Other simple repetitious tales with which you probably are familiar include "The Three Billy Goats Gruff," "The Little Red Hen," and "The Little Gingerbread Boy."

Another type of story that children three years and older love to hear is stories from your own childhood. "When I was a little girl my mother worked at an olive cannery where they had great big barrels where the olives floated in salty water to make them taste good to eat. And there among the barrels my mother found a little gray kitten. . . . Well, what do you think we named her?" These stories, which have their basis in your own experiences, can also stimulate *your* imagination, so that you start telling a whole made-up series of stories about the adventures of the kitten named "Olive." Imagination isn't just for kids!

In stories for young children, although the animals might be personified (like Mrs. Duck), it is best if they are still true to their natures and their lives in the natural world, which the child is coming to know and love. Cartoon characters represent an adult level of sophistication that goes beyond the world of early childhood.

Children also love to hear stories about themselves, especially about when they were a baby (now that they are so grown up!). They like to hear about things they said and did, the time they went to grandma's house, and so on.

When is your child old enough for stories? Obviously it takes a certain maturity of language development for a child to listen to a story. Until that time children are still totally immersed in experiencing the things themselves. Take your cues from your child, and start with very short stories as described above, gradually working through longer ones with repetition, and then into simple fairy tales.

## THE INNER MEANING OF FAIRY TALES

When the child is about four years old, you will find he will be fascinated by fairy tales told or read. A simple story like "Sweet Porridge" from Grimm's collection will delight even a three-year-old. They enjoy hearing of the little pot, so full of abundance, which overflows until stopped by the right phrase. At this age the children themselves have a sense of life's eternal abundance, which one child expressed when her mother told her that she did not have enough time to take her out to play: "But Mother, I have lots of time. I'll give you some."[9] Then a simple story such as "The Star Child" can later be followed by longer ones such as "Goldilocks" and "The Hungry Cat." Some fairy tales are so rich and complex that they can nourish children right up to the age of eight or even nine.

Bruno Bettelheim, who became interested in the psychological value of fairy tales through his work at the University of Chicago's residential treatment center for severely emotionally disturbed children, wrote the award-winning book on the value of fairy tales entitled *The Uses of Enchantment*. He says that "when children are exposed to children's literature, fairy tales consistently have the greatest appeal."[10]

Most parents today are unfamiliar with real fairy tales as literature, having grown up with only the cartoon or Disney versions or the stories "as retold by" someone who took great liberties with them. Such renditions are of questionable value, and I found that reading the English or Germanic tales in their original, unedited versions was an entirely different experience. As I became open to their possible inner meanings and read them with new eyes, I found a great wealth in their images.

Fairy tales have gone in and out of fashion over the centuries. During the age of rationalism they were dismissed as nonsense, and were a dying oral tradition when the Grimm brothers and others made their collections by visiting village storytellers in the late 1800s. The title of their well-known collection of stories in German is called *Kinder und Hausmärchen* (*Children's and Household Tales*), which indicates their original nature as tales or "little reports" that were commonly repeated in the home and told to children. The tales rarely had to do with fairies, but they did seem to talk about a world different from our everyday one, yet somehow strongly connected to our inner life.

Today there is renewed interest in fairy tales through the work of psychologists such as Carl Jung and Bruno Bettelheim, and by writers such as Rudolf Steiner and Kornei Chukovsky, whose important book on language and stories in early childhood, *From Two to Five*, is now available in English.[11] Jung speaks of fairy tales as projections of the collective unconscious in trying to explain their crosscultural similarities. Rudolf Steiner states that fairy tales are like "readings" or reports from the childhood of humanity, a time when people participated in a dreamlike, experiential consciousness which radiated feeling and was filled with images. This preceded the development of our scientifically critical, observant, awake consciousness which is filled with ideas.[12] Both Jung and Steiner agree that all of the characters in a fairy tale are elements within each individual person, aspects of our own selves and our destinies here on earth. Prince and princess, animus and anima, spirit and soul, all are metaphors for our own striving to achieve a sense of union (marriage) of the parts of ourselves.

Miriam Whitfield, in her valuable booklet *Fairy Stories . . . Why, When, How*[13] gives excellent examples of ways of interpreting fairy tales. For example, many stories echo our process of incarnation and subsequent return to a state of union with God. This we see in tales that begin with a king, queen or princess—someone who owned much, who is in possession of cosmic wisdom; i.e., the human being before leaving Paradise, before incarnating on earth, one who is still in union with God.

> Then, from this state of cosmic wealth, the hero is often plunged into great misfortunes and trials. He or she is tested to his utmost

endurance and has to rely on his own inner powers. These powers are often brought to him by some helpful being. It may be an old woman in the woods (wisdom from the past); it may be an animal who has been helped by the hero's kindness and wishes to repay by some magic gift (heart forces). All the while, witches and sorcerers, wild animals and mighty giants are trying to waylay his quest, but with endurance and courage he wins through.[14]

She also gives examples of how fairy stories can echo the evolution of humanity through the gradual rise of individual consciousness in which we live today.

The king stories take us back to our own—and humanity's—distant past. The nobleman, the merchant, the craftsman are characters much closer to our present era. The tailor cuts up cloth and fits it to your size. He can be thought of as the modern mind which uses its analytical powers to assess a situation. The "little tailor" (because although we think ourselves very clever, we are only at the beginning of the development of our conscious forces) often has to outwit the giant. Well, the giants are those great archetypal nature forces which are part of humanity. They are in the unconscious and—if not awakened and recognized and tamed—tend to overwhelm us. Are not jealousy, hatred, sloth or greed, giants who tend to overwhelm us? And don't we need all the cunning and smartness of the [clever] little tailor to overcome them?"[15]

If we read and ponder a fairy tale such as "Hansel and Gretel" with these thoughts in mind, a deeper pattern emerges, so that the story can be seen as a parable of our life's journey from the home of our "heavenly father" to the earth. The earth can be seen as our stepmother, in the sense that the material world presents trials and difficulties for the spirit who has had to leave its original home. The children, who can be seen as representing spirit and soul, are at first guided in the forest by a white bird, that messenger of the spiritual world we have encountered before. But Hansel and Gretel lose their way and are distracted by many temptations to the senses, culminating in the candy house which, like the body, poses the danger of becoming a prison to our higher nature, just as the witch imprisons Hansel.

Once Hansel and Gretel overcome the witch, they are able to take the jewels, the fruits of earthly life, with which they fill their pockets. On their return to their father's house, they are again guided by a white bird, a duck who can take them across the water. In this homecoming, the stepmother is gone and the children are joyously welcomed into the state of union they have achieved.

The richness of the story in its original version cannot be done justice by a short description such as this, but perhaps such a summary can encourage you to read and ponder the fairy tales with a new openness to their inner possibilities.

To the extent that we as adults can "live into" the inner richness of a fairy tale, we and children will be the more nourished by it. We would never want to give explanations to a child or ask him to explain, "Why did Goldilocks go into the house? How do you think she felt when she woke up and saw the three bears?" Fairy tales should not be reduced to intellectual or emotional levels. They do not need any explaining or rationalizing to be appreciated by the child. Just as humanity has passed through various stages of consciousness, so children are passing through these same stages. For this reason, they live with the fairy tale images and are warmed and fulfilled by them again and again. When we tell a fairy tale with an inner understanding and appreciation of its deeper meaning, it is as if the young child feels, "Ah! You understand, too!"

### The Question of Cruelty and Evil in Fairy Tales

Many parents question the violence in fairy tales, and certainly a Hollywood rendition of a story can scare a young child and give him nightmares. However, when fairy tales are told in a melodic voice, without emotional dramatization, the moral pattern of the fairy tales emerges. In the journal *Ethics in Education*, Diana Hughes states that fairy tales speak directly to the natural morality in the child and to his or her sense of moral order in the world. When the good wins and the evil is punished, a child is visibly satisfied.[16] The cruelty of having the witch dance to death in red-hot shoes or the wolf drown from the weight of the stones in its belly does not upset children, because there is a certain rightness to the fact that evil is naturally the cause of its own undoing and is overcome. Through the adventures and triumphs of the main character and as a report that evil is always self-consuming, fairy tales are usually a source of reassurance and comfort to a child. A more subtle theme in several stories is that when one recognizes the potential for evil, it loses its potency. For example, once Rumpelstiltskin and his equivalent Tom-Tit-Tot have been correctly named, they lose their power, and their temper.[17]

Bettelheim states, "It is not the fact that virtue wins out at the end which promotes morality, but that the hero is most attractive to the child, who identifies with the hero in all struggles."[18] There is not a fairy tale known that doesn't end with successful growth and resolution by the hero or heroine.

Steiner recognized that the world of the fairy tale and the world of the young child are essentially the same. Both worlds share moral absolutes, mobility of imagination, and limitless possibilities for transformation.[19] Bettelheim states that fairy tales can often help children resolve fears and build feelings of competence.[20] Neil Postman, in *The Disappearance of Childhood*, praises Bettelheim's demonstration that the importance of fairy tales "lies in their capacity to reveal the existence of evil in a form that permits children to integrate it without trauma."[21]

If *you* have trouble with a fairy tale or its images, skip that one and choose another, but don't change parts of it as you go along. The "true" fairy tales are artistic wholes in which actions and descriptions are very precise. They should be told as accurately as possible, without emotional dramatization. The report of the witch locking up Hansel and later getting pushed into the oven by Gretel will not frighten a child if *you* are not in conflict about the story!

## Sharing Fairy Tales with Young Children

It is important that you be comfortable with a fairy tale and at least open to and appreciative of its deeper meaning. If a particular story pushes your buttons, don't share that one with your children. Rather, choose a fairy tale that speaks to you, one you can meditate on and try to penetrate to its mood and inner meanings. You can gain a familiarity with various approaches to the interpretation of fairy tales by reading some of the books listed at the end of this chapter, but ultimately you will need to let the fairy tale speak to you directly. Try reading it to yourself every night before you go to bed. By taking it into your sleep, you will gradually gain insight into it.

Choose an anthology of fairy tales that is as close to the original as possible (not "as retold by . . ."). A complete edition of *Grimm's Fairy Tales* can be purchased for around $10 and has more than two hundred stories suitable for all ages; Jacob's *English Fairy Tales* are appropriate for children around age seven; the French and Russian fairy tales tend to be suitable for even older children.

Whether you are reading or telling a fairy tale, repeat the same one over and over for your child. Children love repetition, and this gives them time to really live into the images and revel in their familiarity. In the Waldorf kindergarten, I would tell the same story every day for two to three weeks. Sometimes it could have gone on longer, but *I* got bored, not the children! Whenever you are sharing a story with a child under the age of seven, it is best to leave out emotional dramatization. This is very different from how librarians are taught storytelling, but their method is more appropriate for the school-aged child, with his developing inner emotional life. The young child lives more in the cadence and rhythm of the language, and in fact can become frightened or develop nightmares if too much emotion is put into the rendition of a story. However, if you tell or read the stories in a melodic voice, as if you were reporting what you were seeing, the young child will take everything in and be able to digest it and be nourished by it.

In addition to reading stories to your child at bedtime, you might want to memorize and tell a story for a group of children, a birthday party or a special treat. Weaving the storyteller's web is different from reading the same story—it involves more of your creative effort and has a different effect on the children. Memorizing and telling stories is not as difficult as it might seem—and it's never as hard as it is the first time. To memorize a story, read it out loud several times. Then visualize the scenes where the action takes place: "First they are by the well. Then after the frog gives back her golden ball, they are in the castle eating dinner. Then they move to the bedroom. Finally Faithful Henry comes and takes them away in the coach." Now as you read and practice retelling each part of the story, picture it unfolding in front of you. Do this when you tell it to the child. It is not necessary to memorize a story verbatim, although I have found that memorizing the first few sentences can help me find my way into a story.

Whenever possible, incorporate hand gestures into the story, keeping them always the same so they will help the child come to know the story. Udo de Haes writes, "When we consider the child to be ready for fairy-tales, our storytelling must address *the whole human-being* and not merely the head. We are then not expecting the child to discover the story purely through the words but are guiding him along a living experience which leads to the meaning of the fairy-tale. We should relate with the facial expressions and gestures called forth by the story itself, in a manner that is free of sentimentality and 'realism,' for it is through these [expressions and gestures] that the tale can become alive for the child."[22]

One way to match fairy tales to the age of the child is to look at their degree of complexity. In almost every fairy tale there is either a problem that must be solved or a confrontation with evil. The milder the problem, the more appropriate the tale for younger children, and conversely, the greater the evil, the more appropriate the tale is for older children.[23]

Similarly, there are often several trials of varying complexity. In "The Three Little Pigs," the pig is too smart for the wolf three times before he finally overcomes the wolf. The tasks are not really very ominous and are met with a fair amount of humor, making this tale well-loved by most four-year-olds. In contrast, the sister in "The Seven Ravens" must journey to the sun, the moon and the stars in order to free her brothers; this is a tale for five- and six-year-olds. Even more complex tales, such as "East of the Sun and West of the Moon" are appropriate for school-age children.

The following list is adapted from Joan Almon's in "Choosing Fairy Tales for Different Ages."[24] She reminds readers that you will have to make your own decisions based on a particular group of children or an individual child. Book references are contained in parentheses—see the end of this chapter for useful references. ("Grimm 103" refers to #103 in the anthology of Grimm's tales.)

**1.** Simple or sequential stories (three-year-olds):

- *Sweet Porridge* (Grimm, 103)
- *Goldilocks and the Three Bears* (Voland)
- *Little Tuppens* (Voland)
- *Little Louse and Little Flea (Spindrift)*
- *The Turnip* (Russian)
- *The Mitten* (Russian)
- *Little Madam (Spindrift)*
- *The Gingerbread Man*
- *The Johnny Cake* (English)
- *The Hungry Cat* (Norwegian, *Plays for Puppets*)

**2.** Slightly more complex stories, but cheerful without too much struggle (fours and young fives):

- *Billy Goats Gruff* (Norwegian, Voland)
- *Three Little Pigs* (English)
- *The Wolf and the Seven Kids* (Grimm, 5)
- *The Pancake Mill*
- *Mashenka and the Bear* (Russian, *Plays for Puppets*)
- *The Shoemaker and the Elves* (Grimm, 39)

**3.** More challenge and more detail; although obstacles are encountered, they do not weigh too heavily on the soul of the individual (five- and six-year-olds):

- *Star Money* (Grimm, 153)
- *The Frog Prince* (Grimm, 1)
- *Mother Hölle* (Grimm, 24)
- *Little Red Cap* (Grimm, 26)
- *The Bremen Town Musicians* (Grimm, 27)

- *The Golden Goose* (Grimm, 64)

- *Spindle, Shuttle and Needle* (Grimm, 188)

- *The Hut in the Forest* (Grimm, 169)

- *The Queen Bee* (Grimm, 62)

- *The Snow Maiden* (Russian, *Plays for Puppets*)

- *The Seven Ravens* (Grimm, 25)

- *Snow White and Rose Red* (Grimm, 161)

- *Little Briar Rose* ("Sleeping Beauty") (Grimm, 50)

- *The Donkey* (Grimm, 144)

- *Rumpelstiltskin* (Grimm, 55)

- *Snow White and the Seven Dwarves* (Grimm, 53)

- *Hansel and Gretel* (Grimm, 15)

**4.** Tales in which characters have a personal experience of suffering or sorrow (six-year-olds in the kindergarten or first-graders, to match their sense of departure from the heart of early childhood):

- *Jorinda and Joringel* (Grimm, 69)

- *Brother and Sister* (Grimm, 11)

- *Cinderella* (Grimm, 21)

- *Rapunzel* (Grimm, 12)

Almon points out that if a fairy tale is widely known in the society, children are often ready for it at an earlier age. Also, if the storyteller particularly loves a fairy tale, she can often tell it successfully to younger children. With children of mixed ages (such as three- to six-year-olds in a Waldorf mixed-age kindergarten), stories will still be successful if they are appropriate for only some of the children (the rest will listen as if carried by these other children). Udo de Haes points out that you needn't worry about toddlers in a family hearing stories that are being read to an older brother or sister. In such cases, the toddler will be most interested in the closeness of sitting with the mother and listening to the cadences of her voice and will not pay the same kind of attention as the child to whom the story is addressed.[25]

## CURATIVE STORIES

While fairy tales provide one kind of nourishment for the child, your own efforts provide another. As your child becomes older, the stories you make up can become more complex. With sufficient inspiration, you might find yourself hitting upon a main character who has various adventures. The adventures of "Princess Trueheart" were a favorite of my oldest daughter and went on for many months. Aside from the sheer delight of making up and listening to stories, it was also possible to incorporate episodes that mirrored difficulties my daughter might be having in her day-to-day life and show how the princess resolved them.

Similar made-up stories can be told to a child or group of children who are exhibiting a particular problem or behavior that you hope will change: the group may be excluding one child; a child may be telling fibs or not wanting to share. Such a *curative story* is one that presents a problem and its successful resolution in imaginative form. You can describe the situation in a slightly disguised form. Animals can be used, or a child of the opposite sex, or someone from a different time, or whatever comes into your mind. In the story the main character exhibits the problem and then either successfully overcomes it, plays it out to its ridiculously exaggerated conclusion, or in some other way sees the folly of her ways and discovers other ways of behaving. Such stories work on the inner life of the child and are effective for the same reason that Jesus taught in parables: images and stories help to educate our emotional lives, which often respond better in that way than they do to reason, threats or promises.

We used curative stories in the kindergarten about unruly horses or chatty squirrels. Once my assistant made up an elaborate story for a six-year-old boy who couldn't keep his temper under control. It was about a young knight who was given the task of staying and waiting when he really wanted to go off to battle with the others. Although it was so difficult for him, the lad managed to stay at his post, and had his own adventures and rewards. The boy for whom this story was intended was so absorbed in it that when another boy across the circle started to laugh and fool around in the middle of it, he leapt across the circle before we could blink and throttled the other child for interrupting the story. I was amazed at how deeply involved this boy had become in the story, and saw that one curative story was obviously not going to be enough!

## THE HEALING POWER OF PUPPET PLAYS

When stories and fairy tales are translated into cartoons or movies, they lose their evocative quality and are often too powerful or too inane for young children. But when the stories are acted out in front of the children, using stand-up puppets or silk marionettes, the experiences can have a very calming and healing effect on the children.

Such puppet shows for young children can be easily produced by spreading some colored silk or cotton cloth on a table or on the rug and using the stand-up dolls/puppets described in the preceding chapter. Scenery is built up by assembling pieces of bark, cloth, pine cones, shells, stones, unspun wool and similar materials to suggest the various areas of forest, home, castle— whatever the story needs. The scene is covered with a thin chiffon or gauze cloth which is carefully removed as if lifting a veil, revealing the scene in all its wonders. Then you simply tell the story while you move the puppets. You can have someone help by reading the story and playing a children's harp if you have a play group or preschool or birthday party.

Bronja Zahlingen, who has been a Waldorf early-childhood teacher for more than fifty years, and who is a master puppeteer, comments:

> It is also important for the right development and activity of the child's senses that he can watch such a play take place in actual space—length, breadth and depth; otherwise his sense organs are

easily stupefied and made passive. Pictures of action which appear to be moving on a flat screen, brought about artificially by technical skill, confuse the young child's eye, his sense of direction and movement, and often even his mind.

If the child can see the stories unfold step by step, grow and change in the simple but beautiful way described, the pictures can be taken right into the stream of his life forces, without creating hard and fixed impressions. . . . The simplicity and transparency of our table plays call forth the child's powers of imagination, and he is right in the midst of all that takes place. Through this, the creative power for his own play as well as for his own movement and language development are stimulated. In this way the child can also be helped to become a person of independence and creative activity in later life.[26]

The young children won't be bothered by seeing you move the puppets, because they are so interested in what is happening. And the image of an adult making things happen is an image of security for a young child.

You can easily make flowing silk marionettes, like the ones in the photo at the beginning of this chapter. They are moved by three strings on your fingers without any sticks to introduce jerky movements. The silk marionettes are made like the knot dolls described in Chapter 7, with the addition of small stones sewn into the hands to give them weight and strings sewn onto the hands and head. Detailed instructions are given in *Making Soft Toys* by Freya Jaffke. Again, the performing adult is visible, giving the child a sense of the world being guided and directed from above. You move the puppets as you tell the story, or you can have someone sit by the side and play the children's harp and then read the story while the puppets move through the scenes spread out with cloths on the table or floor.

The young child follows the colorful marionettes as they glide through the colored silks and veils and is engaged in a healthy way with both her senses and imagination. Zahlingen states, "An inner activity is created that works in a refreshing and enlivening way into the very breath and blood circulation. Color, movement, gesture and language shape a unity, and fitting music can envelop the soul in warmth and safety. It can also give joy and pleasure. . . . One finds that the adults, too, cannot resist the magic of such a play. The child in us loves to reenter this world of creative imagination, which releases a higher vision out of the sense experience."[27]

Rudolf Steiner gave many indications for marionette work with the fairy tales, including special attention to the color of materials chosen and the quality of voice of the narrator. He was invited by a group of adults headed by an artist/sculptor to help with marionette productions at a daycare center in Berlin just before the end of World War I. In alluding to the healing power of marionette plays he stated, "We must do everything in our power to help the children to develop fantasy."[28]

Helmut von Kügelgen, head of the International Association of Waldorf Kindergarten Teachers, states, "This picturesque, educational medium, the living play imbued with inner imagination and fantasy, should be offered in many styles as a way of activating the creative powers of children. The joy and animation of young viewers, who gladly turn their attention and love to the marionettes performing the fairy tales, develop into building stones for life in the course of a child's education."[29]

I had always wanted to be a puppeteer as a child and had even followed incredibly difficult directions to sew a marionette when I was ten years old. But moving it was so complicated that it soon went into a box to rest. If anyone had shown me these simple, flowing puppets, you never would have seen me again—which brings us to the fact that older children and adults can have a great deal of fun making the puppets and bringing them to life for the children. With my kindergarten and preschool classes, I would tell a fairy tale for almost three weeks and then end with three days of letting the children see it as a table puppet or marionette play. I know both the children and I were nourished by the wonderful mood the puppets evoked.

Children love to imitate and make puppet shows of their own. With the table puppets, sometimes I would leave the scene set up for them to use in their free play. But more often they would create their own scenes and stories from the stand-up puppets and other characters always available on the shelves. Simple marionettes can be made out of large squares of cotton cloth, which are more durable than silk for children's play. The children can then put on their own shows using blanket stands or sitting on chairs with cloths in their laps.

## RECOMMENDED READING

### Anthologies of Stories

*Classic Children's Stories* (Voland Edition, from Rand McNally). A reproduction of this classic volume for children.

*The Complete Grimm's Fairy Tales* (Pantheon Edition). More than 200 stories from which to pick and choose.

*Norwegian Tales* told by Asbjornsen and Moe.

*Plays for Puppets and Marionettes* (compiled by Bronja Zahlingen, available from Acorn Hill Children's Center, 9500 Brunett Ave., Silver Spring, MD 20901).

*Spindrift*, a volume of kindergarten stories and songs gathered by the British Waldorf Kindergarten Teachers (available from the Rudolf Steiner College, 9200 Fair Oaks Blvd., Fair Oaks, CA 95628).

### About Fairy Tales

*Bildsprache der Marchen* by Friedel Lenz. This excellent book is being translated into English; contact the Waldorf Kindergarten Association, 9500 Brunett Ave., Silver Spring, MD 20901.

*Fairy Stories . . . Why, When, How* by Miriam Whitfield. (Available from Joan Treadway, 1920 Thumb Butte Rd., Prescott, AZ 86301.)

*From Two to Five* by Kornei Chukovsky (Berkeley, CA: University of California Press, 1963).

"The Interpretation of Fairy Tales" by Rudolf Steiner (New York: Anthroposophic Press, 1943).

*Lifeways* by Gudrun Davy and Bons Voors (IBP, SG). Contains two chapters on the inner meaning of fairy tales.

*The Wisdom of Fairy Tales* by Rudolf Meyer (SG). Interpretations working out of the indications of Rudolf Steiner.

*The Young Child: Creative Living with Two to Four Year Olds* by Daniel Udo de Haes (IBP, SG). Focuses on stories for the young child, signs when a child is ready for fairy tales and the inner meanings of the tales.

# 9 | *Developing Your Child's Artistic Ability*

## THE EXPERIENCE OF COLOR

Children have natural artistic ability that can easily go un-developed or become stifled by inappropriate activities; this often results in frustration and beliefs such as, "I can't draw." Helping your child's artistic ability to unfold is a great gift you can give him—not that a child will necessarily grow up to be an artist, but that he will maintain a living relationship with color, that he will be able to appreciate the play of light and shadow with a sensitive eye and that he will feel confident about expressing himself through some artistic medium and find enjoyment in the process.

The world of color is directly related to the way we feel. Colors affect our attitude to life and our moods, which are then expressed in colors. Even our speech reflects this relationship— "green with envy," "feeling blue," "livid with rage," "seeing red," "rose-colored spectacles," "jaundiced view." You could say that the very substance of the soul is color. Color is to the spiritual life what food, air and water are to the physical life. As these nourish our bodies, so color nourishes the soul and spirit.

The world of nature is bathed in color. Color comes and goes seasonally, and indeed each day with the coming and going of the light. Just as sunrise and sunset express their own moods through color, so the mood of spring, with its cold earth and moist air, is very different from the mood of fall, with its warm earth and cool dry air.[1]

Children love colors and unite with the colors that flow toward them from their surroundings. Children's feelings are also strongly affected by colors, so that one color may produce a feeling of well-being, while another calls up a feeling of discomfort. Because children are so much more receptive than adults, their experience of color is all the more intense.

In the first seven years the young child takes in everything with her total being; body, soul and spirit are still united. The young child is completely open to experiences of color in her environment, and for this reason we need to create environments that reflect her sensitivity to good artistic qualities—colors, forms, wall decorations, sounds and toys. This achieves a deeper effect than "art education" offered in a few spare hours.

The psychological effects of color on people are now being recognized, and are beginning to be put into practice in such places as hospitals and mental institutions. When we consider the psychological effects of color on children, Steiner says that the complementary color must be taken into account up to the age of nine:

> A "nervous," that is to say excitable child, should be treated differently as regards the environment from one who is quiet and lethargic. Everything comes into consideration, from the color of the room and the various objects that are generally around the child, to the color of the clothes in which he is dressed. . . . An excitable child should be surrounded by and dressed in red and reddish-yellow colors, whereas for a lethargic child one should have recourse to the blue or blueish-green shades of color. For the important thing is the complementary color, which is created within the child. In the case of red it is green, and in the case of blue, orange-yellow.[2]

I saw this phenomenon in my kindergarten when each day the largest, rowdiest boy would immediately head for the costume rack and put on a red satin shirt. When he had it on, he was somehow more settled within himself. The explanation that the complementary color works more directly on the young child was one I was unaware of until I read about it in Steiner's writings. As adults we experience the phenomenon only briefly if we stare at a bright red circle and see a green circle when we look away. According to Steiner, the inner experience of the complementary color is stronger for the young child than the experience of the external color; only in the course of time does he come to experience colors as a grownup does.

Ordinarily we think of colors as attributes of objects. But to the inward vision of the soul, the essential natures of the colors can be revealed. Goethe's *Theory of Color* forms a basis for much of Steiner's writing on color.[3] Steiner states:

> Goethe draws our attention to the feelings which the colors arouse in us. He points out the challenging nature of red, and his teaching is as much concerned with what the soul feels when it beholds red, as with what the eye sees. Likewise he mentions the stillness and contemplativeness which the soul feels in the presence of blue. We can present the colors to children in such a way that they will spontaneously experience the shades of feeling engendered by the colors, and will naturally feel the colors' inner life.[4]

Therefore parents and teachers are advised to let the child live and work in the world of color as soon as possible, immersing himself in the feelings it engenders. Brunhild Müller, in *Painting with Children*, states, "Not only do children perceive the color but at the same time they sense its quality, they feel in themselves its intrinsic nature, and they are conscious of the non-material essential being of such color. This consciousness is lost as the child grows older, and by the time children go to school they experience colors as attributes of objects (the blue ball, the red roof and so on)."[5]

Therefore it is appropriate to expose the young child to activities such as painting and crayoning when they emphasize the experience of color and are not approached as "lessons" in which the child has to imitate the adult or achieve an end-product or finished form. Such experiences of art are valuable for the young child as pure color experiences. Such experiences can also lead to abilities that can be transformed throughout the child's life.

# WATERCOLOR PAINTING WITH YOUNG CHILDREN

One of the best experiences of color for the young child comes through painting with watercolors on wet paper. Colors are in their own true element in water. Their waving, shimmering and streaming nature is manifest the moment they lose their heavy and earthy hardness. Rauld Russell, who wrote *How to Do Wet-on-Wet Watercolor Painting and Teach Your Children*, explains: "A wet paper surface lends flowing movement to color. Color in a thin sea of water can move, mingle, change, lighten and darken, just like feelings and emotions. To fix all the richness of inner life, all the potentiality, into a rigid form with hard boundaries (as one would do in 'dry' painting) can evoke 'hardened' images of life. The application of wet-on-wet most truly corresponds to the soft, unfinished, still growing nature of the child."[6]

No one paints like kindergarten-age children, because they are totally unself-conscious. If you are not familiar with children's paintings done in this wet-on-wet technique, two inexpensive books with color illustrations of such paintings are *Painting with Children* by Brunhild Müller and *Echoes of a Dream* by Susan Smith, both listed at the end of this chapter. You can easily do this kind of painting with your child, and the results are beautiful!

## Supplies

The thought of going into an art supply store may be overwhelming to you, but you only need three tubes of color! In Waldorf preschools we only use the primary colors red, yellow and blue with the young children, allowing the infinite number of other colors they form to appear on the paper under the child's excited eye. Russell reminds us that, "Because watercolor painting reaches into the deep psycho-biological processes that affect a child's growth, for a very young child you will want to choose a bright medium golden yellow, a cobalt or ultramarine blue, and a rose-crimson red. The purity of the color is essential. . . ." He recommends Stockmar, Grumbacher, Winsor Newton or other artist's grade watercolors. (Acrylics will not work.)[7]

It is also worthwhile to invest in some good-quality paper such as Grumbacher or Aquabee all-purpose paper or Strathmore 80- to 90-lb. painting paper. Less expensive paper will not bring out the luminous quality and intensity of the colors and will shred into paper-towel consistency before your child finishes a painting. Large sheets of paper are expensive, but can be cut into four pieces, and you and your child only need to paint one picture each session. This kind of painting is special—it's not like covering as many sheets of typing paper as possible with paints from a box!

While you are at the store, buy yourself and your child a large flat brush (at least three-quarter-inch wide) rather than a pointed brush. The flat brushes give more of an experience of color and discourage outlining.

THINGS YOU WILL NEED FROM HOME INCLUDE:

- A set of three baby-food-sized jars for each painter.

- Pint-sized jars for premixing and storing colors (you may need to store them in the refrigerator if they spoil easily).

- Similar jars for rinsing brushes between colors (the advantage of jars over cans is that they don't rust, and the child can see the changing color of the water as he paints—fully as interesting as the painting itself!).

- Because the paintings need to be kept horizontal to dry, a wooden or masonite board (16" × 20" × ¼") is handy for painting on and drying.

- A clean sponge used only to wipe off the wet paper before starting.

- A sponge or cloth for each painter to wipe her brush on.

- Smocks or painting shirts.

## Preparation

Children love to help with the preparations for painting. Putting on your smock and getting out the materials will almost always produce a willing helper.

- Prepare the paper by cutting it to size (a two-year-old will need a smaller piece than a five-year-old). In the Waldorf early-childhood programs we always round off the corners of the paper because the rounded form is more suitable for the young child than the square geometric form. The rounded form also frees the children from painting around the outline of the paper, which many will do with square sheets.

- Put the individual sheets in water to soak. A sink will do; a plastic tray is helpful if you have lots of children painting.

- Squeeze some color from the tube into your mixing jar and add water to dilute it to a light-syrup consistency. You'll need more color with yellow than you will with blue. Then put a small amount of this pre-mixed color (one-half inch) in each painting jar so it won't be wasted if it becomes muddied or spilled. You can store the extra and refill the small jars as needed.

- Let your child help put the painting boards down and fill the water jars. Arrange the three paint jars on each board and give a dampened sponge to each painter to wipe her brush on. Keeping the brushes until everything else is ready will help prevent premature enthusiasm from carrying everyone away.

- Now put a sheet of paper on the board and wipe it off with the sponge that is reserved for this job. If the paper is too wet, the colors will float away and dry into puddles. But don't wipe it too dry, either!

### Starting to Paint

The first time you use these techniques with a young child, you can just mix up one color. Then, over the first several sessions, the child will experience what yellow, blue and red have to tell him when each is used all by itself.

You will want to demonstrate for your child how to wipe the brush dry on the edge of the jar and on the sponge before it is dipped into the color so that later on greater control can be achieved.

When you introduce two colors, demonstrate how the paint brush needs to be rinsed before changing colors. I often said something like, "Peter Paintbrush needs to take a bath and wash his hair before he puts on his new clothes. And he needs to dry his hair on the sponge first to see if it is clean." We would look at the sponge to see if it was clean, and if so, Peter would go into the next color. Wiping the rinsed brush on the sponge both tests for cleanness and removes excess water. That simple technique is all you need to teach during painting—you don't need lessons or themes—but don't expect young children to remember always to rinse their brush. Simply let the child experience the colors as they unfold in his painting. Because young children are so imitative, it is best for you to do a similar kind of color painting without trying to bring form or meaning to it. Let your child lead *you*, rather than producing an adult painting with meaning. When you start working with two colors, your child will be delighted to discover what happens when yellow plays with blue, for example. The children's experiences with color are alive and active when they paint in this way, so they will have had a living experience rather than an intellectual idea that "yellow and blue make green." Not having had the experience of such things myself as a child, I can recall being ten years old and trying to remember whether yellow and blue made green or blue and green made yellow. Children who paint in this way never have that intellectual dilemma!

You can introduce yellow and blue, yellow and red, and red and blue before you put out all three colors at once. You won't need more than the three primary colors until your child is in grade school. For suggestions on how this approach to painting can evolve with older children, see *How to Do Wet-on-Wet Watercolor Painting and Teach Your Children* or *Painting with Children*, listed at the end of this chapter. From a foundation of having experienced the colors, older children are gradually able to bring forms out of the colors, rather than trying to paint forms based on outlines like a coloring book.

## Children's Experience of Painting

The preschool child best learns to paint as he learns every other skill—through imitation. Therefore if your child can watch you or an older sibling paint, he will soon grasp the techniques without instruction. Just be sure that you are always careful to wipe your brush on the side of the water jar and on the sponge before dipping it into a new color. Avoid the temptation to pinch the brush with your fingers unless you want your child to do the same. In a similar way, your child will help with setting up and cleaning up with you if you give him things to do.

The preschool- or kindergarten-age child does not need explanations or themes to follow. As the child becomes older, stories and fantasy-filled words can be used by the teacher or parent to introduce painting sessions related to various themes such as the fall colors or a spring meadow. But the younger child needs only the opportunity to experience the colors and to paint what comes from within himself. The colors talk to the young child and unfold their secrets before him.

Three-year-olds are often satisfied with a single color, and they are finished painting only when their color jar is empty. It is not possible for them to guide their brush in a directed manner. They may move their brushes enthusiastically or timidly back and forth on the paper, and you can see that movement and the color it produces are the most important aspects for the very young child. If the child has a low table at which he can stand to paint, his body is more free for movement; if not, sitting at the dining room table is certainly all right.

If a three-year-old is given two or three colors at the start, he will probably paint the colors over top of, rather than next to, one another, and a muddy surface will result. But if you begin with a single color and only gradually add the second and the third, your child will soon learn to paint by laying the colors next to one another.

Four- and five-year-old children paint with the colors next to each other on the paper, and will happily share their discoveries of the new colors or the forms that have appeared on their paper. Five- and six-year-olds will approach painting with more of a plan, just as they now approach free play with an idea of what they want to do. Before they dip their brushes into the first color, they often have an image of a definite color they want to use or an object such as a tree, rainbow or heart they want to paint. The watercolors and damp paper make it difficult to paint solid outlines, which is good for the further development of the child's fantasy forces. Many times when the children add a new color to the already started form, they will have a new sense-association which will interact with their fantasy. These older children will gladly tell you or another child something about their picture—which color they especially like or what content they discover in the painted picture.

Be receptive to any comments your child makes, but refrain from asking, "What is it?" or "What does it mean?" The child has had a color experience that may or may not arrive at any completed forms. Also, it is better to praise the beauty of the colors or the nature of their interaction rather than the artist. This postpones self-consciousness and the element of judgment.

A child who is precocious or "overly awake" can be helped by the fluid qualities of painting. Von Heydebrand states, "Color surfaces or waves of color flowing into each other, not strengthening or crystallizing into too hardened forms, bring the over-precocious or too clever child back into the right condition of the more dreamy atmosphere of childhood."[8]

Having already put up favorite paintings on the refrigerator or walls, you will soon have a wonderful, growing stack that you can use for other purposes: as birthday invitations, place cards, gift wrappings, crowns, book covers or origami figures. Even those paintings that don't appear very interesting often have areas where the colors flow beautifully and which can be cut into wondrous things.

### Metamorphosis in Later Stages of Life

In addition to the wonderful present-time activity of painting, there are other benefits. When a child finds the colors in this way true to his own inner experience and being and then finds them again in nature, he will look at them with more sensitivity to the interplay of light and color. Even if it is not his destiny to become an artist, he will have a greater understanding and appreciation of the world, having been awakened to reverence.

There are other benefits, less directly related to the artistic experience, but of great value in a person's life. These qualities in later life that were unconsciously influenced by the young child's experience of painting are discussed by Freya Jaffke in her article "About Painting and Human Development Through Art."[9] For example, painting includes such processes as being careful, paying attention, waiting, following the course of the work, experiencing the laws of color mixing and applying color in varying strengths.

> All of these activities give ever-renewed stimulus to the gradually awakening soul of the child, helping him to grasp his physical body and make his sense organization and his limbs ever more responsive. One who at an early age has learned to pay attention to the strength or delicacy of color and to gradations in applying it, will later find it easier to apply the same soul capacities in social situations, for example in self-assertion and in acquiescence or in the ability to hold conversations in which he brings forth his own arguments and is yet receptive to the responses of his partner. In a similar way, the adult process of logical thinking is helped by the inner order in the sequence of the steps of painting.[10]

As Jaffke points out, "sequencing" is best learned by the young child through *doing,* not by talking about what we did first, second and last.

Jaffke concludes by saying, "Naturally, the child is not conscious of this. He does not reflect on what he is doing, but lives intensively in the activities. In this way he has experiences at deep levels which can wait there to be grasped by him consciously in later stages of life and to find expression in an ability to lead his own life. These effects reveal the true human justification for artistic endeavors in the preschool. Art is not an aesthetic add-on to 'real life,' but as an exercise of continual striving it can become the foundation of a truly human mastery of life."[11]


# COLORING WITH CRAYONS

## *Understanding Children's Drawings*

A child often starts drawing before the age of two, either enthusiastically or tentatively grasping the pencil or crayon for the first time. But once he joyously discovers the potential involved, he will be delighted to color frequently and on any surface that presents itself! At whatever age within the first seven years that the child starts drawing, he will begin at the two-year-old scribbling stage. If the child is already past that age, he will go through all the earlier stages in rapid succession, and stop at the motif corresponding to his own development. What are the stages and motifs you can watch for in your child's drawings? It will strengthen your appreciation for the being of your child when you observe her development as reflected in her drawings.

The following information is taken from the excellent book *Understanding Children's Drawings* by Michaela Strauss,[12] based on a lifetime of observations by Hanns Strauss, who left behind a collection of more than six thousand young children's drawings that he had assembled and annotated.

Children's drawings can be roughly divided into three stages, similar to those found in their play and their painting. In the first phase, before age three, the child creates purely out of the movement that carries her. The process of creation arises in a dreamy way, out of the rhythms and movements coming from within her own body, so if you ask a very young child about her drawing, she will usually be unable to explain the content to you.

In the second phase, between ages three and five, the child lets the arising picture take hold of her imagination. While she draws she will tell you about the picture as it unfolds in front of her.

After the fifth year, the child often approaches coloring with a definite idea or picture in mind, "I am going to draw my dog, Blacky, chasing a rabbit."

Within each phase, certain motifs predominate, and the new ones don't appear until the child has reached the next developmental stage. For example, two types of movements dominate the drawings of children under three. These are a spiral movement and a pendular or vertical movement. At first the movements are very large, even larger than the paper, which barely seems to contain them. Strauss observed that until the age of three, spirals are always drawn from outward to inward, only gradually forming a center that reflects the child's growing realization of self between ages two and three. The flash of ego consciousness is documented by the ability to draw the form of the circle which, even if the child says "I" earlier on, rarely appears in drawings before the third year. It is also interesting to note that monkeys are quite good at drawing like young children—certainly their jumping and swinging gives them an inward propensity toward movement and they have the interest and dexterity to use a crayon or brush—but they are unable to make a connected circle out of the spiral movements they have in common with the child under three.[13]

Strauss suggests that the spiral movements in "scribbling" are echoes of the movements of the cosmos and of the flowing rhythms of the fluids within the young child's own body. Similarly, she suggests that the vertical element that appears along with the spiral one is an expression of the child's own recent achievement of standing upright.

At the same time a child is able to form a circle, he will probably be seen to make a crossed horizontal and vertical line for the first time. Soon the cross will be drawn *inside* the circle, and circles will also be drawn that have a dot inside them. Both cases reflect the child's first experiences of inner and outer in his increasing consciousness during the third year.

After the third year, the circle and crossed lines are fused into a unity, and they appear in the most diverse variations until the fifth year and beyond. However, changes continue to occur during this time. The point and the cross, having crystalized as "I" symbols, begin to transform and to radiate from the center outward. At first the radiating lines will stop at the edge of the circle, then reach out like feelers beyond the edge of the circle.

As the child continues to develop, houses, trees and people are frequently drawn. Strauss shows how the forms of a tree and a human being are the same for a young child and represent his own changing awareness of his body. First the focus is on the head, with a trunk extending down from it (a floating tree or "pillar person"). It is not until the child is older that the legs become divided and firmly planted on the ground. Around the age of four the child's focal point shifts from the head to the trunk, and a ladder pattern emerges in children's drawings, like the branches of a tree or the branching of the spinal column and the ribs. Drawings now for the first time have left-right orientation around an axis of symmetry, like the body around the backbone.

Children at this age also draw people with arms coming off of the head or huge fingers, reflecting their increasing connection with the world: reaching out and getting into everything. The feet take the longest time to be developed in drawings and are thick and heavy, becoming rooted to the ground. The child draws the human being, not as we see it, but as he experiences his own self and body. The inner life processes, not the external form, are the determining factors.[14]

The house is another theme through which the child represents her changing relationship between self and world. Drawings of a very young child often show a circle or "head person" inside a larger circle, like the child in the cosmos or the baby in the womb. As the close unity between self and world gives way to separate individuality, the spherical, "cosmic" house becomes more square in form and anchored near the bottom of the paper. In the third year, the form of the square or box appears for the first time surrounding the person. The narrowing down in the perception of cosmic realms through the acquiring of selfhood— the process of becoming an "I"—resembles an encapsulating of the soul. A child may draw a person looking out of the house, and the connections between inner world and outer world can be seen in the doors, windows and chimneys that now begin to appear.

Color as a new means of expression is added to the drawing of lines in the middle phase, ages three to five. Before the third year the child tends to use color mostly to emphasize the line. But toward the fourth year a new element appears, drawing color for its own sake. Strauss writes, "Touched by the nature of colour, the soul of the child becomes creative. When the world of feeling comes into drawing, the world of colour comes into it too."[15] Before the child uses color for drawing objects, he uses it in drawings to cover a surface, exploring the qualities of colors by filling in areas in a dramatic or more symmetrical "checkerboard" fashion. It is just at this age that block crayons (see next section) enable the child to cover large surfaces and increase his color experience.

Around the age of five children will start making illustrative drawings and wish to represent objects and scenes from life or stories. These narrative-illustrative drawings will start to wrestle with the elements of space and changing perspective; the profile of the face appears for the first time. The triangle also appears for the first time and can become the focus of multicolored geometrical designs which kindergarten children love to make.

When elementary-school-age children draw a tree and a house, the forms look more as we have come to expect them to look. But close observation of such drawings can also reveal interesting things about the inner life of the older child. One very dreamy boy never drew his people touching the ground, even as late as second grade. And a kindergarten boy in my class drew a sad figure between two houses. He said that one was a house and one was a fire station, but from the interview with his mother I knew that his parents were divorcing and he was spending time with both his mother and father—a sad little boy feeling himself on the road between two homes.

The relationship of children's art to their developing consciousness parallels the developing consciousness of humanity as expressed in primitive art and its evolution over the centuries. Just as the first babbling of a baby is unconnected with particular racial or national characteristics, this first picture writing is also universally human. In this early period of the first seven years the language of symbols is the same the world over. Both Strauss's book and *The Incarnating Child* provide many illustrations of children's drawings, which can become another pathway to increase your understanding of the changing consciousness of the young child.

## Coloring with Block Crayons

Using block rather than stick crayons enables your child to cover an entire page with color with very little effort. By using the flat edges rather than the corners of the block crayons, bands of color rather than outlines are made. Within these broad bands of color, forms spring and grow naturally. The yellow streams down and outward; the red is concentrated and strong; the blue gently curves and surrounds. Into these gestures of color spring forms, without demanding precision and intricacy.

When you make a picture in front of a young child, every breath, every thought, every peaceful, careful stroke you make feeds and instructs the child. A picture you carefully and lovingly make for your child is a gift on many levels. It need not be great art! If at night you make a picture for your child from her own experience of the day's activities, with what wonder your child will wake up to this gift, just as the "Rhyme Elves" often left a little poem and drawing of important events for Sylvia in the *Seven-Year-Old Wonder-Book*.[16] Such pictures can be kept in a special collection, perhaps in a special box or drawer.

As you can see, one of the added benefits of doing these things with your children is that you can nourish your own inner child and your innate artistic ability, which was probably squelched through lack of use or beliefs such as, "I can't draw or paint." One of the most exciting things about the Waldorf teacher training is the rehabilitation of your own childhood and artistic ability. All children have this innate artistic ability. If they are given watercolors rather than marking pens, if they can color on blank sheets of paper instead of "keeping within the lines," this ability is more likely to stay alive and accessible to them throughout their lives.

The block crayons used in Waldorf Schools are made of sweet-smelling beeswax rather than paraffin and can be purchased through Hearth Song. If you don't want to order them, *Echoes of a Dream* suggests a way to make your own block crayons. First make little boxes about the size of ice cubes from a double thickness of aluminum foil. Place one to two large stick crayons without their papers in each box (a great way to recycle old broken crayons). Place the foil boxes on a pan and put in a preheated oven (225°F) for about five minutes, long enough for the crayons to melt. Remove from the oven and allow to cool completely. After you take off the foil, you can smoothe the edges with a peeling knife.[17]


## MODELLING WITH BEESWAX

Another artistic activity your child will enjoy is modelling with colored beeswax. Beeswax has several advantages over clay—it smells nice, isn't messy, can be used over and over and involves warmth. The child must take a bit of colored beeswax and warm it with his hands, with both his hands and the beeswax becoming warm in the process. Clay, on the other hand, is cold earth and tends to rob the body of warmth; for this reason, clay is often used with children over nine and beeswax with younger children. With very young children or in very cold weather, the beeswax may be too hard for the child to soften; then it can be warmed a bit by your own efforts or by setting it next to a heater to give the child a head start in softening it.

Colored beeswax as used in the Waldorf schools is available from Hearth Song and makes a wonderful birthday present or holiday gift. To use it, warm a piece in your hands while your child does the same. This is a good time to tell a little story. Then start to make something. As with the other artistic activities, let your child make whatever comes to him without instruction. For preschool children, art is an expression of their inner experience, and it is inappropriate to try to make it conform to ideas imposed from the outside. Remembering the principle of imitation, do your beeswax modelling along with your child. I always found that by finishing last I was able to see the children's creations without them wanting to make what I had made, or wanting me to make the same thing for them! Very young children will simply enjoy the texture of the beeswax, pinching and stretching it. As a fantasy element enters in, they will tell you what it is they have made (even though there may be no resemblance that you can discern). As they turn four and five they can become quite skilled and creative in what they make, and the figures can be placed on a little log in a special place to be played with or to wait until next time they are warmed and transformed into something else.

Another product for modelling is Alpena, which has the advantage of never hardening, but, unlike plasticene, is made of natural ingredients. It is also available from Hearth Song. Having worked with these natural materials, I have grown to prefer their feel to Playdoh or other products—and they don't crumble onto the floor! Flour, water and salt can also make a play dough that will afford your child hours of enjoyment. You'll need to experiment with the proportions.

# MAKING THINGS WITH CHILDREN

Making things with your child or letting him imitate things he has seen you make are artistic activities that encourage creativity, dexterity and aesthetic judgment. Because the preschool children often saw me sewing, they loved to work from their own sewing basket, and a couple of them made dolls that were much more creative than mine because they lacked the conscious element of how a doll "should" look. If you find yourself starting to make dolls and toys suggested in this book, set up a sewing basket for your child. Imitating real work is one of a child's greatest delights.

Similarly, the children loved to embroider, at first using large plastic needles with yarn on burlap placed in embroidery hoops. We were able to make designs on placemats, bookmarks and "nature bags," which we used for gathering treasures on walks. The older children were able to use embroidery floss and sharp needles, and soon learned how to handle safely the sharp scissors for making dolls.

Other projects with yarn include making twisty-twirlies. Tie several colors of yarn to the back of a chair or a door knob. Let your child twist them around and around. Then bring the end up to the beginning and pinch them together. The two thicknesses will wrap around each other into a thicker rope, which can be used as horses' reins, a purse handle, a belt or a dog's leash. Other projects with yarn, such as finger crochet, are described in the books listed at the end of this chapter.

You and your child can also make things out of bark, branches and slices of logs—boats to sail, bird feeders or doll furniture from wood and spools. The act of creation through the transformation of materials is one of the fundamentally human acts. Actually making something is so much more satisfying for children than cutting out shapes or fitting square pegs into round holes. Many wonderful ideas for craft projects can be found in the books listed next.

# RECOMMENDED READING

## About Drawing and Painting

*Echoes of a Dream* by Susan Smith. Available from the Waldorf School Association of London, 838 Wellington St. North, London, Ontario, Canada N6A 3S7.

*How to Do Wet-on-Wet Watercolor Painting and Teach Your Children* by Rauld Russell. Available from the author at The Iris, 1820 Stock Slough Road, Coos Bay, OR 97420.

*Painting with Children* by Brunhild Müller (SG).

*Understanding Children's Drawings* by Michaela Strauss.

## Craft Ideas to Do with Children

*The Children's Year* by Cooper, Fynes-Clinton and Rowling (IBP, SG).

*Echoes of a Dream* by Susan Smith. See address above.

*Festivals, Family and Food* by Diane Carey and Judy Large (IBP, SG).

*Making Soft Toys* by Freya Jaffke.

## Source for watercolors, beeswax crayons and beeswax for modelling

Hearth Song, P. O. Box B, Sebastopol, CA 95473.

# 10 | *Your Child's Musical Ability*

## MAKING A JOYFUL NOISE

Children love sounds. They love to make them—with their own voices, by banging a spoon on a cooking pot, by blowing into a wooden flute. And they love to hear sounds, because sounds give them exciting news about the inner structure of an object. They unconsciously absorb the sound that manifests the nature of the object when it is touched, knocked or dropped. The baby with a rattle is expressing its nature to be in movement, but it is also listening to the sounds its movements produce that stop when it stops moving.

Movement is interwoven with sound for the young child. Neurologists have found that a child who is unable to make certain movements is unable to make certain sounds. The young child is naturally in movement. The child's movement often remains free-flowing until school age if it has not been repressed by the environment. The movement forms itself into long and short rhythms, but doesn't manifest what we call *beat* (regular emphasis every so many counts) until the child turns nine. Around the age of nine, the child enters a new relationship with the world and is able to feel and understand triads and scales.[1]

Speaking of the inner musical nature of the young child, Rudolf Steiner states, "We shall then notice that it is man's nature, up to a point, to be born a 'musician.' . . . It is a fact that the individual is born into the world with the desire to bring his own body into a musical rhythm, into a musical relationship with the world, and this inner musical capacity is most active in children in their third and fourth year."[2]

Seeing to your child's musical and movement activities in the preschool years might or might not make him a great musician in later life (that depends on musical talent and destiny), but it *can* lay the foundation for healthy development, which has ramifications in all spheres of life. Julius Knierim, a music specialist working with children with special needs, reports that "in curative education we often have children whose weak powers of concentration and whose unrest are due to their not having fully lived through their need for movement in early childhood. But we also have children who are damaged by 'music,' who too early have had to take in the 'blessings' of our civilization in the form of 'musica ex machina' [music out of the machine] and who did not come with sufficient constitutional protection against such attacks. Their unrest and lack of motivation, when the challenges of school work arise, have opposite causes."[3] Knierim is here distinguishing between live music, from singing or playing a musical instrument, and recorded music, which can have a damaging effect on the development of the young child, whose senses are so completely open.[4]

## SINGING WITH YOUR CHILD

One of the simplest and best musical things you can do with your child is to sing. This can begin prenatally and continue through lullabies and special songs that you make up for your baby. Once your child becomes verbal, she will love to sing with you, the more so if you add gestures and movements to match the words. Singing involves the breath and the middle heart/lung sphere, whose development is emphasized between the ages of three and five. Its proper development forms the basis for later health and balanced overall development. Rudolf Steiner said, "You will be fostering all this if you give the child plenty of singing. You must have a feeling that the child is a musical instrument while he is singing. . . . Every child is a musical instrument and inwardly feels a kind of well-being in the sound."[5]

Knierim observed that children before the age of nine mostly sing much higher when by themselves than the pitch of music they have heard in their environment. They will also sing faster than an adult's rhythmic sense would dictate. Much of their singing is not yet rhythmically "correct" because their pulse/breathing ratio has not yet settled at the 4:1 ratio that characterizes an adult's; and their voices are still light, nonresonant, hovering and silvery. Children lack the complexity of adult experience and feel completely satisfied and fulfilled with simple melodies, whereas an adult would feel something was lacking and might long for more complicated harmonies and rhythms.[6]

It is difficult to simplify enough for the young child. Even a song with one note can be completely satisfying. Here is one that I made up while looking out the window. It can have hand movements like falling rain and a circle formed by the arms for a puddle.

*See the rain-drops fal-ling down! Mak-ing pud-dles on the ground.*

When in doubt, choose the note *A* above *Middle C*. The qualities of this note are associated with the sun and are especially suitable for early childhood, according to Steiner. Here's a song that goes up and down from the *A*.

*I can run in the sun. I can fly in the sky!*

If you take off running and flying, your child will delightedly be there with you.

You can also make up songs to go with activities around the house, such as stirring or sewing, and songs can also ease transitions, such as cleaning up the toys or going upstairs to nap. The following song is by Mary Lynn Channer, a Waldorf teacher, and is used with permission.

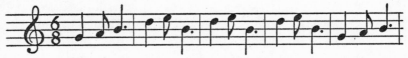

*May I ride piggy-back, piggy-back, piggy-back? May I ride*

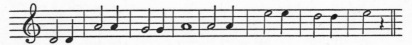

*piggy-back? And then I'll take my nap.*

When you are telling fairy tales, remember how simply key phrases can become a song, like the following from *Briar Rose* ("Sleeping Beauty").

*Mirror, mirror on the wall: Who's the fairest of them all?*

Many favorite folk songs and holiday songs that are part of our culture become "old friends" for your child when they come around each year with the cycle of the seasons. Some traditional songs contain the same kind of folk wisdom we found in the nursery rhymes. For example, "Rock-a-bye-baby," according to Eileen Hutchins, "tells of the child cradled in the mother's womb and surrounded by the world of spirit (for spirit literally means wind). But the time of birth draws near and child and cradle (or caul) are cast into the world."[7]

Singing with your child is one of the joys of parenting. If you can't remember songs from your own childhood, several excellent anthologies are listed at the end of this chapter.

# MOVEMENT GAMES AND FINGERPLAYS

As an adult who hadn't moved for a few decades, I found putting movements to songs and verses not my strong suit as a new early-childhood teacher. I could remember "I'm a little tea pot" from when I was three years old, but that was about all. But I decided to continue inwardly trying to understand the *gesture* of various activities (the movements that express the essential nature of an activity). Gradually the children taught me, and I began to understand more and more. Now I can do appropriate preschool movements to any song or verse, but I certainly felt awkward and self-conscious when I started! Seeing how imitative young children are and how much it is part of their nature to move along with the words helped me rediscover this childlike part of myself.

Start with fingerplays and movement verses from your own childhood or from the ends of Chapters 4 and 5. Perhaps you remember "The Wheels on the Bus" or "Six Little Ducks" or "Where is Thumbkin?" The interaction with your child, the engaging of the faculties of imitation and the musical elements all unite in this kind of play that has delighted children for centuries and that has great value for their development as well. Steiner points out how fingerplays and other tasks such as knitting, which develop dexterity in the fingers, help with brain development and later facility in clear thought.[8]

Circle games are also an ancient part of early childhood that delight young children. Modern ones like "Motorboat, motorboat, go so slow . . . Motorboat, motorboat, go so fast . . . Motorboat, motorboat, step on the gas!" are fun for their quality of changing speed and movement, but they lack the musical element. Older circle games such as "Ring Around the Roses" and "Sally Go Round the Sun" provide a picture in movement and song of the child's incarnating process. Jane Winslow Eliot, in her book on circle games, writes:

> Watch when a child falls on the ground. The shrieks are out of proportion to the damage done. It is because the little one has been shocked out of an enveloping cloud into a sudden realization of the solidity of the earth. The soul resents this. When you ritualize this happening in the garment of a game such as the lovely *Ring Around the Roses*, you lead the child lovingly, gently down to earth

and she begins to enjoy the fun of it. Bit by bit the children don't mind staying.[9]

Ring games are joyful, sociable, simple and yet they have all the solemnity of a ritual in the way they are repeated over and over. A traditional game like "Go In and Out the Windows" has one child weave in and out through the other children's upraised arms. Then she is directed to "stand and face your true love," then "take him off to London" (or New York in the American version). Each verse has the refrain, "As you have done before" and can be interpreted to represent in game form the process of coming into and going out of earthly life or, according to Hutchins, "the alternating condition between sleeping and waking when the windows of the senses reveal the outer world. Then comes the search for the soul mate and the journey to London which symbolizes the achievement of the chosen earthly task. Pedants are often puzzled that such apparently trivial verses have survived the ages, but it is now commonly recognized by folk-lore students that these old songs and games have a ritual quality."[10]

Circle games contain rhythms that affect the beat of the children's pulses; they sometimes incorporate the ability to do tasks without self-consciousness, as in washing the clothes or brushing one's hair in "Here We Go Round the Mulberry Bush"; others deal with the interplay between the individual and the group, as in "The Farmer in the Dell" (which is a game that can be too strong for three-year-olds, who don't yet like being singled out and standing alone at the end). A child who does not want to be chosen should never be forced, for games that single out individual characters are too self-conscious for the very young child. The five-year-old, on the other hand, loves to be the Farmer or the Cheese or to be caught in the games "London Bridge" or "Oranges and Lemons." Younger children will enjoy these games if they can participate as part of the circle without being singled out before they are ready.

Steiner comments about the value of rhythmical games for young children:

> For early childhood it is important to realize the value of children's songs as a means of education. They must make a pretty and rhythmical impression on the senses; the beauty of sound is to be

valued more than the meaning of words. The more vivid the impression made on the ear, the better. Dancing movements in musical rhythm have a powerful influence in building up the physical organs and this should likewise not be undervalued.[11]

*Eurythmy* is an art of movement to speech and tones developed by Rudolf Steiner that has application in both regular and special education. It is especially suited to the musical nature of the young child and is done in those Waldorf kindergartens and nursery programs fortunate enough to have a trained eurythmist in the area. For more information on eurythmy, see Appendix C.


## PENTATONIC MUSIC AND THE "MOOD OF THE FIFTH"

The pentatonic scale has five notes instead of the seven we are used to in our normal diatonic scales. For example, a pentatonic scale built around *A* would have the notes *D, E, G, A, B* with no half steps (so the notes *C* and *F* are not included). If you look closely at children's songs and folk songs, you will see that many are written with this simpler scale that does not include the notes *C* or *F*.

Pentatonic music has the characteristic that it can go on and on without having an ending note that gives it a feeling of being finished (provided the song doesn't end on *D*, which changes the key from D pentatonic to G major). According to Steiner, these types of songs that are not grounded by a resolving note at the end are very appropriate for the young child, who is not yet "firmly on the ground." Such music encourages the young child to stay in a dreamy state, so the greatest amount of energy is available for the healthy forming of the physical body. If this is done in early childhood, then the child can later wake up intellectual capacities while still maintaining a strong contact with wonder, beauty and creativity. In the Waldorf schools, pentatonic songs are used until third grade, when the children have developed an inner emotional life that makes the major and minor scales more suitable for them.

The pentatonic scale was once used by most of humanity; the Greek scale was pentatonic, and it was used in Europe up to the Middle Ages. The Chinese scale is pentatonic, as was the ancient Egyptian. The quality of consciousness of ancient cultures was close to that of the young child—less earth-bound, still on the threshhold of two worlds. Pentatonic music and "music in the mood of the fifth"[12] can have a healing influence on the young child by not rushing the child into fully incarnated earth-bound consciousness and experience.

A *kinderharp* (children's harp or lyre) is a small hand-held harp that can be tuned to the pentatonic scale, which enables anyone to play beautiful music on it; all the notes sound harmonious together and the quality of the sound is ideal for the young child. Such instruments, without sounding boxes, give a very pure experience of each note, without harmonic overtones. This simple, pure experience of the tones is ideal for young children and is recommended by Steiner over more complex instruments like the piano.

Kinderharps are lovely instruments for naptime and bedtime. Their music is very "angelic," and can really help to calm a child and lull him or her to sleep. As children get older, they also like to pick out tunes on the kinderharp. Such instruments are used in Waldorf early childhood programs for the children to play (very carefully) and for the teacher to play at circle time, or at naptime in afternoon programs.

Kinderharps range in price from $65 to $250 and can be purchased from the addresses listed at the end of this chapter. In addition, Choroi makes other pentatonic instruments such as a recorder made out of pear wood, and a *klangspiel* (xylophone or *glockenspiel*). Percussion instruments are not generally recommended for young children because a beat that is too strong can drive children too deeply into their physical bodies. This is in opposition to the fluid molding of their inner organs that occurs during the first seven years. Rock music has an especially strong beat and should be avoided for the young child.

# WHAT ABOUT MUSIC AND DANCE LESSONS?

Young children are naturally musical. Steiner describes it: "The musical element which lives in the human being from birth onwards and which expresses itself particularly in the child's third and fourth years in a gift for dancing, is essentially an element of will, potent with life. . . . If people had the right agility, they would dance with little children, they would somehow join in the movement of all children. It is a fact that the individual is born into the world with the desire to bring his own body into musical rhythm, into musical relation with the world, and this inner musical capacity is most active in children in their third and fourth years."[13]

Is it, therefore, best to start music and dance lessons at a young age? Unfortunately, most teachers of young children don't understand the principles of imitation and the importance of play and fantasy. They teach cognitively, and put pressure on the child to learn a lesson or to do it right. Such a direct approach is far too self-conscious and can be stressful for the young child. While children need *play* that incorporates dance and music, most lessons are designed for older children, even though they may indicate that they are for four- or five-year-olds.

Elkind, in *Miseducation: Preschoolers at Risk*, develops a strong case that any kind of lessons place preschoolers at risk with no real gain.[14] Waldorf teachers would agree that most lessons are inappropriate for the young child. If you do consider any kind of lessons for your nursery or kindergarten-age child—swimming, gymnastics, modern dance, sports—be sure to *observe* the classes *before* you decide whether or not to enroll your child. Does the instructor teach from imitation? Are the things that are asked and done clothed in fantasy? Or is there instruction appropriate for a much older child? Does your child really feel comfortable being away from you? Would the classes be enjoyable or stressful for your child? Would classes be taking away time from play or just being at home (especially important for children who are in programs all day because their parents work). Don't sacrifice the present level of your child's development for some future achievement. If it isn't fun, it is better left undone at this age!

Steiner made two recommendations that aren't going to win him any points with parents today. He recommended that children avoid ballet and soccer. In ballet the fixed and artificial positions are foreign to the fluid and changing nature of the growing child. And ballet affects the same kind of vital energy involved in growth and reproduction, as evidenced by the high rate of menstrual irregularities in professional ballerinas. The discipline and fixed positions of ballet are very different from the rhythmical movement which Steiner recommends for "dancing with children." In soccer the exclusive use of the feet and the head in hitting the ball puts undue emphasis on the extremities at a time when the grade-school child is centered in the middle sphere, the heart/lung area.

With regard to music lessons, unless your child is a musical genius who clearly needs a tutor at age three, there are many reasons to wait until elementary school before beginning music instruction. Unfortunately most people who work with preschool children don't know how to teach from imitation and start by teaching how to read music. Even the idea of *having to learn* a lesson through imitation is too direct an approach for a young child. While the Suzuki method does work through the principle of imitation, the emphasis on tape-recorded music is not consonant with the young child's need to hear live music and simple tunes. Better to save the recordings of classical music until after age seven. Performing at young ages introduces pressure and self-consciousnes into the dream-like world of early childhood. In the Waldorf schools children don't present anything before an audience until they are in the grades, when the classes share their poems, plays, songs and recorder music with one another and the parents at school assemblies.

Playing the wooden recorder is begun in first grade in the Waldorf schools, but the children learn strictly through imitating their teacher. Reading music isn't introduced until third grade, when the child has reached a certain level of maturity and eye-hand coordination and is ready for the full range of musical experience. Most music we hear today is in the diatonic, rather than the pentatonic, mode, and relates most strongly to the feeling life, which only gradually unfolds in the child during the elementary-school years. If you think of the rich and often turbulent inner life of the adolescent, it is easy to see the contrast with the essentially happy life of the young child, whose emotions are more like ripples on a pond. The young child is able to easily change from tears to smiles and lacks the inner emotional complexity of the adolescent or adult. The changes in the emotional life between ages seven and fourteen are dramatic and go beyond the scope of a book on early childhood. But they are mentioned here to point out that there is a time for study of each topic and each area of development, and early childhood is not the recommended time for individual music lessons for most children.

Everyone wants his child to develop according to his full potential. But an understanding of the inner development of the child leads to the realization that certain subjects and certain skills are most beneficial when introduced at the age that corresponds to the child's inner ripeness for them. "Do more sooner" is a symptom of our spiritual materialism which can lead to skipping steps and hastening a child's development in one sphere without realizing the possible ramifications in another. These comments are not meant to provide a list of "Thou shalt nots," but to encourage you to trust your own knowledge, combined with your heart sense, to form an intuitive perception of what is best for your child. If parents do this, they won't subject their children to the Super Baby syndrome at the expense of the important years of early childhood.

## RECOMMENDED SONG BOOKS

*Clump-a-Dump and Snickle-Snack* by Johanne Russ. Pentatonic children's songs from Mercury Press, 241 Hungry Hollow Rd., Spring Valley, NY 10977.

*Gateways* and other volumes by Margret Meyerkort. Six booklets of songs and stories collected by Waldorf kindergarten teachers in Great Britain. Available from the Rudolf Steiner College, 9200 Fair Oaks Blvd., Fair Oaks, CA 95628.

*Pentatonic Songs* by Elizabeth Lebret (IBP). Contains many songs for the seasons and holidays.

## Other Selections

*American Folksongs for Children* by Ruth Crawford Seeger (Doubleday).

*From Ring Around the Roses to London Bridge is Falling Down: Some Incarnating Games* by Jane Winslow Eliot. Published by The Rudolf Steiner School Press, 15 East 79th St., New York, NY 10021.

*The Laughing Baby* by Anne Scott (Bergin and Garvey).

*150 American Folksongs* by Peter Erdei (Boosey & Hawkes).


## PENTATONIC INSTRUMENTS
## (kinderharps, recorders)

Choroi, Karen Klaveness, 4600 Minnesota Ave., Fair Oaks, CA 95628.

Harps of Lorien, Raphael and Lorna Weisman, 610 North Star Rte., Questa, NM 97556.

Hearth Song, P.O. Box B, Sebastopol, CA 95473.

Song of the Sea, Ed and Anne Damm, 47 West St., Bar Harbor, ME 04609.

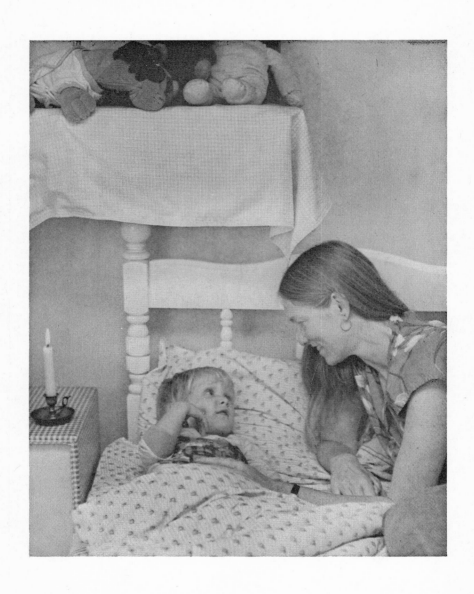

# 11 | *Rhythm & Discipline in Home Life*

## DISCIPLINE WITH THE YOUNG CHILD

### *The Question of Discipline*

The very fact that the issue of discipline is a question to parents is symptomatic of our times. Many parents know more of what they *don't* want to do regarding the discipline of their children than what to do, or what the results of their approach will be. We need to discuss with one another questions about creative discipline and ways to raise children—but not in front of the children! It is important for couples to discuss their ideas about bringing up children and how they feel about the ways their own parents raised them. Children deserve the security of feeling that mom and dad are united and know what they are doing, otherwise they quickly learn how to get around one parent by going to the other.

Many parents don't want to be authoritarian, and they question whether they should insist that their child obey. Studies have shown that among authoritarian, authoritative and permissive parents, the children whose parents are *authoritative* do best. That means effectively and consistently setting limits for the child. Parents have a natural authority with their children because the parents are adults, so children naturally look to them as knowing more about the world than they do. Children "come to earth" only gradually, so the adult must provide the ego force for the child that will direct his emotions; they must make decisions based on a mature viewpoint, rather than on the child's own likes and dislikes. This is also true for the teacher, who must "hold" the class with the strength of his or her own being, or be overrun by a group of children who know that the teacher can't manage them.

It is necessary and appropriate to correct children's behavior—to insist on what I have come to call *right action*. But you can't expect young children to remember what they're supposed to do the next time! It is necessary to repeat right action over and over again with emotional equanimity. Understanding that we need to correct actions *in the present moment* without any hope of the young child's remembering it the next time can help us to keep our own tempers and to model the right behavior over and over again. Firmness permeated by love provides the child with the kind of guidance he needs to grow from baby to adult.

Discipline means more than correcting undesirable behavior. It also means guiding the child to develop in a healthy way physically, emotionally and mentally. We guide the baby largely by nurturing his physical body; we lead the toddler by ordering the rhythm of her day; as the child becomes older we take her by the hand and try to be an example ourselves. Once the child reaches school age, he is guided most by stories and the spoken word.[1] How to guide a child depends on his age, personality and the nature of the parent-child relationship. Even within the same family, differences due to temperament and age mean that all children do not have to be treated in the same way—only *fairly*.

It is impossible to speak about disciplining a baby in the sense of correcting or making her do the right thing, because the baby's will is both so strong and so unintentional. A baby doesn't do things in relation to us and can't change her behavior because we want her to, or insist upon it. According to Steiner, will begins as instinct in a baby, and gradually changes over the years into urge, then desire, then motive. Urge is still strongly connected to the body (biological urges). They will further metamorphose into desire when the emotional element enters around the age of two or three. At this stage parents often think they can start discussing with their children what they do and don't like, what they want to do, or why they did a certain thing. However, children of this age have not yet developed the faculty for motives; only an awakened self has a motive for doing something. A three-year-old is incapable of acting with reflection, so we are asking something of which the child is incapable, although the articulate ones will start giving us all kinds of creative answers! Steiner states that you *might* be able to appeal to reason in a child in adolescence, but not before. When you constantly reason with a young child to have her do what you want, you end with a five-year-old who has learned through imitation to do the same with you, all of the time.

## Imitation and Example

Instead of getting angry *or* reasoning with your child, keep in mind the principles of example and imitation with the child under the age of eight. If you want to teach a certain behavior to your child, one of the best ways is to actually do it in front of (or with) him. This demands that we as adults get up and actually do something, rather than giving the child orders or directions. For example, instead of correcting the child by saying, "Don't eat with your fingers," pick up your spoon and very purposefully go through the motions yourself while saying, "We eat with our spoon." Or instead of saying, "Go clean up your toys," we need to go with the child and do it together while we might say, "It's time to put your toys away."

Movement combined with the smallest amount of fantasy or good humor can go a long way toward getting the child to do what you want. For example, with cleaning up, you can ask the truck driver to steer the truck to its garage or get the cowboy to ride the stick horse over to the stable. Another example is to join in the children's fantasy, rather than interrupting it. So if the children are involved in play, ask the train drivers to move the train out of the walkway while you start moving the chairs with them instead of breaking their fantasy by telling them to move out of the way. Similarly, if you want to have tiny bits of paper cleaned up from your newly vacuumed floor, call on all the little mice to bring the grains of corn to you while you start putting bits into your hand. Your helpers will have the job done in minutes!

What about things you've told a child a hundred times? For example, you've told five-year-old Ryan at least that many times, "Don't slam the screen door!" but to no avail. Try gathering your intention, *meeting him* at the door and saying, "We close the door quietly," while you move his hand through the motion of gently closing the screen door. That will probably do it. If not, a second time is probably all that is necessary. Movement and stating what it is you want to have happen communicate with children in a way they can understand.

Whenever possible, state the positive: "Pet the kitty gently," while you show how to do it rather than shrieking, "Don't hurt the kitty!" Sentences with "don't" will communicate your displeasure, but the brain often doesn't process every word, so the message may in fact register as, ". . . hurt . . . kitty!" It's a lot more effective to be saying, ". . . gentle . . . kitty," instead!

### Not Expecting Results

It isn't until elementary-school age that a child is ready to respond consistently to authority that is expressed only through the spoken word without being accompanied by actions. With the preschool-age child, you need to correct and demonstrate the right behavior again and again, but you can't expect children to remember it. Their memories simply aren't that mature yet. There will be slow improvement over time, but the "learning" that does occur takes place through gradual maturation and the repetition of actions that form habit patterns. For example, early in the year at our Waldorf preschool, several children couldn't sit calmly during snack time. "We sit with our feet in front of us," we repeated again and again as we reseated the child or showed our own straight way of sitting. After several months the children were older and more able to sit calmly during snack time, and the lesson had been repeated so many times that it had begun to penetrate the body. Gradually the child who couldn't stay in his chair could calmly eat and wait for "Red Bird" to come and choose who would blow out the candle, signifying everyone could go and play. But it took a month or two of constant repetition.

Only around the age of five does the child have enough memory and distance on the world to *begin* to remember what he should and should not do. I saw this stage with a little boy in the preschool who was corrected nearly every day for rough behavior toward the other children. We tried everything! As he approached five he started to remember *after* he hit someone that he wasn't supposed to do that, and he began to feel regret both for the action and the discipline that would follow. But it took even more maturity for him to be able to start remembering *before* he struck out; because of his temperament it was more difficult for him to get control of his emotions than for many children. It was a real effort and test of patience to work with him and to constantly insist on the right behavior that took him so long to be able to produce.

Steiner describes the change in a child around age five: "Previously, unable to understand what it ought or ought not to do, it could only imitate, but now, little by little, it begins to listen to and to believe in what its elders say. Only towards the fifth year is it possible to awaken in a child the sense of what is right or wrong. We will educate the child rightly only if we realize that during the first seven-year period—that is up to the change of teeth—the child lives by imitation, and that only gradually will it develop imagination and memory as well as a first belief in what grown-ups say."[2]

Steiner gives another example of a young couple who were distraught because their young child was "stealing" money from a jar in the cupboard. Steiner explained that the child was only imitating having seen the mother take money from the jar. He explained that only after the age of five can the child *begin* to have concepts of right and wrong sufficient to support or avoid the idea of stealing. Prior to that time the child is acting out of imitation.[3]

### When You Say "No!"

Despite moving with your child and stating things positively, there will be times when you need to say no and your child needs to know that you mean it. Elisabeth Grunelius, the first Waldorf kindergarten teacher, said that she found only three reasons for having to say no to a child:

1. When what he wishes to do would be harmful to himself—for instance, to go out on a cold day without a coat.
2. When what he wishes to do would be harmful to others—for instance, to make a noise when the baby is sleeping.
3. When what he wishes to do would result in real damage—for instance, to use his crayons on the wall.[4]

Even in these instances it isn't necessary to start out with a head-on confrontation and battle of the wills. In the first case, you simply help the child put his coat on; in the second, you could suggest that he can play quietly inside or go outside and play; and in the third case you give him a piece of paper and try to switch his activity into more appropriate channels.

Deciding when something will be harmful to a child requires judgment, and the more you can fine-tune your judgment, the better for your child. If we can support our children in getting their own experiences without excessively saying no and without interrupting them, they will learn a great deal about the world and about their own abilities. Climbing trees is an example. Yes, there is a certain amount of danger, but if I hadn't let my daughter climb trees I never would have known that she really should have been born into a circus family that performs high-wire acts. She climbs up fifty feet and sits and plays her wooden recorder! Once when she was four she got stuck up in a tree and my husband was away, so I had to get a neighbor to climb up our forty-foot ladder to help her (not for me, thanks!). The neighbors were hysterical and kept calling up to her, "Don't be afraid!" I had to explain that she wasn't afraid, just stuck! She did fall once, but it only slowed her down for a few hours.

It is important before you say no to a child that you be sure what the child intends and sure of your answer. Sometimes it is good to pause for a moment and decide, because if you change your mind when you realize how intent on a thing your child is, you can confuse him and encourage a habit of pleading until you change your mind. Keeping discipline simple and consistent is important so that your child knows you mean what you say, and that your word is followed immediately by action.

## Negative Emotions

Many parents ignore their child's negative behavior until they either give in or lose their temper. For example, a lady with a baby and a two-year-old in one shopping cart and groceries in the other was ignoring the crazy behavior of her two-year-old, who became more and more annoying, trying to get a reaction. By the time we were both at the checkout stand, he was in a full-blown fit. Although she was still able calmly to ignore it, we need to recognize that it is frustrating to children to be allowed to get crazier and crazier as they keep "upping the ante." There were a lot of calm but effective things she could have done along the way, like stopping the cart and saying it doesn't move unless he's sitting down; singing to him; engaging him by saying she'd let him get the pineapple juice, putting five things in the cart on the way to the pineapple juice, then letting him stand up and pick it off the shelf; asking him to watch in the produce section and tell her when he saw the carrots. Children don't have to be crazy or drive us crazy, but they do require creative interaction.

However, no one is all sweetness and light in correcting her child. Sometimes a sharp no is called for, and a child who continues to raise a fuss can be removed from the action until he is ready to do what is needed (play nicely, take turns or whatever is at issue). Usually three minutes is about all it takes for a child to get himself back together and be ready to try again. If a child is really "out of himself," it may take longer or repeated episodes of "time out" before he is ready. Getting him interested in something that is going on can also help him to reintegrate into social activity if he is having a particularly difficult time.

With negative behavior such as biting or hitting, again it is best to emphasize the positive actions, "We need to be gentle with our friends." "We need to share the toy." If possible, put energy into the child who has been wronged rather than putting your attention into the offender. Obviously, spanking or hitting the child is providing a model of the thing you are trying to get him to stop doing. It gives a really mixed message, because our actions speak to a young child much more powerfully than our words.

Many parents talk to their children about the emotions they are experiencing and encourage them to express their frustration by screaming and yelling instead of hitting. Because many parents went through growth work or psychotherapy during the seventies, they don't want their children to be "repressed." However, emotions for the child under the age of seven lack the complexity that they have for an adolescent. Usually tears or being afraid will quickly pass. They may require hugs or distraction in the moment, but we don't need to dwell on the upset, talk about it, practice having other emotions or all of the things that make emotions far too conscious for a young child. Children whose parents do these kinds of emotional exercises with them usually become very aware and very verbal at a young age. They easily learn to play the verbal games and come up with answers the parents want—after all, it's a major way of relating with the parent. But the young child's emotions are much more present-time oriented and are much easier to deal with if allowed to pass without a great deal of comment—while right action is being insisted on. Remember the young child is centered in the *will*, in movement and doing.

Because children are so imitative, we need to monitor our own emotions and actions when disciplining them, for our actions speak louder than our words. How can we keep our own tempers when we might like to throttle our children, or at a minimum yell uncontrollably at them? Understanding that we need to correct actions in the present moment without any expectation that the young child will remember it the next time can help us keep our own tempers and model the right behavior over and over again. One of the keys to discipline involves bringing one's own consciousness and objectivity to the incident—talking in a quiet voice, sticking by what you say, repeating it if necessary and, whenever possible, actually moving *with* the young child. This will be easier if you have realistic expectations and feel that you can be effective in eliciting right action from your child. Too many parents are silent until they overreact from a string of annoyances that have been building and smoldering. In consequence, the child is running circles around the parent and making life miserable, while the parent is feeling overwhelmed or angry much of the time. If this is happening to you, get some help. You and your child deserve it! Find a friend you can talk to, or a family counselor who can provide a more objective viewpoint, or attend parenting classes. You need some new knowledge and new perspectives, as well as ways of defusing your own emotions. Living with young children is both demanding and rewarding. It requires attention to create a harmonious life, and there is often very little time for other activities (this is where extended family or support systems are a must). Children are young only once. They will soon be away at school and there will be much more time for one's own activities. Understanding the nature of the young child can help you to raise a happy and well-behaved child, as well as a bright one, and can help you to have fun and find satisfaction in it while you continue in your own growth.


## RHYTHM AND DISCIPLINE IN HOME LIFE

Some of the suggestions just given can be helpful when problems arise, but the real key is creating an environment in which problems don't arise. The Waldorf nursery or kindergarten looks effortless; it looks as if the teacher isn't doing very much. Up to twenty children play harmoniously and move from one activity to the next throughout the morning without the teacher having to stop to solve major problems or interruptions. While it may look easy, a great deal of preparation has gone into creating an environment that fits the children and planning a rhythmical series of activities that allow freedom of movement within a structure that holds and supports the children. The rhythms of the day and the week help with the transitions from one activity to the next, so that a short song or similar sign from the teacher is all that the children need to move on to the next activity.

Attention to rhythm and the environment can work similar wonders in home life, helping to avoid most discipline problems and direct confrontations with your child. Because the young child is so centered in the body and in imitation, rhythm is one of the most important keys to discipline. It both guides the child's life by creating good habits and helps avoid arguments and problems. So much of discipline for young children involves self-discipline on the part of the adults: keeping regular rhythms in the home life, working on your own patience and emotional responses, being there when your child needs interaction. (For example, playing with your child *first* can free up an entire twenty minutes to read the paper, whereas telling him you'll do it in ten minutes can result in all kinds of emotional disasters.) Grunelius states:

> Much of a child's happiness depends on our success in conducting the daily life with and around him with a minimum amount of friction. Every time we may feel like stepping in with advice or an order or a correction, we might well pause for a moment to do two things: firstly, to ask ourselves whether our interference at this particular instant is really necessary; and secondly, to find out what the child is actually trying to do.[5]

## The Need for Rhythm in Daily Life

We are surrounded by rhythm in nature: the alternation of day and night, the phases of the moon, the cycle of the seasons, the ebb and flow of the tides. Our bodies are permeated by rhythm, in the beating of our hearts, the breathing of our lungs, women's cycles of fertility and the circadian rhythms of our metabolism. But as modern human beings, we have also established a life that is removed from the rhythms of nature. Through electric lighting we can work well into the night; we can shop at twenty-four-hour supermarkets; we can fly strawberries to Minnesota in January. Through technology we can live outside of most of the rhythms of nature. As a result, we have often become unaware of the messages and rhythms of our bodies and have forgotten the importance of rhythm in daily life. Steiner describes it as follows:

> Rhythm holds sway in the whole of nature, up to the level of man [*sic*]. Then, and then only is there a change. The rhythm which through the course of the year holds sway in the forces of growth, of propagation and so forth, ceases when we come to man. For man is to have his roots in freedom; and the more civilized he is, the more does this rhythm decline. As the light disappears at

Christmas time, so has rhythm apparently departed from the life of man. Chaos prevails. But man must give birth again to rhythm out of his innermost being, his own initiative.[6]

The baby, who has been surrounded by the mother's heartbeat and rocked by her breathing in the womb, emerges into earthly life and must find its new rhythms, gradually developing from the fast and irregular heartbeat and breathing of the newborn to the rhythm of one breath to each four heartbeats of the adult.

A regular lifestyle, like the pattern of life in the womb, offers a stable environment during the rapid growth and changes in rhythm of the body during childhood. Children provided with this regular life feel confident about their world and are not concerned by uncertainty about when the next thing will happen. Rhythm in home life can also help to calm a nervous or difficult child by turning the child's life into a series of events in which he participates, and from which he gains a sense of security. Regular mealtimes and regular nap- and bedtimes help to start orienting the child to a natural feeling for the passing of time. They go a long way toward preventing discipline problems, because bedtimes become something that happen as regularly as the sky turning dark—there is no one to argue with or complain to each night.

Elisabeth Grunelius summarizes, "The rhythm then becomes a habit, is accepted as self-evident and will eliminate many difficulties, struggles and arguments about eating and going to bed. . . . Regularity should prevail in as many of the child's daily activities as possible. It is the key to establishing good habits for life."[7]

Grunelius gives an example of how supportive rhythm is for young children and how much they learn through it. She tells about taking care of a two-year-old child whom she bathed each day in the same way—first soaping her hands, then her arms, then her neck, and so on. When she took care of the child again after several weeks, the child spontaneously asked, "May I wash myself?" and proceeded carefully and happily through the whole sequence exactly as it had been done so many times before. The child was extremely satisfied with herself![8] This example amazed me, because it never occurred to me to wash a child in a regular fashion, thus providing the child with something it would then be possible to learn.

Andrea Gambardella, a Waldorf teacher, explains, "With the young child and the elementary-school student this requirement for an outer structure continues to be vital to growth and emotional well-being. Learning that there is 'a time for all things' is a life's lesson. Now is a time for you to play and do as you will, now for a meal, now for homework, now to prepare for bed."[9]

Rhythm is also a blessing for parents, because it enables the daily activity of life to flow more smoothly, require less energy and become a platform that supports the family, its activities and interactions. Many mothers don't discover the secrets of rhythm until they have two or more children, and suddenly there isn't enough time *not* to be organized! Regular meals prevent constant feeding and cleaning up or overhungry and whiny children; regular bedtimes suddenly free the evening for *adult* conversation and life again as a couple. The benefits are many, and yet it is sometimes difficult to create rhythm in family life—it requires an inner discipline of its own! Creating rhythm in one's life doesn't mean to be rigid and dogmatic. There is still plenty of room for special activities and surprises (and sometimes the piper to pay the next day when a child has missed a needed nap or had a late, exciting evening—but it's worth it!). But freedom is not without form, and one is truly free when not hampered by a disorganized life. The rhythmic structure imposed on a young child and permeated with the parents' love is a discipline in the most positive sense of the word. And as your children become older, they will transform this outer structure into an inner self-discipline that will be invaluable for homework and getting other jobs done. Putting attention into these areas can help the quality of life for both you and your children from the time they are toddlers until they leave home.

## A Word of Caution

Before reading the following practical suggestions, remind yourself that I'm not suggesting you have to do all these things to be a good mother! Rather, by mentioning so many things in so many areas, I hope that you will be sparked to consider adding even one rhythmical element to even one area of your child's life. Most women are too busy to have *every* part of the day be a wonderful time for their children. In my house, breakfasts are efficient, but without frills; there's no way, during the school year, that I'm going to put special place settings on the table! So I put my attention into bedtimes. But for someone else, early mornings might be a real time for their family to be together, especially if evenings are shortened by dad working late.

Once they come to appreciate the value of rhythm, some women feel guilty because they don't provide a rhythmical home life, or they reject the whole idea out of annoyance. My suggestion is that you consider just one area after reading this chapter. You might want to focus on an area that is going the least smoothly in your life. It might be naptime, or it might be dinner, or it might be getting the children out the door in the morning. Whatever the area, think about what happens now, and how you could make things go more smoothly by applying some of the suggestions or by inventing some of your own. Having a regular rhythm, adding a bit of ritual like a song or verse, and avoiding too many choices can transform a hectic part of family life into an activity or transition that flows smoothly. Discuss your ideas with your partner, agree on a new series of actions for an activity and then start doing them with the children. You'll be amazed by the results!

## Mealtimes

Eating together is a major part of family life and can be a valuable cohesive force in bringing people together. However, attention needs to be put into mealtimes so they don't turn into times of tension or chaos or disappear because everyone has grabbed something to eat on the run.

When do meals occur? Who is present? There are no right or wrong answers when you look at rhythms and family life. You need to look at the configuration and the needs of your family members and decide what works for you. The important thing is to bring your consciousness to seeing your situation and working toward what feels best. We know a family where the father and three-year-old had breakfast together weekdays before he went to work while the mother got some extra sleep. It was a special time for the two of them that they really cherished. Similarly, work schedules will probably determine what time dinner happens and whether children will need to eat earlier. Whatever you work out for your family, having meals at a regular time (and regular snacks for the children as needed) is helpful for creating rhythm in family life.

Now look at the setting. Do you have a table around which the family can gather? Any little touches you add to meals, like a candle or fresh flowers, can help to make meals a special time for the family. I found, in the summertime, that by setting the break- fast table the night before, even *I* felt nourished and cared for by waking up to a table that was inviting. And family members, who tended to get up and eat at different times during the summer, all felt "held" by the family, even though no one else might be at the table with them.

Next, consider the atmosphere. Are mealtimes relaxed and conducive to digestion? Small children especially need to eat in calm surroundings, without television and radio. (The six o'clock news is enough to give anyone indigestion through the graphic reports of murders and other atrocities.) Similarly, the adults should be careful not to be negative about people or to dwell on disappointments of the day. Children take everything in and are unable to disconnect emotions from their body's functioning.

Conversation at meals changes with the arrival of children. It becomes impossible to conduct adult conversation in the same way, and children need to be accepted as conversationalists. Meal- time then becomes a time for listening, sharing and balancing conversations so that each child can bring something of himself or herself to the family's time together. The essay on "Family Meals" in *Lifeways*[10] contains many ideas for harmonious meals with growing children.

Beginning the meal with a spoken or sung blessing encour- ages feelings of thankfulness and assures that everyone starts to- gether. Young children are especially nourished by whatever ritual you develop around your family's mealtimes. But you need to bring feelings of gratitude, not empty words said in haste! If you don't have any graces from your religious background, here are two that give a feeling for the connectedness of life and gratitude for our sustenance:

*Before the flour, the mill,*
*Before the mill, the grain,*
*Before the grain, the sun and rain,*
*The beauty of God's will.*
(Unknown)

*Earth, who gives to us this food,*
*Sun, who makes it ripe and good,*
*Dear Sun, dear Earth, by you we live,*
*Our loving thanks to you we give.*
(Christian Morgenstern)

It is important for children to be grateful for their food and for the efforts of the cook in preparing it. Such an attitude will be fostered by the care we take in preparing and serving the food. This is another area where working on our own gratitude and appreciation for the gift of life will communicate most strongly with our children. How you handle a child and foods he doesn't like requires some creative thinking. You will need to set your own table rules about what can be said about food and what needs to be eaten before a child can leave the table or have dessert.

Certain behavior can be insisted on so meals can be a calm and harmonious experience for everyone. If a young child who is whiny or who throws a fit is immediately taken out by a stern adult as described in Chapter 5, he will probably change his behavior within three minutes. No one wants to be away from the action!

Do your dinners have a formal ending, just drift off, or degenerate rapidly? Having children ask to be excused at the end of a meal is not an old-fashioned formality, but a useful way to keep track of who's finished. Some families prefer that everyone stays at the table until a song or short verse is said to end the meal.

Mealtimes change as your children grow older. They are different with toddlers, teenagers or mixtures of a wide range of ages. But gathering around the table for meals and participating in the family's evolving rituals can be an important part of your family's life.

## Nutrition

While it is important for parents to be aware of nutrition, it is just as well to leave young children unaware of the intricacies of vitamins and minimum daily requirements. When a child is really allergic to something like milk or peanuts, he needs to be able to tell people so he won't inadvertently eat those things. But analysis of ingredients or search for refined sugars makes preschoolers pick apart and analyze everything on the table, rather than feeling that what they are being served is good. *Allergic* becomes a synonym for "I don't like," and any kind of common snack becomes impossible because Billy doesn't eat dairy and Jane doesn't eat wheat and Joey is allergic to peanuts and Mary can't have anything with sugar in it.

Trusting that what you give your child is good for him is most important for the child; excessive consciousness among three- and four-year-olds is only divisive. One time, two kindergarten boys at the lunch table noticed that one had a huge lunch with a big thermos of milk, two white-bread sandwiches, potato chips and a fruit roll-up, while the other had carob soy milk, a whole-wheat sandwich with tofu and sprouts, a piece of fruit and a granola bar. These children, starting to be self-aware and aware of the world around them, noticed the discrepancy. One said to the teacher, "My mother says that milk is good for you and helps your bones and teeth."

The other said, "My mom says that milk gives you mucus!"

"Who's right?" they asked together.

The kindergarten teacher wisely replied, "Your mother is right." And both boys were satisfied.

We found our preschool children had become so picky nutritionally that any kind of common snack was impossible. The social element of eating together was tentative at best!

Children instinctively feel that the world is whole and good and that whatever their mother gives them is good for them. It isn't necessary to tell your child more than is minimally necessary for health or for philosophical distinctions like vegetarianism. What you do will be more important than long explanations. "Our family doesn't eat meat" is usually enough for a child to know, and *your* telling friends and teachers will help keep the child from having to make choices. With something like trying to avoid sugar, if you feed your child wisely at home and tell grandma that you wish she would put away the candy jar before visits, then you may decide the little bit your child eats at a birthday party or a friend's house may not be worth all of the intellectual and emotional investment required to tell the child he can't have things. These are issues you have to discuss with each other as parents, and decisions you will have to make based on your medical and philosophical convictions. I can only tell you as a preschool teacher that the awareness and misinformation children have about nutrition these days reflects an increased consciousness of the metabolic sphere that wreaks havoc with the unitive worldview of the young child.

## Nap or Quiet Times

Young children need restful or quiet times during the day as a means of being restored for play. Like the rhythm of breathing, the child's activities alternate between active play, in which the full body is in motion, and quiet times for a snack or a story. Focussing attention on something close at hand, such as making something, coloring or modelling with beeswax, brings the child into himself and balances the active play in which he is totally in movement.

Many children today sleep very little and seem ready to give up afternoon naps at an early age. However, the afternoon nap is of great benefit for a child in "digesting" the impressions of the day, and it provides a welcome time for parents as well. The time can be used for sleep or just as a quiet time in which the child has to stay on his bed or in his room. If the rhythm of a daily rest is maintained, the child will learn that this is a time to be by himself and not to call on mother. All the kindergarten and nursery children who stay afternoons in our Waldorf program lie down on cots; then a story is read or told, and the kinderharp is played. Many of the five-year-olds do in fact fall asleep, even when they wouldn't ordinarily nap at home. And the others rest while playing silently with a favorite doll. Again, the same song is used each time to start and end naptime—and the ending is especially welcome because "Red Bird" (a felt bird on a stick) comes and wakes the children or lets them get up to play.

Recognizing the value of a quiet time for preschool children is the first step in instituting one. An hour in the afternoon without the children can also be a valuable time for a mother to center and refresh her energies by resting or doing something she wants to do. If your child is not used to a quiet time and you want to start having one, think it through first. What time will work for you? What are the parameters of acceptable behavior? You can tell the child that he doesn't have to sleep, he just has to stay on his bed, for example. What kinds of dolls or toys will you make accessible to him, if any? What needs to be done in preparation? Going to the bathroom, washing hands, putting shoes neatly under the chair? Will you sing or tell a story? A kinderharp is wonderful for calming a child and helping him go off to sleep. If you want to sit with your child until he falls to sleep, look and act very sleepy yourself—eyelids heavy, not talking or answering questions, letting sleep ooze from your pores. Putting your hand on a child's head or back can also be very calming. Sleep or rest time is a valuable part of your child's day, through kindergarten age. If you don't have such a time, you will probably find that your child comes home from a morning school program and just wants to sit or play alone for a while after lunch anyway. The children have been so active in a group during the morning that a more inward time is a needed balance.

## Bedtimes

What is bedtime like at your house? Does the evening have a rhythm to it, ending in going to bed at a regular time and according to a regular set of activities? A regular bedtime preceded by a set ritual can help calm your child and prevent arguments. It can also help him to learn to do more and more of the activities involved in getting ready for bed by himself as he becomes older. It can help him to feel more secure when you have a babysitter if the sitter is taught to do things in the same order.

How a child enters sleep is important for refreshing the spirit as well as the body. Falling asleep and waking are portals to the spiritual world, the world of dreams and inspirations. How we and our children enter sleep and wake up can affect the quality of both sleeping and waking life. With a young child, the entire time after dinner is often focussed on leading toward bedtime. Quiet play can be followed by straightening up the room, then by a bath when necessary or washing up, brushing teeth and putting on pajamas. Talking slowly or singing softly can help set a quiet mood for bedtime. Lighting a candle in the room and then whispering as you enter with the child who is ready for bed can help create a mood of calmness and sharing. A few songs, a story, a verse or prayer which unites the child's soul with the divine can help a child to drift peacefully into sleep. You might play some music on the kinderharp if you have one. If you have used a candle, you'll want to blow it out before leaving the room, but its warm, soft light can be very calming during songs and story. If your child has difficulty going to sleep, many more suggestions can be found in the essay "Sleeping and Waking" in *Lifeways*.[11]

Children love consciousness and cling to it, and thus will stay up to the point of becoming overtired. They really can't be depended on to go to bed when they need to! When I first enrolled in the teacher training program at the Waldorf Institute, my children were in kindergarten and second grade and were going to bed at 8:30. One of the instructors talked about sleep and suggested that my children could easily be going to bed at 7:30. I thought, "Not my kids! Eight-thirty is hard enough!" But I decided to try his suggestion to see if it would work. To my utter surprise, the children went to bed an hour earlier without a fuss and slept an hour longer at night, even though they hadn't seemed to be tired on the old schedule. I was dumbfounded! I have had similar experiences, suggesting that preschool parents start their child for bed at 7:30 instead of putting him to bed at 11:00. To their surprise it took less than three days for the child to get into the new rhythm, so that one boy even told his babysitter that it was time for bed in the early evening.

If your child goes to bed early, will he wake up at the crack of dawn? You will have to try it and see. A preschool child who wakes up bright and smiling with the sun can't understand why adults want her to go back to sleep! But most children will not wake up so early, and they can be taught to put on a robe and slippers, if it is cold, and to play in their room (often with something that has been set out after they have gone to sleep) if you need to sleep a little longer.

## Mornings

The transition out of sleep is also an important time, and putting attention into this time of day can help both adults and children. How do you wake up? Many mothers have found that getting up a half-hour before the rest of the family gives them a quiet, centered time in the morning that affects their whole day. Or if they don't get up early, they arrange as many things as possible the night before: what clothes each child will wear, jackets or snowsuits and mittens if needed, bags for school, lunches, the breakfast table and whatever else is needed. The biggest problem with mornings is being rushed, which makes children move even more slowly and puts everyone in a bad mood.

Assuming you wake your child, how do you do it? Margret Meyerkort reminds us, "It is important for both children and adults that the experience of the night-consciousness be allowed to stay more or less actively for a while just below the level of the day-consciousness. For here rest the hints, understandings, reassurances and sense of the spiritual world. Therefore the alarm-clock needs to be kept well away from the young child, for it is such a cold, stern and literally shocking awakener. After such an awakening, the child could be disgruntled for hours afterwards. Instead the parent can hum a melody or sing a seasonal or morning song."[12] Holding a young child up to a window to see the light of the new day is also a nice way to start the morning.

Because a child is still in a kind of night-consciousness after awakening, he often can't cope with any kind of questions for the first ten or fifteen minutes. He simply doesn't have the day-consciousness to come up with the answer, so try to avoid questions and choices. Make your choices together the night before, about what to wear and so forth, so that morning doesn't have to become a battleground of the wills.

Once your child is fully awake, do the events of getting ready for the day have a particular order? Remember that doing things in an orderly way gives a child something to learn and makes it much more likely that your eight-year-old will remember to brush her teeth and hair before taking off for school, or won't forget it even though it is Saturday. Think about your mornings: getting dressed, eating breakfast, brushing teeth, brushing hair; what about making the bed (together at first)?

Greeting the day is something that children love to do with a verse or a song. If you don't know any, here are two suggestions:

> *Morning has come.*
> *Night is away.*
> *Rise with the sun*
> *And welcome the day!*
> (Elisabeth Lebret)

> *Good morning, dear earth; Good morning, dear sun!*
> *Good morning dear stones and flowers every one!*
> *Good morning dear busy bees and birds in the trees!*
> *Good morning to you and good morning to me!*
> (Unknown)

Here is a verse given by Rudolf Steiner that can easily have hand gestures added as you point to your eyes, your heart, make a circle like the sun and put your head on your hands in a resting gesture.

> *With my own eyes*
> *I see the world,*
> *The lovely world of God.*
> *My heart must give thanks*
> *That I may live*
> *In this, God's world,*

*That I may wake*
*In the brightness of day,*
*And may rest at night*
*In the blessing of God.*[13]

Such a verse would not be taught, but said with the child until gradually he learned it by hearing it and beginning to say it with you each day.

## Daily Activities

Giving a child a small task that he can do every day, like feeding the fish or watering a plant, is especially good if it can be done with him at the same time each day. Again, rhythmical care for the world around him is being taught—certainly good preparation for the rest of life!

Think about your child's day. If he goes to preschool, what are his needs for lunch, rest, play in the afternoon or any special things that you do together? Do the activities "breathe," offering balance between exertion and rest, expansion and contraction of attention and movement? If your child is home with you each day, you will need to think about the entire day, taking into account your child's natural rhythms and needs for eating and sleeping during the day.

Helping your young child achieve a sense for the rhythm of the week is more easily accomplished if special activities regularly occur on a specific day. If you tend to go to the park once a week, going every Wednesday will give your child a sense of this activity as a punctuation mark for the week; it will also help you to organize your other activities if you can plan them around certain fixed activities. If you paint with your child, you could do it every Monday, adding another rhythmically recurring event to your child's life.

In former times work was done according to the days of the week as expressed in this traditional verse:

*Wash on Monday*
*Iron on Tuesday*

*Mend on Wednesday*
*Churn on Thursday*
*Clean on Friday*
*Bake on Saturday*
*Rest on Sunday*

This kind of rhythm is still observed in the Amish communities and, rather than being boring, creates for them a pattern in the chaos of having so much to do in daily life. While most of us no longer live according to such rhythms of work, if we appreciate their value for the young child we can do certain activities on set days, or shop together on a certain day, so the child starts to feel at home in the week and its recurring nature.

Within the pattern of the week, something needs to be said about the Sabbath, which used to be a very special day in which no work or play occurred during the observance of religious practices. If your family doesn't go to church or temple, Sunday (or Saturday) may have lost its sense of a day for inwardness, for communion with God, oneself, nature or the family. Think about what your family does on this day. With or without going to church, would it be nourishing to do something regularly, like having a special breakfast, getting out into nature, having spiritual study for adults with Bible stories told to the children? What would be meaningful for your family?


## THE RHYTHM OF THE YEAR

As we live through the changing cycle of the seasons, we can gain an appreciation for nature and the rhythm of the year through the analogy of breathing. In summer it is as if the earth breathes out, creating the myriad forms and colors of summer foliage and the feeling of being right out there in the stratosphere when you lie on your back and look into a summer sky. Winter, on the other hand, is like an in breath; the cold brings a contracted quality, and much of life becomes dormant and sleeps in burrows or as seeds in the earth.

We can also experience the year through the waxing and waning of the light in the sun's cycle and recognize how we echo within ourselves the changes occurring in nature. As the days grow cooler in fall, they become shorter and darkness increases. As life draws inward with the waning light, it is necessary that we strengthen our inner life of thought and resolve. It is common to find that you think more clearly on a crisp fall day, or that you can finish a project much more easily during the winter months than during the summer.

When the winter solstice is reached in late December, the light begins to gain strength again. The increasing strength of the sun in springtime warms the earth and awakens the sleeping trees and flowers, so that life springs forth again in all its glory. At the summer solstice in June (also called Midsummer), the sun is at its strongest, and the leaves and fruits soak up the warmth of its rays, ready to give back their summer experience of the sun in the richness of harvest and the flaming fall colors of the trees.

All of the major religions acknowledge and incorporate our experience of the year into the celebrations of their festivals. Thus in the fall, with the decline of the outer light, we have the need to kindle our own inner light and resolve to transform the unredeemed qualities in our own souls, manifested through the image of St. Michael and the dragon (September 29 is Michaelmas). In the fall many countries have festivals that bring together this juxtaposition of outer darkness and fire or inner light: the bonfires of Guy Fawkes Day in Great Britain (November 5); our own Halloween Jack-o-lanterns; the traditional lantern walks in Germany on St. Martin's Day (November 11); or the Santa Lucia festival of lights in Scandinavia (December 13), in which the youngest daughter wears a crown of burning candles and brings special cakes to her family members for breakfast.

In Judaism, Hannukkah is a Festival of Lights that occurs at the time of greatest darkness in December. In Christianity, the four candles of the Advent wreath prepare the way for the "Light of the World," whose birth is celebrated just at the turning point of the year in relation to the sun.

Similarly, the image of the resurrection of Christ is echoed in nature through the rebirth of the world each spring. To complete our cycle of the major festivals of the calendar, we need to mention St. John's (June 24), which has traditionally been celebrated in European countries with bonfires at this time of the sun's greatest strength.

## CELEBRATING FESTIVALS AND THE COURSE OF THE YEAR

Many people today feel a need for festivals and meaningful celebrations or rituals in their lives. If they have turned away from the religious upbringing of their childhood, they are nonetheless seeking new ways of celebrating meaningful events in their lives (such as marriages), or finding new ways to approach the meaning of Christmas despite all the commercialism that surrounds it today. The celebration of festivals is not only important in individuals' lives, but it is important socially and for the possibility it provides us to step out of "ordinary time" and be connected with something more abiding. Steiner felt that renewed awareness in the celebration of festivals could form a valuable link between the earthly and the divine worlds.

Whatever your heritage, I encourage you to look toward the festivals of the year within your religion and find ways to celebrate them that are meaningful to you and can nourish your children. Because I come from a Christian background, my greatest familiarity is with the Christian festivals; but I have learned a great deal through the Jewish parents of my students, who have brought the Jewish festivals to their children in a living way and have shared their efforts with our classes. Excellent sources within Judaism include *The Jewish Holidays*[14] and *The First Jewish Catalog*.[15] *Celebrating Festivals with Children*[16] and several other books listed at the end of this chapter can provide helpful background on the inner meaning of the Christian festivals and ways to celebrate them.

*Festivals, Family and Food*[17] gives numerous stories, recipes and craft ideas for celebrating the major and lesser-known festivals of the year with children. Remember that, with young children, the preparation for the festival is as important as the celebration itself—the baking, making of special presents, decorating and singing of special songs year after year. Be sure to include your children in all of the preparation activities! In trying to convey the inner spiritual realities of a festival to a young child, remember that what you do speaks more loudly than what you say. The care you put into making a present teaches more about giving than a lecture on divine love. In bringing festivals to a young child, tell the story in simple images she can follow. Then the story, like the one of King Hamen and Mordecai accompanied by noise-makers and *Hammentaschen* cookies, will be a wonderful celebration for the young child. An example related to Easter comes through a story from the Waldorf kindergartens in Britain about a caterpillar who wanted to be like a flower and worship the sun.[18] Mother Earth told him that there was a way of transformation, but it was almost like dying and being born again in a new form. The brave caterpillar becoming a flower that can fly is an image of the resurrection in which nature mirrors the miracle of the resurrection of Christ and our own potential for inner transformation.

Christmas is a festival that young children relate to naturally because Jesus as a baby is very near to them. The celebration of Advent with children makes a time of inner preparation more visible both to them and to us. The Advent calendar, with its magic windows, and the Advent wreath which can be lighted each night as a story is told, can help keep the inner side of Christmas from getting lost in the flurry of activity.

In addition to whatever religious festivals you celebrate with your children, you can enrich your own and your children's lives by observing the passing of the seasons. Seasonal songs, foods prepared in special ways and seasonal activities all help to raise our awareness of the changes in nature that surround us. Both *Festivals, Family and Food* and *The Children's Year* suggest a wealth of things to do with your children.

You can bring a bit of nature into your home through a *seasonal table*, a place where you can keep special things, like the shells collected at the beach during the summer or a special birthday card from grandma. The colors of the cloth on this little table can be changed with the seasons, just as the objects on it change to reflect the changes in nature.

# BIRTHDAYS

Children's birthdays are special festivals that parents can either find delightful or a real strain. In planning celebrations for children, remember *the simpler, the better*. Try to avoid sensory overload. If *you* don't actively enjoy being in a place, chances are your child shouldn't be there either. (So many parties for young children now occur in pizza or ice-cream parlors with blaring music, nauseating clowns or "singing" mechanical characters and video games.)

Many suggestions for delightful birthday celebrations at home can be found in *Festivals, Family and Food*. With a group of children you can do some movement games, or try decorating "treasure bags" and taking a walk in the woods, or making a "fairy garden" out of moss on a paper plate which is decorated with acorns and a pretty stone that the child finds.

A birthday celebration, even just within the family, is a way of saying, "We're glad you were born!" Ways of letting the child be special that day can include having a special drawing or crown at her place at breakfast, letting her choose what will be cooked for dinner, or whatever you devise. Think of traditions you might want to start: making a card for your child each year that includes several photos of major events that year—riding a tricycle, getting a new kitty, going on a trip. Such cards can become things that will be saved and treasured when the child is older.

For the young child, a birthday story that tells of her coming down to earth over the "rainbow bridge" is fitting, because the young child is still very connected to the spiritual world. Birthdays provide us with an opportunity to note the passage of time, which seems to go by so quickly when we see how our children grow and change in the course of a year. Birthdays, holidays, the changing seasons, all provide a familiarity and rhythm that can nourish us as well as our children. On a daily basis, a rhythmical lifestyle is one of the greatest gifts we can provide the young child.

# RECOMMENDED READING

*Celebrating the Festivals with Children* by Friedel Lenz (IBP, SG).

*The Children's Year* by Cooper, Fynes-Clinton and Rowling (IBP, SG).

*The Cycle of the Year* by Rudolf Steiner (AP).

*Festivals, Family and Food* by Diane Carey and Judy Large (IBP, SG).

*Festivals Magazine* provides many suggestions for family celebrations of religious and other festivals. Available from Resource Publications, 160 E. Virginia St., San Jose, CA 95112.

*The First Jewish Catalog*, Richard Siegel, et al.

*The Jewish Holidays*, by Michael Strassfeld.

*Lifeways* by Gudrun Davy and Bons Voors (IBP, SG).

*Punishment in Self-Education and in the Education of the Child* by Erich Gabert (AP).

For seasonal songs, see the list at the end of Chapter 10.

# 12 | *Cognitive Development & Early Childhood Education*

Parents naturally want to give their children the best start in life and do everything they can to assure their intellectual development. In earlier chapters we have indicated that the best thing you can do for your baby's cognitive development, once he starts to crawl, is to childproof your home and let him explore freely while he is near you. The baby needs to move and to explore, and the objects in your home provide better stimulation than many expensive educational toys.

Once your child becomes verbal and begins to ask endless questions, there is a tendency to start providing rational and scientific answers. In *Miseducation*, Elkind points out that we must constantly remember that young children's verbal skills far outpace their conceptual knowledge. Because children's questions sound so mature and sophisticated, we are tempted to answer them at a level of abstraction far beyond their level of comprehension. Children are really asking about the purpose of things, not about how they work.[1] For example, when your four-year-old asks, "Why does the sun shine?" he is quite satisfied by the answer, "To make the plants grow and keep us healthy." He doesn't need an answer about burning gasses and ultraviolet rays, which introduce concepts he has no way of understanding.

Grunelius agrees that concepts are products of the mind at a more advanced age level, while images or additional observation will lead the child to arrive at his own answer. She gives the following example:

> Coming home from the beach, a six-year-old child may ask, "Why are there waves on the ocean?" Instead of explaining, we may say, "Come, let me show you," fill the wash-basin with water and blow on it. The child will see the waves, repeat blowing on the water several times and get what is for him a more perfect answer than any explanation could furnish.
>
> Speaking about the child's reaction to the ocean, he will notice that the sea at times rises higher and at other times recedes, and ask about it. To answer him by telling him the influence of the moon is not to answer a child at all, who is not ripe to comprehend any more than the rhythmic sequence of the up-and-down movement of the water.
>
> We answer him with complete accuracy, however, if we let him hold his own hand over his breast so as to feel his inbreathing and outbreathing, and then tell him how the rise and fall of the sea resembles that breathing movement in his own body.[2]

Both Maria Montessori and Rudolf Steiner recognized that the young child should not be taught cognitive work directly. Montessori said that the child should be taught through the body; hence the wealth of special equipment (not called *toys*) in a Montessori program, for teaching such concepts as geometric shapes, weights and so forth. Steiner went even further and said that *concepts* shouldn't be taught at all to children before the change of teeth. He placed the emphasis on creative play, imagination, imitation, movement games and fingerplays, crafts and artistic activities until the physical body is more developed and the energy needed for its intense early growth is freed for forming mental pictures and memory work.

In noting the tremendous changes that occur naturally around the age of seven, Steiner gave indications of the problems that could arise by introducing early cognitive learning to children. While it is possible to speed up development in certain areas with some children, tampering with nature's timetable can result in negative effects in other areas. Whenever you call directly on the intellect and memory of the young child, you are using energy that is needed for physical development during the first seven years. The same forces that are active in the physical development of the young child are used later for intellectual activity. Attention to this factor in development during the early years can form the foundation for health and vitality throughout life. Obviously the child is learning a tremendous amount and developing cognitively during these years. Steiner simply means not to address the intellect directly, but to encourage the child's learning through direct life experiences and imitation. He explains:

> In the human embryo the eyes are protected and the external physical sunlight must not work upon their development. In the same sense external education must not endeavour to effect a training or influence the moulding of the memory, before the change of teeth. If we, however, simply give it nourishment and do not try as yet to develop it by external measure, we shall see how the memory unfolds in this period, freely and of its own accord.[3]

## THE VALUE OF PRESCHOOL

Today virtually all children attend kindergarten and nearly forty percent of all children have attended preschool classes before starting kindergarten. This is more than triple the 1965 rate, and it will probably become larger as an increasing number of school systems provide programs for four-year-olds. With nearly sixty percent of mothers with children five and under in the work force at least part-time, most children have some kind of daycare or preschool experience. Burton White suggests that the pressure to fund public preschool is actually the result of the lack of quality daycare—public or private—since "there is no mandate in the law for child care and there is a mandate for education."[4]

Even mothers who don't need to work like the social and learning experiences a part-time preschool program provides for their child, and the free mornings can give them needed time away from children or time alone with a new baby.

Long-range studies, like the one at High Scope Educational Research Foundation in Ypsilanti, Michigan, have shown an advantage in attending play-based preschool *for children from low socioeconomic backgrounds.* Following one-hundred twenty-three poor black youths with low IQs from the age of three or four up through age nineteen, this study compared the group who attended the preschool program at Perry Elementary School and had home visits from trained staff with a group who received no preschool education at all. Those who attended preschool went on to spend less time in special-education classes, have higher attendance rates and graduate from high school in greater numbers; fewer received public assistance, were arrested or became pregnant before age nineteen.[5]

However, "for children from emotionally and financially stable homes, the advantages of preschool are less evident. While many experts believe that the early years are an enormously fertile time for teaching little children . . . some think that they learn best at their own pace at home. 'School for four-year-olds is indefensible on educational grounds,' says Burton White, author of *The First Three Years of Life.*"[6]

The experiences of life provided in a nursery or kindergarten can often be provided as well at home as in a formal program. There is no need to seek out preschool if you and your child are doing well at home; there is also no need to avoid it or feel guilty if your child is eager to play with other children and welcomes the activities a guided program can provide.

## Evaluating Early Childhood Programs

When you first begin to investigate early childhood programs, you will find they vary greatly in their philosophies and activities. Many tend to be much more academically oriented than kindergartens were thirty years ago. With the launching of *Sputnik* in 1957 and the consequent pressure on American education, the age of formal learning has steadily been pushed down, so that many kindergartens are now doing what was once a first-grade program, while nursery-age children have taken on tasks previously meant for older children. This push toward early academics has been fueled by parents in their late thirties, who pushed their "baby boomlet" children toward early success with such programs as baby flash cards, classes and academic preschools to get them into the "best" private elementary schools. However, the Super Baby syndrome with its inherent difficulties seems to be abating. In February 1987, *Newsweek* reported: "Now the pendulum may be swinging away from 'hothousing,' as the academic preschool phenomenon has come to be known. After years of internal debate, the early-childhood establishment has rallied against formal instruction for very young children on the ground that it can lead to educational 'burnout' and a sense of failure."[7]

Parents need to investigate preschool and kindergarten programs in which they are interested to see that they are *not* teaching children to read, do workbooks or work with computers, and to make sure that ample time is allowed for play that is self-directed and serves no other motive than the child's own.

When you look for a daycare, preschool or kindergarten for your child, here are some things to consider.

- Is there a rhythm to the day, providing a structure within which there is time for large movement as well as guided activities?

- Is there an appreciation of the importance of imaginative play, and toys to support it?

- Do the children play outside every day? What equipment is available?

- What is the teacher's background, training, philosophy, experience in teaching and/or in mothering?

- What does the teacher hope the children will learn? Early reading, deskwork and workbooks don't match the young child's needs.

- Are there artistic activities—painting, coloring, crafts?

- What role does music play in the program? Is it all from tapes and records, or are there singing and movement games?

- Do the children watch television or play with computers? High tech is best avoided with young children.

- How many children are there? How many teachers? Does it feel calm or hectic?

- What is the environment like? Is it safe? Is it beautiful? Warm?

- Does the teacher love the children?

## THE WALDORF EARLY-CHILDHOOD PROGRAM

Waldorf early-childhood programs provide a nurturing environment based on an understanding of the young child's special developmental needs before the age of seven. Sometimes they have separate nursery and kindergarten classes, but more often there are mixed-age kindergartens with children from three to six years old in one group. The Waldorf program is modelled after a good home environment. The mixed-age kindergarten has the advantage of being even more like a large family; the older children provide a model for the younger ones and help them, while the little ones bring a softer element to the five- and six-year-olds. And as they stay in the kindergarten for two or three years, those who were younger get to experience being the bigger children for the new ones.

Over the past ten years, interest in Waldorf education in North America has exploded, with many new preschools being founded each year. Since the pressures of today's world often make it impossible for a child to stay at home, such nursery schools are a necessity. Often they have the added task of healing the effects on the young child of our technologically geared society. Many early-childhood programs are associated with existing Waldorf schools (K–8 or K–12), while others are separate early-childhood centers that later may grow into full elementary schools. A complete list of schools can be obtained from the Waldorf Kindergarten Association of North America, 9500 Brunett Avenue, Silver Spring, MD 20901.

The description of the Waldorf early childhood program given here may serve as a more detailed guide for things to look for, even if you do not have a Waldorf school in your area. The understanding of the young child and the activities suggested by Waldorf education can be incorporated into home life or into existing daycare or preschool programs. Or, a reader may become so inspired that he or she will want to find out more about the full training to become a Waldorf early childhood teacher!

## The Activities

Let's take a look at a child's day as it might occur in a Waldorf program. The morning typically consists of creative play, an artistic activity, a story, singing games and fingerplays, snack and outside play.

*Creative Play:* As the children arrive, they hang up their sweaters, say hello to the teacher and happily become engrossed in their favorite play. We might see several boys and girls in the home area, cooking and playing with the dolls. Nearby, three children are moving blanket stands to make a house covered with a sheet. Another child has put on kitty ears and and is mewing at their door. Another boy arrives, puts on a cape and crawls under the table with two standup dolls. Two other boys have taken their backpacks off the hook and are being scuba divers. One child sits next to the teacher, who is cutting fruit for snacks, and helps her. As more children arrive, the room becomes filled with the sounds of their play. Two children have become engrossed at the workbench. Now several children are sliding down and jumping off of the wooden indoor slide. Two children have put embroidery hoops over their heads for dog collars and tied on yarn to be taken for a walk by their owner. The transformations are endless as the children's play unfolds over forty-five minutes to an hour.

The room could seem chaotic to a casual observer as the children experience the world through their inner-directed play. The teacher and her assistant watch attentively and help as needed by tying on a costume or helping two children to take turns with a contested object. They are happy to be brought things as part of the children's imaginative play and will interact with them, but they don't get down and play with the children or interrupt them except as necessary for safety or to resolve conflicts that the children don't work out themselves. The teacher remains aware of everyone in the room while she is busy preparing the snack or sewing a new toy for the children. In this way the children not only see a model of creative work, but her activity can also be transformed by them in their play.

*Story Time:* A song tells the children it is time to put all the toys away, and the little gnome comes out of his house to see what good workers they are. When everything is in its place, another song brings the children to morning circle.

Through verse and song the children greet one another and the day and then listen attentively as the teacher begins to tell a story. She has already been telling the same fairy tale for a week-and-a-half, and some of the children join in with the hand movements it contains.

*Snack Time:* After story it is time to wash hands and set the tables for snack. The children eagerly help to put around the napkins and placemats. Today there is fruit salad, which the teacher and her helpers have been making during free play. Another day there might be hot cereal, wholegrain crackers or bread the children have baked. The children sing a song of thanks for the food, and then talk with one another while they eat. When they are finished, they sing, "Red Bird, Red Bird, who will you choose today?" and eagerly wait for the red felt bird suspended from a stick to visit the nests they make with their hands and to nibble at the crumbs. He chooses a lucky child at each table to blow out the candle and then dismisses the children one by one to go and play.

*Artistic Activity:* After the tables are wiped, preparation is made for the day's activity. With this group, Monday is painting day, Tuesday is beeswax, Wednesday is baking, Thursday is crafts and Friday is coloring. Today is crafts, and the teacher brings out pine cones and feathers to make birds. Several of the children immediately come over and watch her place small pieces of beeswax in the sides and stick feathers into it for wings. Another piece of beeswax forms the beak. The children quickly copy. Then the teacher helps them tie on a piece of string so they can fly the birds around. While they are working, the teacher sings a song about a little bird.

The children who are finished fly their birds and some start to play being birds. Other children want their turn, and finally the teacher calls over the last two little boys, who are engrossed in their play, by asking what color feathers they like for their birds.

The project materials are put away, and when it is time for games, the birds all fly to their "nests" in the children's backpacks.

*Movement Circle:* The teacher now begins to sing, "Sally Go Round the Sun" while she takes two children's hands. Soon a circle has been formed, and the children play circle games interspersed with fingerplays and verses with accompanying movements. The circle varies in tempo and loudness, with active games alternating with slow movements or fingerplays. Once a week the eurythmist comes for a very special time of movement with the children. Movement circle ends with a goodbye song, and the children get ready to go outside.

*Outside Play:* The children play outside for about half an hour and are picked up by their parents at noon. They play on the swings, slide, teeter totter and climbing dome. There is also a sandbox and a large horse made out of logs and branches. The children's play area is like a garden and feels enclosed by foliage. Sometimes the children go for a walk with their teacher to the park or the woods during outside time.

Within the rhythm of the day, which holds the children, the specific activities and stories change according to the seasons of the year. This includes collecting things for the seasonal table, baking seasonal foods, making things for the festivals and outdoor activities such as making leaf crowns or planting spring bulbs. Much of the teacher's preparation relates to the rhythm of the year and the children's experience of it. This is reflected in the daily activities, the changing decorations in the room and the special events she plans—such as a field trip to pick apples in the fall, an Advent garden in December or a trip to see newborn lambs in spring.

With a mixed-age group, activities take place on many levels simultaneously, as with a craft project in which the older children can do all of it themselves while the younger ones require help from the teacher. Stories from various levels are told with mixed-age classes. Kindergarteners love hearing again the story of "The Three Little Pigs" while younger children will be carried along by the group when a story for older children is being told.

Direct intellectual teaching does not take place in a Waldorf nursery or kindergarten. There are no exercises in reading readiness or doing pages from math workbooks. Nor are shapes and weights manipulated to learn concepts such as "triangle" or "heavy and light." The child is allowed to take in the world through his senses and to participate in it through movement, making things and play. It is recognized that one of the tasks of early childhood is the healthy mastering of body skills; finger-plays and movement games help to develop coordination and contribute to the formation of speech. They also can form the basis for later mathematical learning by matching rhythmical counting with body movements, forming a valuable foundation in the body for number and rhythm. Similarly, the transformation of one object into another in creative play provides a concrete basis for the more abstract manipulation of symbols involved in reading. Developmental steps are not skipped or hurried. Rather, there is a confidence in the unfolding of the young child according to the patterns of nature and the stamp of the child's own individuality.

Many times children who can already write the alphabet, or even read, enter a Waldorf early childhood program. However, the children are not provided time to practice such skills. Because their days are so full of creative play, stories, puppet shows, crafts and artistic activity, they are fully engaged and often do not even notice that they aren't reading or doing mathematics in kindergarten. And the rich experiences they receive in the Waldorf program can serve as a balancing force for the early intellectual development they have experienced.

## The Setting

Because the environment is so important for the young child, a great deal of care is put into creating a room that is nourishing and inviting to the children. When it is possible to build according to Steiner's indications for architecture, the buildings produced really feel as if they embrace and surround the children with their curves, cubby holes and play areas. However, since it is usually necessary to adapt an existing building for a kindergarten, lights and right angles are often softened by hanging colored cotton gauze or silk in the corners and over light fixtures. I once used a parachute to cover a ceiling in a public school building and create a feeling of clouds instead of steel beams and reinforced concrete. Smaller activity areas can also be created with wood and cloth.

Many Waldorf kindergartens are painted a light rose color that Steiner called "peach blossom." It is a color that reflects the lightness of the young children, who have not yet fully arrived on earth. A special way of painting called *lazuring* uses washes of various colors on a wall to give an impression of depth on a flat surface. Through this technique, murals or images can be painted to suggest forms in a very soft, beautiful way.

The room is decorated with seasonal motifs, such as a nature table, tissue paper pictures on the windows and decorated branches. The attention to detail and beauty will be reflected in the mood of the children and the quality of their play.

The toys are made from natural materials and are arranged in activity areas or little scenes which invite imaginative interaction.

## The Role of the Teacher

Waldorf nurseries and kindergartens often appear deceptively simple. Everything flows so easily and looks so effortless. The tremendous amount of work by the teacher is mostly invisible, except as it is felt by those who know children and who can sense the mood the teacher creates. Someone from another preschool program visited our preschool home and was surprised by how peaceful it was with twelve children in such a small space.

She said to her assistant, "Can you imagine Jane [one of their teachers] here? It just wouldn't be the same!" The being of the teacher and the physical and emotional environment she or he creates are what really nourish the children.

Because the teacher is constantly an example for the children, she pays special attention to the quality of her movements and the tone of her voice. She does many things with the children, such as preparing the snack, telling a story or leading the circle games. But she also does a great deal just by her *being*, by who she is. She tries to put aside her own problems and emotional upsets so that she is as clear as possible when she is with the children. She needs to get enough sleep and to have her own meditative practices to remain centered in the classroom and to keep the rest of her life in order. Her role with the children is similar to a meditative state of awareness: she is aware of everything, totally in the present moment, not thinking about other things—just there with and for the children. Being with young children often involves more being than doing. It's hard to make everything simple enough. We tend to think that we have to stimulate and provide things for the children, when our more difficult task is to provide them with the space to be themselves, to experience and grow and try on the world and its activities within the guidance and protection provided by the adults.

The teacher's attitude of warmth and love provides a calm and healthy atmosphere for the young child. Steiner describes it as follows:

> The joy of the child in and with his environment must be reckoned among the forces that build and mould the physical organs. He needs people around him with happy looks and manners and, above all, with an honest unaffected love. A love which fills the physical environment of the child with warmth may literally be said to 'hatch out' the forms of the physical organs. The child who lives in such an atmosphere of love and warmth and who has around him really good examples for his imitation is living in his right element. One should therefore strictly guard against anything being done in the child's presence that he must not imitate.[8]

Because the young child is an imitative being, the teacher simply begins each activity, and the children follow along. She doesn't announce, "Now it's story time," or "Let's take hands for circle games." Instead, she simply takes two children's hands and starts singing and moving with the intention that everyone will join in, and they do. Story time may begin with the same song every day, or the teacher may light a candle or put on a special storytelling hat and play a few notes on the kinderharp; whatever she has chosen, the children soon learn what will follow.

During the children's free play, the teacher can provide an example of work from real life—sawing wood, gardening during outside play, making something for the preschool. The children can often help with the activity itself, like cutting fruit for snacks or winding yarn. The activity will also appear transformed in their play. For example, if the teacher is sewing, a few children will want to get out their sewing basket, while another might go off and pretend to sew something with her fingers.

The warmth and love of the teacher for the children involves really taking on their care as a trust, in conjunction with the parents. Thus the teacher needs as complete a picture as possible of each child before accepting him or her into the program. She will observe the child if possible and have an in-depth interview with the parents—how was her birth; how did she develop; what does she like to play; are there any health problems; has she been in other daycare or preschool programs; what are the parents' expectations? The teacher needs to feel that she can really take on this child, and that she can work together with the parents for the child's growth and well-being. The parents also need to evaluate the teacher and the program and make sure that this is where they want their child to be.

Once a child has been accepted, the teacher tries to visit the family at home to get a picture of the child in his own surroundings, to meet any brothers and sisters or pets, and to see the child's room. In addition to helping the teacher better understand the context in which the child lives, such a visit provides a wonderful link for the child between home and school, a sense of interpenetration of the two worlds which is very supportive.

The teacher's work does not stop when the children go home. There is not only cleaning up and preparing for the next day's activities, but there is also work with the parents through parent evenings, conferences, toymaking workshops and so forth. At night the teacher visualizes each child and takes the image into her sleep. This practice not only supports the child and his connection with the teacher, but can provide the teacher with inspiration if a child is having particular difficulties.

### The Training of a Waldorf Early-Childhood Teacher

The attitude of the teacher and the understanding gained by working out of the indications that Rudolf Steiner gave about the developing human being are the most important elements of a Waldorf preschool. Simply having dolls without faces or block-shaped crayons does not make a Waldorf program! The activities suggested in this book are appropriate for all children and really fit the young child. They can be incorporated into home life and into existing daycare and preschool programs with very positive results. But one needs to distinguish between "a bit of this and a bit of that" and a full Waldorf program. For such a program, trained Waldorf teachers are the essential element; addresses of training programs are listed in Appendix D.

However, it is often impossible for someone with a spouse and small children to move near a training center for one or two years. It is sometimes possible to do home study while apprenticing as an assistant at an existing Waldorf school. There are also several short courses and workshops available for parents, daycare providers and new teachers; they are listed in Appendix E.


## WALDORF EARLY-CHILDHOOD EDUCATION IN THE HOME

Many mothers who are trying to incorporate these ideas and recommendations about young children into their home life find themselves wanting to start play groups with other parents who share the same interests and ideals. If there is a group of interested mothers, you can take turns being with the children while the other mothers discuss questions they are having about their children and share resources. It is also possible to share craft and festival ideas and to select a book for study and discussion. Several recommended titles are listed at the end of this chapter. If you find yourself alone in working with these ideas, you will need to keep studying and find support through networking while you are looking for more like-minded people.

In many places, Waldorf early-childhood teachers have founded what could be called Waldorf preschool homes, in which a full Waldorf program is offered to a small group of children in the teacher's home. Many times such programs have grown up around an existing Waldorf school, forming a network of pre-school homes that provide support for parents who are interested in Waldorf education. We were fortunate in Ann Arbor to have four Waldorf-trained early-childhood teachers who decided to found such preschool homes, rather than try to establish a free-standing early childhood center when there was no physical room at the Rudolf Steiner School for such a program. We felt that it would be ideal for three- and four-year-olds to be in small groups rather than going to a large center, so the home setting was chosen. Legally the programs come under "daycare," which means the regulations are much simpler than establishing a school or center. In Michigan a person can take care of six children in her home, or twelve if she has another adult helping her. Each teacher had a room in her home which she was able to leave permanently set up with the Waldorf toys; in addition, some of the teachers use their dining rooms or other rooms of their home, depending on the number of children they are working with.

Our experience has been that these children have the best of both worlds—a full Waldorf early-childhood program in a home environment with from six to twelve children. It is a very gentle first introduction to "school" for the young child. It is also ideal for the teachers, both financially and in terms of the minimal amount of administrative work required.

In Ann Arbor, the preschool home teachers meet once a month with the kindergarten teachers and their assistants from the Rudolf Steiner School for study, sharing of ideas, discussion of difficulties and undertaking common projects like large marionette plays or festival celebrations. The faculty of the school also invites the preschool teachers once each month to part of their faculty meeting covering a topic relating to Waldorf education, discussion and an artistic activity; this further helps to increase the communication between the school and the preschool homes.

In our community, mothers who have been associated with the school for several years are now starting to offer Waldorf-oriented daycare programs in their homes, and this is also happening in many other communities. The need for quality daycare still far exceeds the supply and there remains much room for growth in this area.

Many women start taking this approach to early childhood with a group of children in their home, because they want this kind of experience for their own children. When there is no Waldorf School in your area, such a group can also evolve into a "Saturday Club," which provides some of the enriching activities of Waldorf education for older children who are in other schools or who are being taught at home.

Waldorf education was started for the children of the workers in a factory in Stuttgart in 1919; it embraces children of all economic and intellectual levels and welcomes children from all cultural backgrounds. The principles of Waldorf education are not elitist and reserved for the relatively small number of children who live near Waldorf Schools. Its principles are universal and can be applied to all children. In fact, in Bern, Switzerland, public-school teachers attend courses at the Waldorf Teacher Training Program as part of their public-school training.

In our highly technological society, the view of child development and the principles of education initiated by Rudolf Steiner (and further developed by thousands of Waldorf teachers over the past seventy years) need to become known to more and more parents for the healthy development of young children. The quality of life in the home and the preschool environment is perhaps more important than what kind of elementary school the child attends.

If you take care of children in your home, you may want either to incorporate some of these ideas and techniques into things you are already doing from other sources, or you may want to strive to be working fully in the Waldorf tradition. In the first case, you will certainly be enhancing your work with the children. In the second, I urge you to get the most complete training you can, at an established training center if possible. To avoid misunderstandings about Waldorf education, it is best to avoid calling your own work "Waldorf" until you have had sufficient training and developed your professional competence as a Waldorf teacher. However, certification is not as important as the constant striving to deepen your understanding of the young child and to continually improve in your teaching and care of the children.

## RECOMMENDED READING

### Journals on Waldorf Education

*Child and Man*, international journal of Waldorf education published twice a year. Distributed by Child and Man, 6334 Gaston Ave., Suite 212, Dallas, TX 75214.

*Childhood*, quarterly journal on Waldorf principles published by Nancy Aldrich, Rt. 2, Box 2675, Westford, VT 05494.

"Waldorf Kindergarten Association Newsletter," published twice a year from the Waldorf Kindergarten Association of North America, 9500 Brunett Ave., Silver Spring, MD 20901. Back issues available.

### Books on the Waldorf Preschool

*Early Childhood Education and the Waldorf School Plan* by Elisabeth Grunelius.

*Plan und Praxis des Waldorfkindergartens* in translation by the Waldorf Kindergarten Association of North America (see above address).

### Books for Beginning Study Groups

*Lifeways* by Gudrun Davy and Bons Voors (IBP, SG). Chapters deal with issues of family life. Excellent for a mothers' group.

*The Waldorf Parenting Handbook* by Lois Cusick (IBP, SG). An introduction to some of the ideas behind Waldorf education from birth through high school.

*You Are Your Child's First Teacher* (IBP, SG). Share it with your friends!

*The Recovery of Man in Childhood* and *The Way of a Child* by A. C. Harwood. Two excellent introductions to child development and the Waldorf approach that we hope will soon be back in print.

## Waldorf Teacher Training Programs

See Appendix D.

## Seminars on Waldorf Early-Childhood Education

See Appendix E.

# 13 | *Readiness for First Grade*

## WHEN SHOULD YOUR CHILD START SCHOOL?

"School readiness" used to mean readiness for first grade, but it must now be expanded to include readiness for most kindergartens because of the academic pressure placed on the majority of kindergarteners. Due to the downward shift of the curriculum over the past thirty years, it is even more important that children today be *developmentally* ready for school as well as *chronologically* ready. The developmental age of a child can be six months to a year or more away from his or her chronological age. Developmental age is measured by how closely the child's social, emotional, physical and perceptual maturity corresponds to the norm for his age. Just as babies crawl, teethe, walk and become toilet-trained at different ages, older children too remain on their own individual timetables. There is not necessarily any correlation between developmental age and intelligence; a child with a high IQ can be developmentally delayed.[1]

In "Pupil Age at School Entrance—How Many are Ready for Success?" James Uphoff and June Gilmore report marked differences in school performance and emotional adjustment between children with summer and fall birthdays, who were less than five years and three months of age when they entered kindergarten, and those children with summer birthdays who were given an extra growth year and were as much as six years and three months when they entered kindergarten. For example, in a study of two-hundred seventy-eight pupils in the Hebron, Nebraska, elementary school, the young summer children made up seventy-five percent of the school's failure population while *none* of the held-back summer children had failed a grade.[2] While the young summer children in this study had higher average IQs, the less bright but older and developmentally more mature pupils were able to do more with the ability they had than were the brighter, younger ones. Uphoff also found that fewer of the young summer children were perceived as having leadership abilities in later years, and that in studying youth suicides, fifty-five percent of the boys who committed suicide had started school in September when they turned five in June or later, and eighty-three percent of the girls had!

Uphoff and Gilmore summarize their research as follows:

1. The chronologically older children in a grade tend to receive many more above-average grades from teachers than do younger children in that grade.
2. Older children also are much more likely to score in the above-average range on standardized achievement tests.
3. The younger children in a grade are far more likely to fail at least one grade than are older children.
4. The younger children in a grade are far more likely to be referred by teachers for learning disabilities testing and subsequently be diagnosed as being learning disabled than are older students in a grade.
5. The academic problems of younger children who were developmentally unready at school entrance often last throughout their school careers and sometimes even into adulthood.[3]

The Gesell Institute of Human Development in New Haven, Connecticut, is a leading advocate of slowing down the accelerated pace of childhood. Their studies found that only about one-third of the children they tested in grades K–3 were ready for the grade in which their age had placed them. The readiness of another third was questionable, and the final third definitely were not ready. Their recent studies compiled from school districts across the country indicate that as many as fifty percent of students with school problems today have them because of over-placement.[4]

Many school systems still allow children to enter school who turn five by December 31. Fortunately, however, in the last decade at least seventeen states have moved their cutoff date earlier in the year, recognizing that children do better when they are older at school entry. And many school systems are establishing "pre-kindergartens" or "junior first grades" for those children who are developmentally unready for the tasks at hand. However, regardless of a school system's cutoff dates, parents together with teachers must decide if an individual child is really ready for kindergarten or first grade. Giving a child who has a summer or fall birthday an extra growth year can be a lifelong gift that may put him at the head of the class instead of scrabbling to keep up intellectually or socially.

If a child is kept in kindergarten a second year, or needs to go into a "pre-first" program, in no way should the parents regard the child as a failure or learning disabled. Remember that developmental maturity has no correlation with IQ. If the parents feel positive about the change and take responsibility themselves, the child can adapt well and the change can have positive benefits. Parents sometimes find it hard to explain to grandparents why they are having their child in kindergarten for two years, but the advantages for the child are worth the effort if you are feeling pressured to keep your child going through the system when she is showing signs of not being ready.

## WHAT HAPPENS AROUND AGE SEVEN?

Between five and seven you will see many dramatic changes in your child. In terms of the development of memory, your child may say something like, "I can see grandma anytime I want to now," referring to an emerging ability to call up mental images at will. He may also tell you more of his dreams.

You will see a kind of logic appearing in speech that represents a new level of thinking and is expressed in words like *because, so, if* and *therefore*. This new ability is expressed in creative play by the love of tying things together with string, like linking one thing to the next with logic. A growing grasp of, and interest in, time will also be apparent.

In play you may also see intention manifested as things are built *for* other things, as with a sand structure now being built as a garage for a car rather than for the activity itself. An authoritative element enters into group play at this age, with a child sometimes directing and sometimes being told who or what he will be.

In the sphere of drawing, the individualizing element expresses itself in the use of the diagonal line: triangular designs, a ladder leaning against a tree, the stair going up inside the house or the appearance of the arching rainbow.

Physically you will first see the differentiation of the chest or "middle sphere" around age five—the child suddenly loses its round Buddha belly and acquires a waist and a neck, showing how the life forces have completed their work in the rhythmic system. As the shift of the growth forces is made to the limbs, the arms will lengthen during this time. This is why an older child will be able to reach directly over her head and touch her ear, while a younger or less-developed one will not. Finally the growth shifts into the legs, and the child will also often start to eat more, and will sometimes increase in his awareness of digestion (expressed in the frequent stomachaches of some children of this age). At the same time the growth forces are moving into the legs, the features of the face become more individualized and the milk teeth begin to loosen.

The child starts to have real friendships and likes to make and give surprises. He likes to play with words and create rhymes, to play riddle and guessing games, to whisper and to giggle. Meyerkort says, "He feels the future dawning, the new stage coming, he says, 'I hope. . . .'"[5]

All of the changes discussed here should be allowed to become consolidated in a play-oriented kindergarten before the child is called upon to exercise the new faculties that are used in first grade.

Steiner explains the changes around the age of seven as resulting from the life forces completing their work of individualizing the child's physical body: first the head between birth and age three, then the middle sphere between ages three and five, and finally the limbs and the hard, boney teeth. Once finished, the forces are freed for development of the memory and school work. According to Steiner, the way to teach the elementary-school child between the change of teeth and puberty is with images and pictures, through which the child is allowed to take guidance from the inner meaning she discovers for herself in the pictures and allegories. What the child sees and perceives with the eye of the mind is a more appropriate means of education than abstract conceptions for the elementary-school child.

It is upon this ground of imagination that the later powers of intellect, judgment and critical thinking will be based. Therefore, all of the subjects—from reading to mathematics to physics—are taught in an imaginative and artistic way in the Waldorf elementary school, providing a rich and nourishing foundation for the faculty of analytical thinking that arises and can be developed in puberty.

## READINESS FOR FIRST GRADE

No matter what kind of kindergarten experience your child has, the decision about when to go on to first grade is an important one. Each child should be evaluated individually toward the end of the kindergarten year to see if he or she is developmentally ready for first grade. Your child's kindergarten teacher can provide valuable input, and you can ask about the Gesell Readiness Test or the Easter Seal Readiness Test if you are not connected with a Waldorf program. There is no stigma attached to giving a child a growth year that will put him in the top rather than the bottom portion of the class! Some of the signs of readiness to look for include:

MOVEMENT SKILLS

- Can catch and throw a large ball or beanbag
- Can walk forward on a balance beam (wall, log)

- Can hop some distance on either foot

- Can bunny hop (both feet in the air)

- Can play finger games, cut with scissors, sew or do other small motor skills presented in the program

- Often walks in a cross pattern (right arm swings forward with left foot, and vice versa)

- Can reach across top of head to touch further ear

- Can deal with own buttons, zippers

- Should not be unduly restless or lethargic

- Has lost some baby teeth

*Note:* Left/right dominance should be noted, including handedness; eye dominance, by having the child look through a rolled-paper "telescope" or camera; ear dominance, by offering a large shell in which one can hear the sea; and leg dominance, by kicking a ball or seeing which foot leads in going up stairs. Cross dominance (left eye, right hand) should especially be noted for further observation as it has potential significance in learning.

COGNITIVE DEVELOPMENT

- Enjoys stories and listens well

- Remembers broad outline of favorite stories

- Has fluent, rhythmical speech habits and clear enunciation

- Can tell about a recent experience coherently

- Knows by heart some of the songs and rhymes he has heard

- Has a beginning sense of pitch in singing

- Seems interested in books and shows a desire to read

- Knows own last name, address, telephone number

- Recognizes the colors and knows their names

- Is capable of selective attention

- Follows indications of teacher in circle games

- Is able to complete a task from beginning to end

SOCIAL DEVELOPMENT

- Ability to share
- Can play comfortably in a small group
- Can look after own hygienic needs
- Follows instructions
- Joins in offered activities
- Helps with chores and carries them through (sweeping, table setting)
- Is not regularly either an aggressor or a victim and is accepted by most other children

Further information on school readiness and the advantages of making sure children are old enough for what will be demanded of them can be found in *Better Late than Early* and *School Can Wait*, both by Raymond and Dorothy Moore.[6]

The Waldorf schools have always recognized the advantage of delaying entrance into first grade until a child is developmentally ready for school. Children usually have to turn six by summer, rather than December first, and special attention is put on younger children with summer birthdays. Each child is evaluated individually by the kindergarten and first grade teachers and a decision is made together with the parents. Because the Waldorf kindergarten is play-oriented, a younger child can do fine in the program and is often admitted to kindergarten with the understanding that he will most likely spend two years there. In a mixed-age kindergarten, the children typically remain in such a group with the same teacher for two or three years.

# BEGINNING ACADEMIC WORK:
# THE WALDORF APPROACH

In the Waldorf program, reading, writing and math aren't started until first grade. By starting academic tasks when they are developmentally more mature, such children do not fall behind peers who start earlier in other school systems. In fact, there are definite advantages in delaying instruction in the Three R's until around the age of seven.

Writing is taught in the Waldorf first grade through stories and pictures, and then the children learn to read from what they have written themselves. Just as humanity first wrote through picture glyphs before developing the alphabet, so the young child develops the forms and the sounds of the letters through stories and pictures provided by the teacher. The more abstract work of reading begins toward the end of first grade, and the transition to printed books is generally not made until second grade.

Although reading is taught more slowly in a Waldorf school, by the end of second grade most of the class will be reading at grade level, with some children having leapt way ahead. There will also be a few for whom the decoding process has not yet taken hold. These children will probably become readers in third grade without needing extra help, because there is no sense of failure by being relegated to a slow group. Much of reading depends on the inner maturation of the child, and Steiner reminds us that, "That which is asleep will waken." By the end of third grade, the teacher will recommend individual work for the few children who *do* require extra attention. In general, the Waldorf approach to reading reduces the number of children who have difficulties; late starters have fewer failures. It results in the bright children leaping ahead into real literature because they haven't burned out on years of "Dad had a tan pad," or other inanities.

Children who are first taught to read at a later age miss out on years of "I can read" books, but what are they really missing? Bruno Bettelheim, in his article "Why Children Don't Like to Read,"[7] lambasts most of the early readers and texts used in elementary schools as being totally devoid of meaning, content and interest for young children. He points out the constant reduction in the number of words taught to children, so that books become a series of repeated words that lack any relationship to spoken communication and lack a meaning or story line that the child would want to learn to read in order to discover. He states, "Although in the 1920s few children went to kindergarten and little preschool reading instruction was given, by the 1970s, when many children were attending kindergarten and reading was consistently taught there, the first-grade primers contained only a quarter of the vocabulary presented to first-graders fifty years ago."[8]

Bettelheim continues, "It is not impossible to teach children to read while respecting their intelligence and dignity. The primers used in Europe are generally far more difficult than those in use in this country. We believe their success is proved by the fact that at the end of the first grade, the average European child has a larger reading vocabulary than that of the average American child. Moreover, reading retardation, the curse of so many young Americans, is much less common among European children and when it occurs, is rarely as severe."[9] While the above points are certainly significant, it should be noted in all fairness that some European school systems admit children to first grade at age seven rather than six and that English is less phonetic than many other languages. Maturation is clearly an important factor in reading; our public school system violates this rule by moving reading instruction earlier and earlier in the child's life.

Some people have the mistaken idea that there are no books in a Waldorf school. This is far from true! While there aren't readers in the kindergarten, and in the first grade children learn to read from what they have written themselves, books with *real* literary content are introduced from second grade on, and children are never given anything that is condescending in tone or that has been predigested especially for children. Real literature is always used in the classroom, selected according to reading level and the inner maturity level of the children. Waldorf schools have libraries for children's reading pleasure, and for doing research in the upper grades.

Although reading is taught more slowly in the Waldorf curriculum, math is not. Nothing is done until first grade, but then all four processes—addition, subtraction, multiplication and division—are introduced. This is possible because the concepts are introduced imaginatively. For example, there might be a story about four gnome brothers: Mr. Plus is fat and jolly with stuffed pockets; Mr. Minus is thin and sad, and all of his jewels keep falling out of a hole in his sack; and so forth. The children work from the whole to the part, first using chestnuts or shells to see that 8 is 1 plus 7; 8 is 2 plus 6; and so on. They also walk various rhythms and verses that help to make the multiplication tables much easier to learn. When mathematics is made concrete and imaginative, the children take to it with delight.

A complete listing of the Waldorf curriculum for grades 1–8 can be found in Appendix B.

## What About the Advanced or Gifted Child?

Waiting until a child is in first grade before starting academic work has obvious advantages for an average or slow child, who needs the extra neurophysiological maturity before beginning tasks such as reading and mathematics. However, what about the bright child, who wants to start writing letters or learning to read at age three or four, or certainly by kindergarten age? As children become more aware of the world around them, they want to imitate and learn, and many children will show interest in these activities by age five. You can share their enthusiasm and say, "You will learn more about how to do that when you are in first grade!" But you needn't sit down and start lessons then, as it is still too soon to exercise the memory or the intellect directly. There is no critical time when you have to teach a child to read or risk his not being interested later on. On the contrary, telling a child, "That's what you'll learn when you go to the big school," develops eagerness and anticipation, and keeps the young child learning through imitation rather than through direct lessons.

By not being taught to read in kindergarten or before, children miss several years of early readers (which isn't missing much), and they are given the gift of the final year or more of early childhood. Direct cognitive work wakes the child up and brings her out of the magical years of early childhood. Children grow out of these years soon enough on their own. Allowing your child to stay in the magical realm of early childhood without pushing cognitive development provides a sound basis for later health and creativity.

Our oldest daughter, who is quite bright, has a November birthday, so we decided to keep her in kindergarten a second year, following Steiner's indications. She thoroughly enjoyed her second year of Waldorf kindergarten, and by the time she got to school, she was *really* eager to learn. In every grade her attitude could be described as *Give it to me!* She even started doing things at home that anticipated the curriculum about two weeks before the teacher introduced them in class—an indication of how well matched the curriculum is for the children's developmental stages. Although we delayed teaching her to read, by third grade she was reading *Little Women, Tom Sawyer* and books I hadn't read until high school or college. She is still an avid reader at age eleven, in contrast to her older brother who was taught to read at age four and had lost interest in reading for pleasure by fourth grade.

Especially with bright children, it is important to emphasize balance. It *is* possible to teach them intellectual skills at a young age and to put them into academically advanced programs from preschool or kindergarten on. But the result is often the production of a "forty-year-old" in a five-year-old body. Advanced intellectual development in childhood is usually at the expense of the artistic/emotional sphere or the healthy development of the body. Elementary-school education should appeal so much to the child's imagination that the gifted child still feels fully interested and engaged. If that kind of creative education isn't available for the very bright child, you may face some hard choices.

You will need to investigate educational approaches and make your own decisions for your child. I felt it was important to work toward a balanced development of the heart forces, the head forces and the body/will forces, so that a *whole* human being would emerge who would be able to lead a fruitful life and act in service to humanity. The danger in education that emphasizes *only* intellectual development is in turning out thinkers and scientists who are emotionally divorced from humanity and from the consequences of their work for the world. For this reason, I chose for my children an approach to education that emphasized balance, rather than a program designed specifically for gifted children.

## SELECTING A FIRST GRADE PROGRAM

In investigating public and private elementary schools in your community, find out about their philosophy and curriculum, and then try to visit the classroom to observe. Meet your child's teacher and see if you can establish rapport and a relationship based on trust and communication. Stay in touch throughout the course of the year; don't wait until May to learn that your child is having difficulty with a subject or has spent much of the year sitting in the hall!

If the "ideal" situation doesn't exist in their community, some parents decide to join the school board or other committee where they can have some input into education; others work toward starting an alternative school; while others decide it is important enough to move to another city. But sometimes there isn't a lot you can do, and it is necessary to make compromises or sacrifices. The most important thing is to stay involved and to stay connected with your child and his teacher so you are working together and are aware of what is happening. Remember that it is possible to bring some of the elements that may be missing at school to your child through the art, music and stories that you do together at home. This can be enhanced by bringing in other children (and parents!) for activities on a regular basis, such as forming a Saturday Club.

Some parents who don't find what they want in their community opt for home schooling if one of them has the time and inclination to be their child's teacher. Even if home schooling is difficult in your state, most states do not have mandatory kindergarten attendance, so you can work with your child at home during that year before having to deal with curriculums and teaching certificates. Home schooling can be done successfully if the parent-child relationship can support such constant contact and if an effort is made to get together with other children. Waldorf education does not easily translate into home schooling because of the importance of the social element in the child's development and the fact that Waldorf education is not a series of techniques, but an inner way of working to see the world and bring it before the child in a living way. The home schooling curriculum with the most Waldorf elements is the Oak Meadow program, listed at the end of this chapter.

If you are interested in alternatives in education, it is good to start investigating when your children are still young. Forming a discussion and study group will not only help you find out more, but it can also put you in touch with parents who have similar interests. This is valuable as a source of support for your style of parenting, playmates for your children and possible resources for exchanging childcare or providing enrichment for your children.

## RECOMMENDED READING

### School Readiness

*Better Late than Early* by Raymond and Dorothy Moore, et al.

*The Hurried Child* by David Elkind.

*Your Five Year Old* by Ilg and Ames (and other volumes on the six- and seven-year-old; from the Gesell Institute).

*Miseducation* by David Elkind.

"Pupil Age at School Entrance—How Many Are Ready for Success?" by James K. Uphoff and June Gilmore. Authorized copies available from the Waldorf Kindergarten Association, 9500 Brunett St., Silver Spring, MD 20901.

*School Can Wait* by Raymond and Dorothy Moore.

### Waldorf Education in the Grades

*An Introduction to Waldorf Education* by Rudolf Steiner (IBP).

*Rudolf Steiner Waldorf Education* by Brien Masters, Ed. (IBP).

*Creativity in Education: The Waldorf Approach* by René Querido (SG).

*Rudolf Steiner Education* by L. Francis Edmunds (SG).

*Education Towards Freedom* by Frans Carlgren.

### Home Schooling

*Childhood*, quarterly journal on the Waldorf approach, with an emphasis on parenting and home schooling. From Nancy Aldrich, Rt. 2, Box 2675, Westford, VT 05494.

*Clonlara Home Based Education Program* can help parents with curriculum and meet legal requirements of being under a certified teacher. From Clonlara, 1289 Jewett, Ann Arbor, MI 48103.

*Growing Without Schooling,* magazine emphasizing John Holt's work, from 729 Boylston St., Boston, MA 02116.

*Home Education Magazine,* P.O. Box 218, Tonasket, WA 98855.

*Oak Meadow.* Offers elementary-school curriculum and home teacher training; lower grades have a Waldorf influence. From P.O. Box 712, Blacksburg, VA 24060.

# 14 | *More Parenting Issues*

When I speak with parents around the country, similar issues come up again and again as parents consider the approach to the young child suggested in this book. By sharing some of these questions and the reasoning behind my answers, I hope this chapter will spark your own questions and your search for the answers that are most nurturing to you and your family.

*Even if I wanted to provide an idyllic world for my young child, I don't think I could do it. Modern life is just too fast-paced and stressful. Children need to adjust to the realities of today's world.*

The best way to prepare our children for the stresses of today's world is not to expose them to problems early in their life, but to provide them with an environment that is warm and nurturing and that shelters them when they are young from as many of the problems of the adult world as possible. Child psychologist David Elkind has discussed at length the difficulties children encounter when they are hurried to grow up and face adult choices too soon, or when they are subjected to miseducation by too early instruction in academic subjects, swimming, gymnastics, ballet and so forth.[1]

The rushed lives that most of us live make it difficult to provide children with an ideal world for their early childhood years. We tend to move frequently or travel a lot, to work full-time or part-time, to be "too busy" for the tempo of our children. Divorce, single parenting and blended families add to the stresses on a child. And, with the best intentions, many parents push their children to achieve at an early age or to be grown-up emotional companions for them.

Yet there is a great deal parents *can* do for their children by providing an environment filled with love and warmth. By understanding a young child's development and his complete openness to his surroudings, we can do our best to provide a stable and nurturing environment within our current living situation. Children are, fortunately, very giving and forgiving—and fairly resilient.

Now that we have recognized some of the ways in which children differ from adults, how can we let them be children in a society in which changing family, social and academic pressures make them deal with the adult world earlier than ever before? Most of us can't radically change our life situations, even if we wanted to. For the most part we are members of our highly technological, urban, material-minded society. Yet no matter where we find ourselves, ways to meet the real needs of the young child have been suggested in this book. In summary:

- Attend to your own life and emotions. The emotional environment you create for your child is far more important than the material environment.

- Honor the spiritual element in life, especially as it is brought to you by your children.

- Work toward rhythm in family life that can support you and your children.

- Remember that imitation and repetition are the keys to discipline with the young child, not reasoning or punishment.

- Set limits and consistently enforce them; accept that you are the parent.

- Allow plenty of time for your child's creative free play as well as musical and artistic play. Include time for just being home and "doing nothing."

- Buy or make childlike toys, ones that encourage imaginative play.

- Avoid pressuring your child to be an early achiever in academics, sports or the arts.

- Continue to pay attention to what your child experiences, limiting overstimulation from loud music, movies and television.

- Avoid concerning your child with adult problems through news broadcasts, conversations and so forth. Even third graders don't yet need to be taught about AIDS or substance abuse, as they have no way of comprehending such things!

*Your description of a play-oriented kindergarten leaves me wondering whether it really prepares children for the high-tech world in which we live. What about computer literacy? I want my child to have a competitive edge, not be behind the times.*

As with other forms of instruction, there is no demonstrated advantage for a child starting to use computers in preschool over a child who begins at age twelve or fourteen. Computers, as word processors and vehicles for logical thinking through programming, are suited to the realm of the adolescent, not the preschool-age child! Computers as toys are inappropriate, because they present a two-dimensional abstraction of the world to the young child, who should be moving and playing and acquiring a broad base of experiences of the physical world and the world of imaginative play. The visual image on the computer screen is especially hard on the developing eyes of the young child.

Most of the educational programs for young children try to teach concepts at too young an age. Remember that the young child needs to be addressed through movement and imitation. Steiner comments: "Have we the right to believe that with our intellectual mode of knowledge we can ever participate in the experience of the outer world which a child has, the child who is all sense-organ? This we cannot do. . . . It is immensely impor-tant that we do not consciously or unconsciously call upon the child's intellect prematurely, as people are so prone to do today."[2]

We need to remember how the fantasy and play of the young child transform into the artistic imagination of the elementary-school child, the questioning of the teenager and the rational thinking of the young adult. Then we will have confidence that fantasy and imagination, which are so natural for the young child, form a better foundation for later creative thinking than early learning. Creative thinking is more needed in our highly technological world than four-year-olds who can push the but-tons on the computer.

*My five-year-old has always been precocious and already reads. He can outreason me in getting what he wants. If we want to try to encourage his balanced development, what can we do now? He can't go back to early childhood!*

In working toward balanced development, it is necessary to have a picture of your child that includes more than intellectual achievements. What is he like emotionally? Is he happy being a child? Does he relate well with other children, or almost exclu-sively with adults? What is he like physically? Is he at home in his body and well-coordinated? Does he have frequent illnesses and require antibiotics frequently?

Many times early intellectual awakening can result in a weakening of the child's vital forces, manifesting in frequent colds or other illnesses. The dreamy state of early childhood is an es-sential element in the healthy formation of the physical body dur-ing the first seven years. The intellect is crystalline and hardening in its effect. When it is engaged prematurely, it can inhibit the proper development of the physical organs and the unfolding of the fluid emotions. Steiner even relates some illnesses in later life to influences in the first seven years:

> Whoever studies the whole course of a man's life from birth to death, bearing in mind the requirements of which I have spoken, will see that a child who has been exposed to things suitable only to grown-up people and who imitates these things will in his later years, from the age of about 50, suffer from sclerosis. . . . Illnesses

that appear in later life are often only the result of educational errors made in the very earliest years of childhood.[3]

Because the job of the intellect is to analyze and exercise critical judgment, very bright children tend to have difficulty relating emotionally with other children, a problem that can intensify as the child becomes older.

While an awakened child cannot go back to the dreamy world of early childhood, imaginative play and the arts can have a healing influence on the child's life forces, helping to "reweave the web" which protects the child during the first seven years. Images from fairy tales are also nurturing to the unconscious elements of the young child.

While you can't go back in time and do things differently with your child, it is also important not to feel guilty about choices you have already made. You were just as good a parent then as you are now. You made the best decisions you could then, based on your knowledge and perceptions of your choices. Guilt only takes us out of the present moment and makes us less able to see what is needed now, thus perpetuating problems rather than leading to meeting the present creatively. If there is going to be the possibility of healing, it must take place in the present. We make the best choices we can for our children in each moment, just as our parents did for us.

*Why do you suggest eliminating television for young children? We only let Jessica watch educational programs, and she loves them!*

Many thinking parents today justify the time they "buy" in letting their children watch television by saying, "We only let her watch children's shows and educational programming." However, the lack of movement on the part of the child and the poor quality of the sensory stimulation from the television screen make *all* television watching problematical for young children, regardless of the content. Television is an important source of information and diversion for most adults. But children are not in the same stage of development as adults.

In an article on "Children and Television," John Rosemond suggests that you look at your child next time he is watching television and ask yourself what he is doing—or, better yet, what he is *not* doing. He states:

> In answer, the child is *not:*
> * Scanning
> * Practicing motor skills, gross or fine
> * Practicing eye-hand coordination
> * Using more than two senses
> * Asking questions
> * Exploring
> * Exercising initiative or motivation
> * Being challenged
> * Solving problems
> * Thinking analytically
> * Exercising imagination
> * Practicing communication skills
> * Being either creative or constructive
>
> Also, because of television's insidious "flicker," television does not promote long-term attention.
> Lastly, because the action shifts constantly and capriciously backward, forward and laterally in time, not to mention from subject matter to subject matter, television does not promote logical, sequential thinking.[4]

Rosemond notes that the deficiencies listed above are characteristic of learning disabled children, "children who don't seem able to 'get it all together' when it comes to learning how to read and write." While television is not the only cause of the learning problems plaguing our schools, we need to look at the fact that learning disabilities have become epidemic and functional illiteracy among seventeen-year-olds has steadily risen since television became a mainstay of our culture in 1955.

In her article "Movement or Television," special education expert Audrey McAllen also reports that, when the TV set first arrived, she could distinguish the "watchers" in her class from the others by the difference in the way they sat and their lack of limb control. McAllen observes:

> After many years of working with children who have learning difficulties one sees clearly how unconnected the present day child is with the interaction of hands and limbs. They do not bother to lift

their legs high enough to throw a ball under them, the hand collides with the thigh. Also the left leg seems heavier than the right and harder for them to lift. When classes have been screened for learning problems, this symptom of limb heaviness is now general among children. Over the last years it has become apparent that the children born in the 60's take longer to respond to therapy than those born earlier.[5]

McAllen points out that children are always in movement. Even when asked to sit still in church, they still swing their legs, fiddle their fingers, gaze and wonder over the colored windows, count the number of hymns still to be sung and so forth. In contrast, when children watch television, their gaze is riveted, the eyes slightly unfocussed, their natural movement is inhibited, their jaw relaxes, their hands are stilled, and the child's lively fantasy is replaced by images on the screen. And when they are finished watching, their movements tend to be jerky and fidgety—they seem to be "all wound up" from having been so inactive and having absorbed so many impressions.[6]

McAllen states that kindergarten teachers of long experience observe that children today have less initiative than formerly, and expect grown-ups to start something. They wait passively for something to stimulate them when indoors. Their play lacks the imaginative inventiveness children once had.[7] Rosemond reports the same phenomena: "Veteran teachers consistently report that today's children are less resourceful, imaginative, creative and motivated than pre-television generations. They also comment that the average child's attention span seems to have shortened mysteriously since 1950."[8]

The young child wants to run and jump in space, touch and grasp with his hands, hold his breath for the fun of it, jump with joy, experience the world for himself with all his senses. "Can I see it?" means "Can I touch it?" The child is hungry to experience everything as fully as possible. "The growing-up Ego-Being, basically, wants to guide its own sight, its own step, its own hand, in order to enter into a personal and concrete relationship with its environment. Only in the meeting with this concrete objective reality and its fullness of life, as well as through the resistance experienced thereby, can it increasingly grow and eventually come to itself."[9] Seeing something on the screen through the changing viewpoint of the camera's lens leaves the child passive and usually uncomprehending.

One study showed that the ability to interpret the changing viewpoints and sequencing of images in even the "best" educational films required a level of maturity children usually only develop around age eleven:

> The ordinary fare of films, such as we used in our experiments, is as a rule not comprehended as a totality before a child's eleventh year of age, whereas younger children succeed no further than making a sum of individual scenes out of it. That only little of the film's content is grasped appears to have something to do with a general developmental law. That signifies, then, that it's hardly practical to show educational or feature films to children 8 to 10 years old.[10]

I observed something similar when my six-year-old watched a cartoon for the first time. I was about to get my hair cut when the friendly beautician put a "Popeye" cartoon into the VCR for the children. Although my daughter was fascinated, she couldn't make any sense out of it and my ten-year-old had to run constant commentary on it for her. That was the first time I realized how "unreal" the medium is, even for quite bright younger children.

Joseph Chilton Pearce describes the problem with television in relation to brain development. In development of the brain, words are taken in through stories, and then images are developed that connect the intellectual brain to the outside world through the midbrain (limbic) metaphoric structure. Television, however, floods the child with both the sound *and* the image at the sensory motor level. It gives the system a synthetic counterfeit of what it is supposed to *create*. The child's first seven years are devoted to development of the symbolic, metaphoric language structure in the the midbrain, and all future development rests on the functioning of this imagery. Television disrupts this development of an inner imagery by furnishing that imagery from an outside source.[11]

Marie Winn, in her book *The Plug-In Drug*, again emphasizes, "It isn't what your children watch on TV but the act of watching that harms them." She states that with heavy television viewing, the right hemisphere of the brain is developed at the expense of the left. The left hemisphere controls the verbal, rational thought—the ability to read and write, to reason, to organize ideas and express them in speech and writing. Television viewers are bombarded with images that don't require them to think, or even give them time to.[12]

By the time most children graduate from high school they will typically have spent 15,000 hours in front of a television set, compared with only 11,000 hours in the classroom.[13] If you subtract hours for sleeping and doing homework, children are left with relatively few hours spent in reading, playing and doing the other creative activities of childhood. Radically limiting your child's television watching before the age of ten or eleven is probably one of the most far-reaching gifts that you can give him or her developmentally. This may mean putting the television set in your bedroom, if there are shows that you or your partner watch regularly while the children are up, or finding another way to keep it covered or inaccessible if your child is a button pusher. You will probably need to put more time into family activities when you first get rid of the television, but then you will find that the children become self-motivating and that you, as well as they, will have more time to do things alone as well as together. The world without television is very different and very much more in keeping with the developmental needs of the young child.

*I want to change the kind of toys my child plays with, but she always pesters me to buy her the other ones when we go to the store. I can't just throw everything out. Where can I start?*

At first it may be difficult to step outside of the chrome and plastic world of high-tech toys, but as you and your daughter begin to experience more alternatives, it will become easier. Certainly you won't want to take away favorite toys and create lots of strife! Possibly you can make a start by eliminating toys she doesn't play with now. That will clear out some of the clutter and make some space. Then make something, or buy an imaginative toy, and have a special place in her room where it lives or is played with. Invest some energy into the imaginative aspect of it, and make sure that it is put away each day in an attractive manner, ready for the new day. Gradually add other toys of the type that encourage imagination, while you phase out old ones that are no longer played with. You will find that costumes and toys that invite imaginative play in little scenes will easily become favorites.

Increase the kinds of toys you want your child to have by requesting that appropriate catalogs be sent to grandparents and others who send gifts. Some parents have a "rainy day box" for gifts and toys that don't match their values for daily play, but which can be a fine adventure for a rainy day.

Incorporating some of the suggestions in this book into your parenting may involve changing patterns that are already established. Often it is possible to change things gradually, so the child doesn't have a sense of losing things. For example, adding painting and coloring with block crayons and telling stories or reading fairy tales means that activities they are replacing will gradually fade away. You don't need to throw away every children's book, but you might go through the pile with a critical eye and phase out those that were vaguely disturbing to you (and now you know why). Similarly, as you add more natural toys, you will be able to phase out other ones to higher shelves or the basement.

Sometimes it is necessary to go cold turkey, as when we decided to get rid of our television set. We did it at a time when we were moving anyway, so it didn't become associated with patterns in the new house. And I was amazed that the children didn't even complain. (I had been braced for a loud wail!) At first we replaced television time with activities the children were doing at school—knitting, singing, playing recorder and reading stories out loud so they wouldn't go around asking what to do now that they couldn't watch television. We also tried to keep television from becoming forbidden fruit by telling the oldest child that he could watch certain events like special football games at the neighbors if invited. With the younger children, we told the neighbors that we didn't have a television, so they should tell our girls their daughter couldn't "play" if she wanted to watch television instead. I found being tolerant and avoiding being "holier than thou" helped things to go smoothly without a lot of emotional upset.

Sometimes parents are discouraged by their children's playing with neighbors who have very different values. You can't constantly police your child when he is out of the house, so have faith that your values make the strongest impression on your child. What you can do most effectively is make your own rules at your house, and then make your house sufficiently attractive that your children and their friends will play there much of the time.

The issue of play with guns, for example, is one that parents need to discuss together and decide for themselves. I still don't have any clear philosophical or psychological answers as to what parents *should* do on this issue and why; I just knew that I wouldn't buy guns and my children learned that no gun play was allowed in our house. That limited their access without bringing up long discussions or making the neighbors wrong. Children can accept that there are different rules in different places. "This is the way we do it at our house," is enough of an answer to many a why from a young child. Similarly, in the kindergarten, children were told that certain play was all right at home, but not there. They didn't have any problem with that.

*Kidnapping and child abuse are in the news. With so many crazy people today, how should I educate my child about safety and "stranger danger"?*

In recent years there has been a widespread fear of stranger danger, with an abundance of programs and articles on child abuse and kidnappings. Granted that the world seems to be crazier than it was thirty or fifty years ago, still we can't bring up our children in constant fear. Fear attracts that which it fears. And young children need to live in a world of goodness and wholeness. While we need to caution our children from age three on not to get into cars driven by people they don't know, and not to go off with people they don't know for ice cream or candy, that is really about all they can handle comfortably. Child psychologist David Elkind points out that it is *parents'* responsibility to keep children supervised and safe, and the burden of resisting adults and being able to distinguish "good and bad touches" should not fall on the child.[14]

It has become evident that most of the hysteria of the mid-1980s was media hype. In 1984, the FBI listed 350,000 cases of missing children. Of these, only sixty-seven were actually kidnapped by strangers. The remaining children were either abducted by parents or relatives engaged in custody battles, or else were runaways.[15] All of those pictures of missing children on the milk cartons at every meal were finally discontinued because they led to the solving of only six cases.

What we did by all the media coverage was to create a climate of fear and anxiety in our children when there was very little actual abduction by strangers going on. Similarly, most sexual abuse occurs within the family or with people the child knows, not with strangers. It is fairly obvious that if an adult truly wanted to kidnap a child, there is actually very little a child could do to resist effectively, regardless of how much so-called education he had had about it. In our community a child was stuffed into a jeep, sexually abused and murdered—he was thirteen years old and fought with his attacker. All of the reading of gruesome stories about strangers to little children didn't do a bit of good the one tragic time it happened.

The American Academy of Pediatrics now cautions that fingerprinting and other child identification programs are of limited value and tend to create unhealthy and unnecessary anxiety. The report says that parents may be transmitting fear of stranger abduction to their children, and are advised to consider the whole story of the missing-children statistics and the possibility of suppressing the child's developing social skills.[16]

In the preschool, it was obvious from the children's play that they didn't know what to do with all of the input they were getting about strangers. During that time I tried to shield my daughter from all the hysteria, but it was too prevalent in her companions and everywhere we turned. (We changed brands of milk, but then the instant-copy shop had a free flyer she picked up.) The issue resurfaced a couple of months ago at the grocery store. Even though she is seven, she was somehow sitting in the grocery cart and told me proudly, "Two ladies said hello to me and one said I had on a pretty dress, but I didn't say anything to them!" I hated to deflate her, but I had to say, "Jasmine, that wasn't polite. If someone does that, you can say hello or thank you. You don't go in cars with drivers you don't know, and don't take candy or ice cream from people you don't know. But it's all right to talk to people!"

A few weeks later we somehow got into a discussion of what a stranger was. I tried to tell her a stranger was a friend you hadn't met yet. She assured me that a stranger was someone who grabbed little children and hurt them. The discussion went a little further, but I was discouraged by the impossibility of protecting my daughter from the very people who were trying to protect her!

As adults, *we* need to be responsible and know where our children are and that they are properly supervised, but we need to involve the children themselves only in the simplest way by telling them a few specific rules. I personally don't use "Don't talk to strangers," because that's too broad for a child and creates confusion. I can remember as a child walking home from the store in over 100-degree heat and feeling that I ought to refuse a ride offered by a neighbor whom I knew well because I "shouldn't go in cars with strangers." She understood my hesitation and my unspoken dilemma and said, "If your mother has said not to, it's best to go ahead and walk, but ask her about it when you get home." My mother, of course, explained that the rule meant people we didn't know, and I was furious for the misunderstanding and my having had to walk in that heat!

We need to protect our children's world from fear and mistrust while we do what is necessary to keep them safe. Children's books, and theater productions in the schools, present situations and emotions too advanced for the children. They need to be told simple things on the level of action, not all of the intellectual and emotional ramifications involved. If you're going to get gunned down in McDonald's, you're going to get gunned down in McDonald's. You can't live your life in fear of it, and you can't teach your children how to avoid it. The same is true with much of the well-meant but misplaced education about stranger danger.

### What effect will divorce have on my child?

The effects of divorce will vary according to the age and temperament of the child and the animosity or remaining good will between the parents. When parents are going through marital changes, the child is helped most when as few other things as possible change for him. Divorce is often emotionally and financially complicated, but making efforts to uproot the *child* as little as possible will yield positive results while unavoidable alterations are in progress.

Co-parenting can take many forms, from sticky custody battles to amicably continuing to share in the child's upbringing. If the child is under seven, I would advise against her alternately living a few days with one parent and then the other. The young child's sense of well-being is very connected to her environment remaining the same. A very young child usually does best living with the mother, because of the depth of the mother-child connection up to the age of three. Even children over three find it stressful to spend two days in one house and then three in the other, so parents might want to think about less disruptive living arrangements with visiting privileges while the child is still young.

The child in a family going through a divorce is obviously in a difficult position and should be spared as much as possible the parents' negative emotions about one another. If a child always behaves badly after visiting the other parent, the cause could be having his routine changed, as much as the emotions involved in the separation. You can try to arrange for transition times that will help to divert the negative energy and avoid head-on collisions. For example, always doing the same thing when the child comes home might help to ease him back into his routine at your house. Or you might want always to have a quiet dinner as soon as he comes home, or have a story time. Avoid stressful situations (i.e., things that don't seem to have worked so far). If you and your former spouse can talk about the child's needs and behaviors and decide on ways to work together to create harmony for the child, that will be all the better.

Different children within the same family can react very differently to a divorce. Young children are certainly very open emotionally to their environment, but they can also be fairly oblivious and nonreactive. If your child continues to seem happy, don't worry about having to delve for the upset and abandonment he "must" be feeling. On the other hand, if your child starts manifesting behaviors you can't handle and that don't improve with your own improving psyche and situation, you may benefit from professional advice. It is important not to worry or fantasize about what the divorce may have done to your child's psyche, but to be in the present so you can be there for your child and perceive his real needs.

By far the greatest number of divorces end with the mother becoming a single parent, having to work full-time and having difficulty making ends meet, even when some child support is paid by the father. Being a single parent can be very difficult because the parent (usually the mother) feels as if she has to provide everything and be everything for the child. Here is where building a support system is a *must* for both parent and child. Not only does the child need other adults in his life, but also the parent does! One of the biggest problems in single parenting is the lack of perspective—the lack of someone to talk to about the child who can give feedback on one's actions and decisions. Without input and support from another source, your relationship with your child can become very ingrown. The child can often become emotionally manipulative, but this can also happen in two-parent families where the father absents himself from involvement with the children. Because single parents usually have to work, they tend to be very wrapped up in the child at all other times. The result is that the parent never has any time for herself, and the child is often overprotected or overindulged.

Life can be easier for single parents if they put extra attention on rhythm, because there is no time or energy for hassles! Co-parenting with another single parent can also have many advantages. Finding grandparents you can adopt can also be wonderful. You need to explore your resources and create a network through which you can reach out and be supported in return.

*We're expecting a baby in four months. Should I have my three-year-old present at the birth?*

Many children experience the arrival of a brother or sister into the family while they are still young themselves. Children today tend to be much more involved in the pregnancy and the birth than in the past, and this seems to result in easier initial adjustment than when mother went away to the hospital for five or ten days and mysteriously came back with a precious little bundle. However, many parents give much more anatomical information than a young child needs and overlook the spiritual dimension, which can be expressed in images or stories.

There are divergent views on whether a child should be present at the birth itself. Marshall Klaus, who did extensive work on bonding, said he found birth too powerful and upsetting for children under seven.[17] Many midwives, on the other hand, have seen that children seem to do well at births. But one can still ask what the deeper response has been, and I know of no follow-up studies to see whether having been at births has had a positive or negative effect on children, and in particular on girls' self-image as they approach womanhood. What I have repeatedly discovered is that children perceive things very differently from adults.

Just as children would have no way of understanding the noises and the energy of sexual intercourse and would be likely to misinterpret it, they can become upset at a birth by mother's making loud noises or being in pain, or just by the intensity of the energy. Young children can also require attention or energy from the birthing mother or make her feel inhibited. Bringing the child in shortly after the birth still enables him to love the baby and bond with it and to maintain his intuitive awareness that birth is a spiritual process of incarnation. The consciousness of most adults at birth is much more focussed on the task at hand than is the dreamy consciousness of the young child, who intuitively grasps the truth of the incarnating soul who will be his brother or sister.

Parents who have had a child present at the birth of a brother or sister strongly recommend that another adult be there specifically for the child to attend to his needs—and to even miss the birth if he wants to be somewhere else (labor can be boring or overwhelming for young children). Special preparation also needs to be given to reassure a child that blood does not mean you are hurt, and that you may make noises, as you would if you were moving a piano. Labor is hard work, requiring the mother's full attention; she shouldn't have to be reassuring her other children as well!

If a mother miscarries after having told a child that he will have a new little brother or sister, she may wonder what to tell him. Children don't need all of the medical and anatomical facts; something which expresses the spiritual reality will be enough for them. Saying something like, "The little baby changed its mind and went back to heaven" or, "God called that little baby back" can be enough of an explanation. If "Why?" follows, it is all right to say honestly, "I don't know." It is also all right to express your sadness—you miss that child—but your preschooler is much more likely to console you than feel sad herself.

## What should I tell my child about death?

In decades past, death was more familiar to children, since most people died at home. Today most deaths occur in hospitals or nursing homes, places that are often closed to children. Relatives may be buried before anyone even tells young children they have died.

It is important not to ignore children when the death of a family member or close friend has occurred, but it is also important to understand that they don't think and feel like adults. According to Maria Nagy, a Hungarian psychologist who studied children's views of death in the 1940s, young children do not see death as final and irreversible:

> They envision it more in terms of a long sleep or journey, from which the dead person will return. They often think the dead can still eat, talk and play, but that they do it underground or in Heaven. Thus they may take the news of a death quite casually at first.
>
> From the age of 5 to about 10, children come to appreciate the finality of death, but it is often personified, for example, as a modern grim reaper like Darth Vader. Not until they are 10, according to Nagy, do children tend to hold an adult view of death as the irreversible and impersonal end to life activities and appreciate the fact that someday they too will die.[18]

With young children, the care we take in burying a dead bird or a pet who has died can begin to teach them attitudes about life and death through our actions, but they are happy to lie down and play dead and jump up again. "Forever" is a concept without meaning for them.

If a grandparent dies, you need to consider whether you want a young child at the funeral. If so, you should describe the events at the funeral or wake and make sure the child wants to go. You should also have someone who is there for the child and is willing to go out with him if he wants to leave in the middle.

If you decide that the child is too young or for other reasons should not go to the funeral, it is good to do something within the family to commemorate the death and to celebrate the grandparent's life, especially by remembering the good times that were shared together. Be sure to answer your child's questions honestly, including your spiritual beliefs, and to feel comfortable saying, "I don't know" when necessary. It is important to reassure the child that the person died from a very serious illness or accident or old age and that you are not going to die and leave him.

After a death in the family, a child may talk a lot about death or you may see death come up in his play. Remember that these are healthy ways the child has of trying to digest the experience.

When a brother or sister dies, the impact on the family can be staggering, and the children especially need not to be ignored in their grieving process. The child should be reassured that he did not cause the death by misbehaving or wishing the sibling were dead. Never tell a child not to cry over the loss of a loved one; in fact, it is beneficial for children to see your own tears of grief, within reason. If you are too busy dealing with your own grief, see that someone is present to hear your child's feelings and thoughts. *Thumpy's Story,* about a bunny who loses a sister, is an excellent resource to share with children in this situation; *Remember the Secret* by Elisabeth Kübler-Ross is excellent for an older child.[19] In some cities there are resources for helping with childhood mourning, as well as support groups for bereaved parents. If your child does not seem to be adjusting well after a death, it can be good to seek professional help.

*My child often wakes up at night with nightmares and is afraid to go down into the basement. What can I do?*

Many children go through a phase where they are afraid of the dark or wake up with nightmares. While fears are normal and will usually subside as the child grows older, the child needs reassurance in the present moment. It can be helpful to see if there has been any episode on television or the movies or a situation such as being chased by a dog that may have precipitated the fear. However, often no reason will be apparent, although fears sometimes seem to come up in reaction to increased independence and sense of self.

Some fears can be dealt with on the physical level, like leaving a flashlight at the top of the stairs for a child who is afraid to go down into the basement to turn on the light. Other fears can be circumvented through distraction, like a child who is afraid of having her hair washed being coaxed with a little story and song about the mermaids. Letting her lie down rather than dumping water over her head can also help her feel more in control.

Some fears function on a more emotional/magical level, and can be dealt with by entering into the *child's* reality. If the child is convinced that there is a monster under the bed, you may accomplish more by agreeing and then chasing the monster out than by appealing to logic. With many kinds of fears at night, it can be very calming to the child to talk about her guardian angel, whom she may see in her dreams and who watches over her while she sleeps. If you don't believe in guardian angels, you should— they're very calming! I happen to believe in the truth of guardian angels and have collected many newspaper stories in which I feel certain children have been protected by unseen forces. Even Bruno Bettelheim, who takes the psychological approach that angels are projections of the mind rather than spiritual realities, recognizes that it is beneficial for children to believe in them rather than to be limited to a completely materialistic and rational world. He states:

> It is such (partly imagined) security which, when experienced for a sufficient length of time, permits the child to develop that feeling of confidence in life which he needs in order to trust himself—a trust necessary for his learning to solve life's problems through his own growing rational abilities.[20]

*What about immunizations? I've heard some people say that child-
hood illnesses could be beneficial. How could this be?*

While no one wants their child to become ill, many parents
today question whether it is necessary to immunize their children
with the standard array of vaccinations, and at what age the immunizations should be given. Many opposing views exist on the
subject, and parents need to do their own research and make
responsible decisions.

The doctors in Germany who are working out of the indications of Rudolf Steiner will not immunize infants until they are
one year old, and then will only immunize for the more serious
illnesses such as polio, diphtheria and tetanus. They feel that the
childhood illnesses such as measles, mumps, chicken pox and
even whooping cough can have beneficial effects. By activating
the immune system in a natural way, childhood illnesses strength-
en it and can help to prevent susceptibility to other illnesses in
later life.[21]

Most childhood illnesses are characterized by fevers, which
not only activate the immune system, but can have developmental
benefits as well. Pediatrician Uwe Stave reports: "Fever attacks
can affect children in quite a positive way. Even though his physical strength is reduced, the child may disclose a wealth of new
interests and skills. He may find new and advanced ways to communicate, think, and handle situations, or display a refinement
of his motor skills. In short, after a fever, the child reveals a spurt
of development and maturation. Parents, frequently surprised,
fail to mention their observation of such development to their
physician."[22]

Dr. Stave explains this observation by referring to the effect
of warmth on the process of incarnation:

> Fever acts by shaking and loosening up the physical body. Activa-
> tion by heat can help the Ego form and reshape the physical or-
> ganization of the young child. In addition, the physiological and
> biochemical functions of organs and systems are assisted in the
> maturation process through febrile illness, and inner forces gain
> strength and become more differentiated. Although the pediatri-
> cian often shares parental concern that repeated feverous infections
> overstress the young child's fragile organism, fever most often sup-
> ports development and individualization, although it is sometimes

a warning signal, indicating weakness in the child's defense against his environment. As children grow older and learn how to control the will, gradually an "inner fire" replaces the "developmental fever" of a young child.[23]

Many of the childhood illnesses that involve fever, such as measles, chicken pox and mumps, have nearly become anachronisms through routine immunization of infants. Parents who choose not to have their children vaccinated for some or all illnesses need to appreciate the seriousness of the diseases and the child's special need for strict home care and medical help in mustering her forces to overcome the illness. Measles can't be treated like a common cold or flu—it can develop into pneumonia, or worse. Whooping cough requires weeks of convalescence and may require medicine or other remedies to help the child fight the illness successfully.[24]

On the other hand, if you do immunize your child, you need to recognize that introducing the illness through the vaccine is a powerful shock to the body. Dr. Wilhelm zur Linden states that the reason vaccinations are given to babies and infants is because older children can react with cramps, fever, vomiting and confusion. He states, "It is not known that small children react so mildly because they do not yet possess sufficient strength with which to counteract the vaccination."[25] Dr. zur Linden suggests that the homeopathic remedy *Thuja 30X* given morning and evening starting on the day of vaccination can help to protect the child when vaccinations are given. Whether or not to immunize a child, for which illnesses, and at what age, is an individual decision parents must make for their children, weighing the pros and cons as best they can.

### Are there ways to handle a high fever without giving antibiotics or aspirin?

Hippocrates taught that fever is the helpful response of the body to overcoming disease. About one-hundred-fifty years ago this theory was rejected and replaced by the still-prevalent opinion that fever itself is a disease, and needs to be treated as such. The tendency today is to give antibiotics or at least aspirin at the first signs of fever, but during artificially suppressed fever the body's defense system remains inactive. And recent studies showing a possible connection between giving aspirin for viral illnesses such as chicken pox or the flu and the subsequent development of Reyes Syndrome has led the Centers for Disease Control and the Committee on Infectious Diseases of the American Academy of Pediatrics to warn against giving aspirin in these cases.

Fever needs to be monitored and not allowed to get too high, but its course can be a valuable tool for your physician in diagnosing an illness. Fever mobilizes the body's immune system, which is valuable in fighting the disease at hand and is possibly of long-term value in a world with immune deficiency diseases such as cancer and AIDS.

You should report your child's fever to your doctor as part of the observations used in diagnosing an illness. If your doctor advises bringing down the fever, there are techniques that don't involve suppressing it with aspirin. Most people have heard about febrile seizures or convulsions that children can have from high fevers. For information on this, I will quote from "Visit with a Pediatrician" in *American Baby Magazine*, because this is probably most representative of sound mainstream medical thinking. In "The Facts about Fever Convulsions,"[26] Dr. Alvin N. Eden explains that a "simple febrile seizure" is a convulsion from a high fever that comes from an infection anywhere in the body that does not primarily involve the brain. He clarifies, "Therefore, by definition, a child who has a fever during a seizure does not have epilepsy. Furthermore, simple febrile seizures do not lead to mental retardation."[27] If your child has a fever convulsion, you will want to consult with your doctor to make sure that the child doesn't have a "complex febrile seizure" which stems from infection in the brain. But usually what happens is that a normal one- or two-year-old becomes ill, often with a sore throat or ear infection, and starts to run a high fever. If his temperature reaches his threshold for convulsion, there is a seizure. He may start to twitch and then shake violently all over. He loses consciousness, his eyes roll back, and often he foams from the mouth. "These generalized convulsions, called *simple febrile convulsions*, rarely last longer than five minutes and stop by themselves without specific treatment. After it is over, the child frequently goes to sleep, and when he wakes up, he is fine. The first seizure is always a harrowing experience for parents, but no permanent damage results, and the baby will be fine."[28] In almost all cases the fever convulsion will occur during the first day of the child's illness, and there is usually only one convulsion during the same illness.

Whatever *your* child's temperature was at the time of the convulsion is the "threshold convulsion temperature," or the temperature that you want to avoid in future illnesses! One child might have a convulsion at 103° F, while another might be fine until 106° F. The great majority of infants and children never have a febrile seizure.

If your child does have a fever convulsion, Dr. Eden advises keeping calm, putting the child on her stomach with her head turned to one side and making sure her mouth is empty. Once the seizure is over you will want to start bringing down the temperature by giving the child a "sponge bath" with lukewarm water, or you can put the child into a cool bath. If the water is too cold, though, shivering will increase muscular activity and actually raise the temperature.

Dr. Eden naturally recommends that you call your doctor and have the illness diagnosed. However, he warns that, "Some doctors recommend that a child who has had a simple febrile seizure should be kept on daily doses of phenobarbital for a period of two seizure-free years to help prevent any further trouble. If the child is under three years of age at the onset, these doctors recommend that phenobarbital should be given until he is five years old. *Most physicians do not agree with this approach, however*" (italics mine).[29] I cannot recommend strongly enough that if you have a physician advising phenobarbital for fever convulsions, you seek a second opinion and research the matter yourself, rather than accepting a course of action on which even conventional physicians do not agree. I had experience with preschool children on phenobarbital and felt that the drug's effect was almost like a veil keeping the child from really being present in his body. As always, the decision and responsibility for your child rest with you, so become informed of your options and the possible results of various courses of action if your child is ill.

Things doctors recommend to help keep a fever from becoming too high include getting the child to drink plenty of fluids (such as water, tea or juice), keeping the child's room cool, and giving a sponge bath as described above. Alcohol should not be used on babies as a sponge bath because it can cause neurologic damage.[30]

A "lemon wrap" is something that can be done for either an adult or child to lower a fever. It is described in the useful book *Caring for the Sick at Home*,[31] and is designed to draw the heat away from the head and out the feet. It should be used only if the feet are very hot. Strips of cotton cloth need to be available for wrapping the legs. Then a lemon is cut in half and placed in a bowl of warm water. Make slits in the lemon under water and then squeeze it by pressing against the bottom of the bowl. The cotton strips are rolled up and soaked in the lemon water. One set of strips is removed and squeezed quite hard. A towel should be placed under each leg, and the first leg is wrapped, beginning at the foot and wrapping from the inside of the arch to the outside of the foot, all the way up to just above the knee. Be sure to cover the entire foot and leg, without any gaps. Immediately wrap the towel up around the foot and leg, or a wool shawl can be used or strips of wool fabric wrapped over the wet cotton ones, to prevent too rapid chilling. The second foot and leg are carefully but quickly done in the same way, and then the covers should be replaced. The wraps are left on until the wet cotton becomes dry, about twenty to twenty-five minutes. The procedure can be repeated if the fever is still high.

If you don't have the materials described above when your child produces a high fever, you can use a pair of adult cotton tube socks or a pair of your knee socks which will reach well up the child's leg, and you can just cover them with a blanket to prevent too rapid cooling. If you don't have a fresh lemon, vinegar can be used in the water instead.

## How should I care for my child when he is sick?

Before talking about *how* to care for a sick child, it is necessary to emphasize how important it is *that* you care for a sick child. A child needs time and rest to fight off an illness and to consolidate the physical and developmental changes that may be occurring. If given insufficient time to recuperate, the child's system will become weaker and more prone to complications or future infections. Many young mothers are so harried that they don't think to call everything to a halt and get help (with taking the other child to school or going shopping) so they can keep the sick child at home and really attend to his needs. Mothers who have to work are often tempted to give antibiotics immediately (suppressing symptoms) so the child can be back in preschool within twenty-four hours, not realizing that he needs quiet time to regroup his inner forces and to heal. Or working mothers must take their children to unfamiliar daycare centers for sick children if they can't use their own sick days in order to stay home with a child. Clearly our culture is not set up to meet the needs of children and working parents!

When a child is sick, with whatever illness, certain principles need to be kept in mind. The most important is that the child needs less stimulation so that the forces of the body and of the Ego can fight off the illness and go through whatever changes are necessary. This means quiet play, staying in bed if necessary, eating lighter foods (usually less meat or egg during an illness—most sick children know this naturally). Television is especially to be avoided when the child is sick. It is amazing how most hospitals not only pay so little attention to the environment, but also expect patients to get well while watching "General Hospital" on television!

Once you recognize the importance of home care for a sick child, what should you do? One important thing is to observe your child, both physically and intuitively. With an infant, note how he holds his body when he cries; observe the breathing and the nature of the cough; note the child's eyes and facial expression. Try to feel what is happening and whether the child is getting better or worse. All good pediatricians will ask the mother for her observations and intuitions about a sick child and will take them seriously. It is important to try to find a doctor with whom you can develop a relationship of trust, feeling that you are both working toward healing of the whole person. Paracelsus, the renowned sixteenth-century healer, said that, "nature heals, the doctor nurses. . . . Like each plant and metallic remedy, the doctor, too, must have a special virtue. He must be intimate with Nature. He must have the intuition which is necessary to understand the patient, his body, his disease. He must have the 'feel' and 'touch' which make it possible for him to be in sympathetic communication with the patient's spirits."[32] As parents we, too, must develop the intuition and powers of observation that will help us to see our ill children as more than machines that require a quick fix.

There is a lot you can do to help your child's comfort and recovery at home. First, recognize the value of your care and love. The child not only needs to be surrounded by warmth and love, but love and connectedness often tip the scales in the cases of seriously ill infants or premature babies. There is real healing power in love.

Next, you could look at your child's surroundings. Putting the room in order, fluffing the pillows, putting fresh flowers in a vase, all enhance the impressions the child will be taking in. Consider the air in the room, and the amount of light coming through the curtains, and adjust them as feels appropriate. Sometimes putting a bowl of water with a few aromatic drops such as rosemary oil in it can help the air in a sick person's room.

You can turn a straight-backed chair over on a bed to make a backrest and make a small lap table out of a cardboard box if your child is well enough to sit up. Once your child is nearly recovered and wants to do things, you can provide quiet activities like coloring or playing with small figures in the covers.

If at all possible, don't send a child back to school or back to his usual routine until he has really regained his strength after a serious illness. The old adage about one day of rest afterwards for each day of fever isn't bad advice. Sometimes children become ill because they need time to be quiet at home, time to "reorganize" and to make the next developmental move forward. I had this sense with a boy in my kindergarten who tested positive for strep throat but had no symptoms. By law he wasn't allowed back in school until he had a negative throat culture. We laughed because it was clear that this particular child had really gone through some "stretching" to be at kindergarten and to adapt to all the children and activity. He was telling us he had had enough for a while and got ten days at home with no discomfort!

The health and vitality of your children are a responsibility shared by you and your children in conjunction with health-care providers when they are ill. We are a nation prone to the "quick fix." But, if we can take the time for real healing with our own and our children's illnesses, we will have gained a great deal. As parents, there is a great deal we can do to help members of our family when they are ill. Compresses and poultices, herbal teas, and therapeutic touch are all home measures that can be learned to comfort a sick person and aid in healing.

*My husband and I don't go to church, but we want to do something with our child in terms of religious instruction or upbringing. We don't just want to send her off to Sunday School, but what can we do that is meaningful and appropriate?*

Having children usually brings up questions about one's own experiences with religion as a child, one's current spiritual orientation and what one wants for the children. Many times children lead parents back into a relationship with the religion of their childhood, which they rediscover with new depth and meaning. Because the expression of spiritual beliefs is so individual, I encourage you and your partner to discuss them together and to work toward finding or creating an appropriate expression of your beliefs that is suitable for your children as they grow.

It is our job as parents to acclimatize the child to this new land, this new condition of life on earth, but to do this in such a way that the child is not driven into forgetfulness of his true origin and ultimate goal. How can we help our children develop their innate religious sense? How can we feed their spiritual hunger? How can we assist them in developing their spiritual nature? These questions are addressed in *The Spiritual Hunger of the Modern Child*, a compilation of ten lectures by notable speakers representing a variety of religious perspectives including Judaism, Christianity, Subud and Buddhism.[33] In great depth the writers discuss the nature of children, the effect of the home environment, the use of prayer, the power of attraction, heredity and conscience.

All of the writers agree that who you are and what you do around young children are more important than religious dogmas or indoctrination. Reviewer René Knight-Weiler summarized the book's common theme as: "Religion must be caught, not taught, and indeed it cannot be caught from someone who doesn't truly have it. It will be caught through practice, feeling, symbolism, image and spirit in the home."[34]

In one of the essays, the Reverend Adam Bittleston of the Christian Community speaks on the ideas of Rudolf Steiner and echoes the theme that the real work of early childhood is work on oneself: "That is really the fundamental thing to satisfy the spiritual hunger of the child—that the grown-up does not stop working upon himself, that no day does he stop working on himself."[35]

Joseph Chilton Pearce, in *The Magical Child Matures*,[36] emphasizes this same theme: In order for the child to be whole, he must have a model who is whole. While none of us qualify as fully realized human beings (and our children must have known this!), the fact of our striving and our efforts, our awareness and our yearning communicate to the child, and are far more valuable than either complete materialism or sanctimonious piety, both of which children can see through and reject as false.

*From the Well-Springs of the Soul: Religious Instruction for the Child* by Herbert Hahn[37] and *Celebrating Festivals with Children* by Friedel Lenz[38] provide information for parents on a Christian orientation that is consonant with Steiner's understanding of child development. Principles to keep in mind include not calling on the intellect or giving moral exhortations, but providing stories and images that awaken in the child a feeling for the holidays or the qualities one is trying to convey.

Because of the imitative nature of the young child, the child's *experiences* during any kind of Sunday School will have a deeper effect than the words that are spoken, just as what you are and what you do speaks more clearly than your words. Thus it is important to give attention to the quality of this experience in your church or temple. Is there an atmosphere of calm and warmth in the preschool classes? Do the activities and methods fit the nature of the young child? You may find that you have to become a teacher yourself!

According to Steiner, the imitative nature of the young child has a spiritual basis. In speaking of the young child, Steiner says, "He is still filled with the devotion that one develops in the spiritual world. It is for this reason that he gives himself up to his environment by imitating the people around him. What then is the fundamental impulse, the completely unconscious mood of the child before the change of teeth? This fundamental mood is a very beautiful one, and it must be fostered in the child. It proceeds from the assumption, from the unconscious assumption, that the whole world is of a moral nature."[39]

The child gives himself over to the people and objects of the world with the assumption that they are good, and then imitates them. Steiner states, "The child is completely given up to his environment. In adult life the only parallel to this devotion is in religion, expressed in the soul and spirit of man. . . .[The adult's] own soul and spirit are given up to the divine spirit of the world. The child gives up his whole being to his environment. In the adult the activities of breathing, digestion and circulation are within himself, cut off from the outside world. In the child all these activities are given up to his environment and are therefore by nature religious. This is the essential feature of the life of the children between birth and the change of teeth; his whole being is permeated by a kind of 'natural-religious' element, and even the physical body is in a religious mood."[40]

In another lecture, Steiner clarifies, "It is not the soul of the child that is given up to the environment, but its blood circulation, its breathing activities and processes of nourishment through the food it takes in. All these things are given up to the environment. The blood circulation, the breathing and the nourishment processes are praying to the environment. Naturally, such expressions seem paradoxical, but in their very paradox they present the truth. If we observe such a thing with our whole being and not with the theoretical intellect . . ." then we will develop an attitude or mood in being with young children which Steiner calls "priestly."[41] Thus parents, daycare providers and early childhood teachers are like "caretakers of the divine" as they recognize it in the child and introduce him or her to earthly life through the sacred qualities of rhythm, beauty and love.

While I feel it is beneficial to recognize the importance of our role with young children, I am the first to admit shortcomings in my attitudes and actions in bringing up my own children and in being with young children in many given moments. However, we not only try to do the best we can, but we can also strive to do better, for the most important work of the parent with young children is inner work on oneself. The young child accepts us as perfect and good; once he becomes older and sees our imperfections, the most important thing is that the child sees we are striving to do better. Our desire for inner growth (or our complacency) is perceived by the child and has a very deep effect on him.

How can we help the child's natural development of religious feeling? Because the child is so given over to the environment, we help the child by furthering an attitude of gratitude in ourselves and hence in the child for all that the world gives us. "If he sees that everyone who stands in some kind of relationship to him in the outer world shows gratitude for what he receives from this world; if, in confronting the outer world and wanting to imitate it, the child sees the kind of gestures that express gratitude, then a great deal is done towards establishing in him the right moral human attitude. Gratitude is what belongs to the first seven years of life."[42]

Reverence is another attitude important to foster in early childhood. Steiner writes: "If one observes children who, by a right upbringing, have developed a natural reverence for the grownups in their surroundings, and if one follows them through their various stages of life, one can discover that their feelings of reverence and devotion in childhood are gradually being transformed during the years leading to old age. As adults such persons may have a healing effect upon their fellow-men so that by their mere presence, or through the tone of their voice, or perhaps by a single glance they can spread inner peace to others. Their presence can be a blessing because as children they have learned to venerate and to pray in the right way. No hands can bless in old age, unless in childhood they have been folded in prayer."[43]

However, qualities such as reverence and prayer cannot be taught to a young child through doctrine or exhortation. They must live within the parents. If prayer is a living reality for the mother or father, then he or she can communicate that to the child and teach him, through example, about prayer. Think about your own childhood. What experiences carried spiritual reality for you? Which people seemed to have a special quality? Looking at spiritual questions can be a great gift that your children bring to you.

*Conscious parenting seems like a tall order! What can help us on the way?*

Conscious parenting involves keeping perspective—that we don't let ourselves become so bogged down in the day-to-day task of raising our children that we neglect to focus on the larger picture. Part of our task is to see the spiritual in the mundane, to recognize the inner light in a child, or the ways in which a child's drawing, for instance, might give us a picture of his emerging consciousness. Another part of our task is to let the events or experiences of the everyday world lead us to questions and experiences of the divine. As we come to see the relationship of microcosm to macrocosm, to "see a world in a grain of sand . . . and eternity in an hour," we will find ourselves transformed in the process.

Certainly we all have shortcomings and failings; there wouldn't be any growth if we didn't. But we need to have patience and kindness toward our own development and not be self-critical. Practicing kindness toward one's own shortcomings is as important as developing patience with others.

Parenting takes a tremendous amount of energy. If you don't keep your energy replenished, you become frazzled, harried, short-tempered and otherwise hard to be around. Especially while your children are young, you need to make sure that you get adequate sleep. It helps to have some kind of meditation or practice or prayer, even five minutes a day, that can help to keep you centered. Creative activities such as art, music, sculpture or dance are also unique in actually replenishing the kind of energy that children demand. Being in nature also does this. When you're taking the baby out for a walk or taking your two-year-old to the park, cherish this time as something that can help renew *your* energy as well.

Taking parenting seriously can also remind you that what you are doing is important and worthwhile. Because women's work is undervalued and underpaid by our society, we can fall into the same trap of undervaluing it, unless we put intentionality into what we are doing. Peggy O'Mara McMahon, editor of *Mothering*, states very clearly:

> I believe, however, that women will never be satisfied with a life that is an economic imitation of mens' lives. Women must find a

new way, a way of the spirit, and they must insist on an economic reality that acknowledges the concerns of the heart. If women are satisfied only to find success as men have found it, in the traditional marketplace separate from the home, we will never create a better world. When women polarize over daycare and at-home mommies, they polarize over a male model of the separation of work and family that has not worked for men and is not now working for women. It doesn't work not because we need more daycare centers, but because the current social reality we emulate has no heart.

We must seek broader solutions to the economics of family life, and we must be very careful not to fall into the trap of defining ourselves solely by the values of a society in transition.[44]

Viewing parenting as part of the path of love and service can also help get you through the rough spots. Having children certainly opens your heart and makes you stretch, through constantly having to consider the needs of another person who is dependent on you—and whom you must gradually release. Parenting can be a rich source of life experiences in the course of one's development as a human being, if you use what is given to you for self-knowledge and transformation. In her article, "An Ethic of Parenting," O'Mara McMahon describes the inner work of parenting as follows:

> In our society, we are not accustomed to the surrender and service required by the human infant. In order to sustain an ethic of parenting that honors the necessity of surrender and service, we will have to surround ourselves with the kind of support and information that will enable us to overcome the limitations. . . .
>
> Serve your child—for in serving your child, in trusting your child, you serve yourself and give yourself an opportunity to be reparented and reloved. The greatest kept secret of the world is the personal transformation inherent in developing an ethic of parenting that is truly in keeping with the nature of the child. Parenting with this type of ethic releases the full potential of the human being, a force greater than anything we have yet to see on this planet.[45]

# IN CONCLUSION

All parents want what is best for their child. But most first-time parents know very little about children or parenting (I certainly didn't!). Learning as you go is often uncomfortable, but it can provide many opportunites for growth for parents as well as children. As our children's first teachers, we can and must provide the love and warmth, calm and rhythm, interest and enthusiasm vital to their growth. And, they provide us with new areas of study, work and self-examination as we come up against our shortcomings and the dilemmas our children present to us.

What is needed today is not another expert, some new authority to follow or to reject, but a new way of seeing the human being that takes into account all aspects of development—physical, emotional, intellectual and spiritual—so we and our children can meet the challenges of our changing world and fulfill the purposes of our time on earth.

We are living in a time of transition, a time in which the old patterns of society no longer hold us. We are being called upon to approach all aspects of our lives with new awareness. Life in our families, cities, churches and schools is changing at an ever-increasing rate as we struggle to establish or maintain equilibrium and then to create something new.

We can't go back to a milk-and-cookies mentality that denies the changes of the past twenty-five years. But we need to recognize that the world of the young child is critically endangered today, as more and more children are placed in daycare beginning in infancy and academics is pushed onto younger and younger children. It has become even more urgent that we understand that children are not little adults. They do not think, reason, feel or experience the world as an adult does. Instead, they are centered in their bodies, and in the will which manifests in such powerful growth and need for movement in the first seven years. They learn primarily and most appropriately through example and imitation. Repetition and rhythm are also vital elements in the healthy world of the young child and need to be emphasized by parents and others responsible for the care of young children.

The young child takes everything in without blocks or filters, and for this reason we must put special attention into the quality of the environment and the experiences that come to her. There needs to be a balance between stimulating and protecting the baby's and young child's senses. Stimulation from artificial sources (movies, records, synthetic fabrics) has a different impact on the young child than stimulation from your own voice or objects from nature. Because the young child is all sense-organ, we need to be selective in what is experienced and help guard against violating the young child's natural dreamy state.

Everything of life is taken in so deeply by the young child, to be transformed and come out again in creative play. Providing time and appropriate materials for this kind of play helps the child to work his way into earthly life by imitating through his play everything that he experiences. Allowing this natural impulse of creative imagination to flourish is one of the greatest gifts parents can give their child between birth and first grade.

The young child also has a natural artistic and musical ability, which can be furthered by allowing its free expression without lessons or pressure to produce something in a certain way. Songs, rhythmical movement and circle games all speak to the magical world of early childhood.

Just as it is developmentally important that children crawl before they walk (and do not skip steps), so it is important that children not be prematurely awakened from the dreamy, imaginative world of early childhood before the natural time for this, around the age of six or seven. Lessons, workbooks and academic tasks not only take the child away from movement and valuable play, but they also accelerate the child's change of consciousness and rob him of the last valuable years of early childhood—years which are vital to a person's later physical health as well as mental development. Trying to speed up development in young children places them at risk, with no apparent gain to justify such risks.

As our children's first teachers, there is much we can do, and much it is better that we don't do! It is my hope that this book will contribute to parents' understanding the special nature of the young child and her unique needs. If we can take both knowledge and practical experience into our hearts, we will have increased confidence as we develop our own ethic of parenting and make our own best choices for our children. The challenges are great, but so are the growth and the rewards!

# RECOMMENDED READING

(Letters in parentheses refer to mail-order book stores. See Appendix A.)

## Health and Illness

The practice of medicine directly inspired by Steiner's work has mainly developed in continental Europe, with only a handful of practitioners in North America. These doctors and nurses work out of an inner effort to understand the entire human being and the meaning of illness, utilizing many things in addition to standard techniques: nutrition, massage, painting, eurythmy, sculpture, music, baths, herbal oils and so forth. Further reading about this approach can be found in:

*Anthroposophical Medicine: An Extension of the Art of Healing* by Victor Bott, M.D., (AP).

*Anthroposophical Guide to Family Medicine* by Victor Bott, M.D. (SG).

*Caring for the Sick at Home* by Tineke van Bentheim, et al. (AP).

*Health and Illness*, Vols. 1 and 2 by Rudolf Steiner (advanced level) (AP).

"Illness" by Gudrun Davy and "A Sick Child in Hospital" by Stephanie Westphal, in *Lifeways* by Bons Voors and Gudrun Davy, editors (IBP, SG).

*When a Child is Born* by Wilhelm zur Linden, M.D. (AP, IBP, SG) has information on dealing with childhood illnesses.

## Nutrition

Rudolf Steiner also gave many indications regarding the plant and animal kingdoms and nutrition for children and adults. "Feeding the Family" by Wendy Cook in *Lifeways* provides an easy introduction, as does Chapter 10 in *The Incarnating Child* by Joan Salter. More detailed information can be found in:

*Foodways* by Wendy Cook (SG).

*Nutrition* by Rudolf Hauschka (AP).

*Nutrition No.'s 1 and 2* by Eugen Kolisko (SG).

*Problems of Nutrition* by Rudolf Steiner (AP).

*When a Child is Born* by Wilhelm zur Linden (AP, IBP, SG).

## Television and Children

*Amusing Ourselves to Death* by Neil Postman (NY: Viking, 1985).

*Four Arguments for the Elimination of Television* by Jerry Mander (NY: Wm. Morrow).

*The Plug-In Drug* by Marie Winn (NY: Viking, 1985).

*Unplugging the Plug-In Drug* by Marie Winn (NY: Viking/Penguin).

*Who's Bringing Them Up?* by Martin Large (Gloucester, UK: Hawthorn Press).

## Religious Life

*Celebrating the Festivals with Children* by Friedel Lenz (AP, IBP).

*Festivals Magazine,* quarterly magazine with many suggestions for bringing the spirit into family life. From Resource Publications, 160 E. Virginia St., #290, San Jose, CA 95112.

*From the Well-Springs of the Soul: Religious Instruction for the Child* by Herbert Hahn (Rudolf Steiner Book Store, Museum St., London, England).

*Prayers for Mothers and Children* by Rudolf Steiner (AP, IBP).

*The Spiritual Hunger of the Modern Child: A Series of Ten Lectures* by John G. Bennett, et al. (from Claymont Communications, P.O. Box 926, Charles Town, WV 25414).

*Spiritual Mothering Journal.* Quarterly magazine discussing spiritual aspects of parenting. From 18350 Ross, Sandy, OR 97055.

# APPENDICES

## APPENDIX A
## *Sources for Books*

AP: Anthroposophic Press, Bell's Pond, Star Rt., Hudson, NY 12534.

B: Check your local book store; they can special order if necessary.

IBP: Informed Birth & Parenting Books, P.O. Box 3675, Ann Arbor, MI 48106.

MF: Moonflower Birthing Supply, P.O. Box 128, Louisville, CO 80027.

SG: St. George Book Service, P.O. Box 225, Spring Valley, NY 10977.

## APPENDIX B
## *Rudolf Steiner & Waldorf Education*

Rudolf Steiner (1861-1925) spent his early adult years preparing the scientific writings of Goethe for republication. A. P. Shepherd, a canon of the Anglican Church, says of him, "Steiner thought, spoke and wrote as a scientist. . . . Although his own investigations carried him into fields far beyond the range of physical science, he always carried into these investigations, and into the application of them to physical phenomena, the concepts and methods of scientific thought."[1]

At the beginning of this century, Steiner began to lecture and write extensively, imparting a knowledge about the realms beyond the physical and our connection with them. During the last six years of his life, he was active in applying his spiritual scientific knowledge in various fields such as education, agriculture, arts, medicine, theology and so forth. To help carry on his work as a force for personal and cultural renewal, he founded the Anthroposophical Society ("anthroposophy" comes from the roots "anthro," meaning "man," and "sophia," meaning "wisdom"). The society now has working groups and branches all over the free world.

Steiner turned his attention to education after the First World War at the request of Emil Molt, who helped him found a school for the children of the factory workers at the Waldorf-Astoria cigarette factory in Stuttgart in 1919. The impulse for "Waldorf education," as it came to be called, spread throughout Europe, with the first school in America being founded in New York City more than fifty years ago.

The past decade has witnessed a tremendous surge in interest in Waldorf education, making it the second largest private school movement in the world with approximately 400 schools worldwide.

From preschool through high school, the goal of Waldorf education is the same, but the means differ according to the changing inner development of the child. In Steiner's words, "Our highest endeavor must be to develop free human beings, who are able of themselves to impart purpose and direction to their lives."

During the early childhood years, the child is surrounded by a homelike environment and taught through the principles of imitation, movement and rhythm (the program is described in detail in Chapter 12). In the elementary school years (grades 1-8), all of the subjects are presented in a lively and pictorial way, because the elementary-school child learns best when information is artistically and imaginatively presented.

Analytical thinking is developed in the Waldorf high school, where subjects are taught by specialists in their fields, who try to help the adolescents develop their own thinking powers. When the high school students analyze trends in Western civilization, for example, they have the experience to draw on from fifth grade of having heard the myths of Greek civilization, presented some Greek drama, painted scenes from Greek history and so forth. Similarly, when they start to prove the theorems of analytical geometry in high school, they have already had the experience of artistically generating the triangles of Thales' Law in sixth grade.

In a Waldorf school the same teacher stays with the children for the "main lesson" subjects from first through eighth grade. This includes language arts, math, history, science and so forth, which are taught in blocks of three to six weeks during the first two hours of the morning. During the rest of the day, special subject teachers fill out the rich curriculum by teaching the foreign languages, orchestra and other subjects as summarized in the chart of a typical curriculum in a Waldorf elementary school.

A complete list of Waldorf schools can be obtained from the Association of Waldorf Schools of North America, 17 Hemlock Hill, Great Barrington, MA 01230.[1]

| 1st GRADE | 2nd GRADE | 3rd GRADE | 4th GRADE |
|---|---|---|---|
| Language Arts<br>• writing<br>• phonics<br>• reading<br>• fairy tales<br>Mathematics<br>• add./subtr.<br>• mult./div.<br>German<br>French<br>Beeswax<br>  Modelling<br>Painting<br>Knitting<br>Recorder<br>Phys. Ed. | Language Arts<br>• extend skills<br>• legends &<br>  fables<br>Mathematics<br>• +, −, ×, ÷<br>• telling time<br>• money<br>German<br>French<br>Beeswax<br>  Modelling<br>Painting<br>Crochet<br>Recorder<br>Phys. Ed. | Language Arts<br>• extend skills<br>• grammar<br>• letter writing<br>• Old Testament<br>  stories<br>Mathematics<br>• extend skills<br>• measurement<br>German<br>French<br>Farming<br>Painting<br>Crafts<br>Recorder<br>String Instr.<br>Phys. Ed. | Language Arts<br>• grammar<br>• drama<br>• Norse myths<br>Mathematics<br>• adv. skills<br>• fractions<br>German<br>French<br>Zoology<br>Local History<br>State Hist. &<br>  Geog.<br>Embroidery<br>Recorder<br>String or<br>  Wind Instr.<br>Phys. Ed. |

[1]Quoted in Joan Salter, *The Incarnating Child* (Glouc., UK: Hawthorn Press, 1987, p. 146).

| 5th GRADE | 6th GRADE | 7th GRADE | 8th GRADE |
|---|---|---|---|
| Language Arts<br>• extend skills<br>• stories of<br>  ancient<br>  cultures &<br>  Greece<br>Mathematics<br>• adv. skills<br>• decimal<br>  fractions<br>German<br>French<br>Botany<br>Greek History<br>U.S. Geography<br>Crafts<br>Recorder<br>Orchestra<br>Phys. Ed. | Language Arts<br>• biography<br>Pre-algebra<br>Geometry<br>German<br>French<br>Greek & Latin<br>Physics<br>Roman History<br>World Geography<br>Woodworking<br>Recorder<br>Orchestra<br>Choral Singing<br>Gardening<br>Phys. Ed. | Language Arts<br>• biography<br>• drama<br>Algebra<br>Geometry<br>German<br>French<br>Greek & Latin<br>Physics<br>Chemistry<br>Astronomy<br>Med./Ren. Hist.<br>World Geog.<br>Woodworking<br>Sewing<br>Recorder<br>Orchestra<br>Choral Singing<br>Gardening<br>Phys. Ed. | Language Arts<br>• biography<br>• drama<br>Algebra<br>Geometry<br>German<br>French<br>Greek & Latin<br>Physics<br>Chemistry<br>Physiology<br>U.S. & Modern<br>  History<br>World Geog.<br>Woodworking<br>Sewing<br>Recorder<br>Orchestra<br>Choral Singing<br>Gardening<br>Phys. Ed. |

## APPENDIX C
# *Eurythmy*

Eurythmy is an art of movement to speech and tone developed by Rudolf Steiner from his recognition that each sound can be represented by a corresponding movement of the human body. As a performing art it was developed under the direction of Marie Steiner von Sivers at the Goetheanum in Switzerland, and has been performed on the major stages in Europe and more recently in America as well.

As "visible speech" eurythmy represents each vowel and consonant sound as a gesture of the body; similarly, each musical tone has a movement which is its expression in form. Eurythmy is taught in Waldorf schools, beginning with movements to accompany simple verses and fairy tales in the kindergarten and progressing to complicated forms and work with copper rods in the upper grades. Eurythmy is also used in curative work and in special education for the healing properties of certain sounds and movements.

If you are fortunate enough to live near a Waldorf school or Steiner Institute for adult education, you might be able to see eurythmy performed and perhaps do some yourself. Steiner states:

> Parents can do an enormous amount of good, if they only take care to build less on externally induced music than on the inducement of the whole body, the dancing element. And precisely in this third and fourth year infinite results could be achieved by the permeation of the child's body with an elementary Eurythmy. If parents would learn to engage in Eurythmy with the child, children would be quite different from what they are. They would overcome a certain heaviness which weighs down their limbs. We all today have this heaviness in our limbs. It would be overcome. And there would remain in the child when the first teeth are shed the disposition for the complete musical element.[1]

Eurythmy with nursery and kindergarten children lets them live freely and naturally in their joy of movement and at the same time stimulates their imagination. If you do not have the opportunity to encounter eurythmy, the best way to foster this musical element with your child is through rhythmical movement and circle games, as described in Chapter 10.

## APPENDIX D
# *Waldorf Teacher Training Programs*

*Programs in English-speaking countries include:*

Rudolf Steiner Centre, P.O Box 472, Station Z, Toronto, Ontario, Canada M5N 2Z6.

Rudolf Steiner College, 9200 Fair Oaks Blvd., Fair Oaks, CA 95628.

---

[1]Rudolf Steiner, *Practical Course for Teachers* (London: Rudolf Steiner Press, 1937, p. 19).

Waldorf Education Program of Antioch College, Pine Hill School, Wilton, NH 03086. Master's level only.

Waldorf Institute, 260 Hungry Hollow Rd., Spring Valley, NY 10977.

Waldorf Institute of Southern California, 17100 Superior St., Northridge, CA 91325.

Emerson College, Pixton, Hartfield Rd., Forest Row, Sussex, England.

Waldorf Kindergarten Training, Margret Meyerkort, Wynstone's School, Whaddon Gloucester, England GL4 OUF.

## APPENDIX E
# Seminars on Waldorf Early-Childhood Education

Acorn Hill Children's Center, 9500 Brunett Ave., Silver Spring, MD 20901, often sponsors weekend workshops by noted Waldorf early-childhood educators.

Informed Birth & Parenting, P.O. Box 3675, Ann Arbor, MI 48106, offers an annual "Magical Years Conference" on Waldorf principles from birth through age six.

Rudolf Steiner College, 9200 Fair Oaks Blvd., Fair Oaks, CA 95628 offers seminars during the summer on early-childhood education.

Rudolf Steiner Institute, P.O. Box 1925, New York, NY 10025 offers a variety of three-week courses each summer (usually held in Maine).

Waldorf Institute, 260 Hungry Hollow Rd., Spring Valley, NY 10977 offers week-long seminars each summer and weekend courses during the year.

## APPENDIX F
# Resources

## Journals on Waldorf Education

*Child and Man*, 6334 Gaston Ave., Suite 212, Dallas, TX 75214.

*Childhood*, Rt. 2, Box 2675, Westford, VT 05494.

*Waldorf Kindergarten Newsletter*, 9500 Brunett Ave., Silver Spring, MD 20901.

## Books on Waldorf Education

Anthroposophic Press, Bell's Pond, Star Rt., Hudson, NY 12534.

Informed Birth and Parenting Book Service, P.O. Box 3675, Ann Arbor, MI 48106.

St. George Book Service, P.O. Box 225, Spring Valley, NY 10977.

## Natural Clothing and Baby Items

See the list at the end of Chapter 2.

## Toys and Natural Craft Supplies

See the list at the end of Chapter 7.

## Children's Harps and Other Pentatonic Instruments

See the list at the end of Chapter 10.

## Beeswax and Art Supplies

Hearth Song, P.O. Drawer B, Sebastopol, CA 95473.

# NOTES

## CHAPTER 1
### *You Are Your Child's First Teacher*

1. Burton L. White, *Educating the Infant and Toddler* (Lexington, MA: D. C. Heath and Co., 1988, p. xvi).
2. Burton L. White, *The First Three Years of Life* (New York, NY: Prentice-Hall Press, 1985, p. 4).
3. *Ibid.*, p. 5.
4. *Ibid.*, p. 90.
5. "The Missouri Project," *American Baby,* April 1986, p. 43.
6. Rudolf Steiner, "The Child Before the Seventh Year," Dornach, December 23rd, 1921. Reported by Albert Steffen, *Lectures to Teachers* (London, England: The Library of the Anthroposophical Society in Great Britain, 1948, p. 39).
7. David Elkind, *The Hurried Child* (New York, NY: Alfred A. Knopf, 1984).
8. David Elkind, *Miseducation: Preschoolers at Risk* (New York, NY: Alfred A. Knopf, 1987).
9. Rudolf Steiner, quoted by Werner Glas in lectures at the Waldorf Institute, October 1980.
10. Fern Schumer Chapman, "Executive Guilt: Who's Taking Care of the Children?" *Fortune,* Feb. 16, 1987.
11. "The New York Times Magazine," August 16, 1987, pp. 40-41, 50.
12. David Elkind, *op. cit.*, p. 120.
13. Rudolf Steiner, *Philosophy of Freedom* (Spring Valley, NY: Anthroposophic Press, 1964).
14. For accounts of the spiritual aspects of conception and pregnancy, see Jeanine Parvati Baker, et al., *Conscious Conception* (Monroe, UT: Freestone Publishing Company, 1986) and Murshida Vera Justin Corda, *Cradle of Heaven* (Lebanon Springs, NY: Omega Press, 1987).

## CHAPTER 2
### *Receiving & Caring for the Newborn*

1. Frederick Leboyer, *Birth Without Violence* (New York, NY: Alfred Knopf, 1975).
2. Hugo Lagercrantz and Theodore A. Slotkin "The 'Stress' of Being Born," *Scientific American,* April 1986, pp. 100-107.
3. Werner Hassauer, *Die Geburt der Individualität* (Stuttgart, Germany: Verlag Urachhaus Johannes M. Mayer GmbH, 1984, p. 57).
4. *Ibid.*, p. 97.

5. *Ibid.*, p. 65. For further information on Steiner's use of the terms *body, soul* and *spirit*, see Rudolf Steiner, *Theosophy* (Spring Valley, NY: Anthroposophic Press, 1971).

6. *Ibid.*, p. 92.

7. Rudolf Steiner, *The Kingdom of Childhood* (London, England: Rudolf Steiner Press, 1974, p. 22).

8. Leboyer, *op. cit.*

9. Maureen Hack (producer), "The Amazing Newborn" available from Polymorph Films, 118 South Street, Boston, MA 02111.

10. See Thomas Verny, M.D., *The Secret Life of the Unborn Child* (New York, NY: Dell Publishing Company, 1981) or contact The Pre- and Peri-Natal Psychology Association of North America, 36 Madison Ave., Toronto, Ontario, Canada M5R 2S1.

11. Rudolf Steiner, course of lectures given in Torquay, England, Summer 1924. Quoted in Elisabeth Grunelius, *Early Childhood Education and the Waldorf School Plan* (Englewood, NJ: Waldorf School Monographs, 1974, p. 42).

12. Rudolf Steiner, *The Spiritual Ground of Education* (London, England: Rudolf Steiner Press, 1947, p. 38).

13. Peggy Eastman, "Your Special Role in Infant Development," *New Parent Adviser*, date unavailable, pp. 33-38).

14. Joseph Chilton Pearce in a lecture at the Magical Years Conference, April 3, 1987, in Ann Arbor, Michigan.

15. Reported in *The Lancet*, Vol. 2, 1983, p. 1014.

16. White, *op. cit.*, p. 19.

17. Rudolf Steiner, *The Education of the Child* (London, England: Rudolf Steiner Press, 1965, p. 24).

18. White, *op. cit.*, pp. 15-16.

19. White, *op. cit.*, p. 16. See also T. Berry Brazelton, *Infants and Mothers: Differences in Development* (New York, NY: Dell, 1986).

20. *Ibid.*, p. 15.

21. Leboyer, *op. cit.*

22. White, *op. cit.*, p. 29.

23. Marshall Klaus and John Kennell, *Parent-Infant Bonding* (C. V. Mosley Co., 1982).

24. Ashley Montagu, *Touching: The Human Significance of the Skin* (New York, NY: Columbia University Press, 1971).

25. Ina May Gaskin, *Spiritual Midwifery* (Summertown, TN: The Book Publishing Company, 1978, p. 251).

26. *Ibid.*

27. Aletha Jauch Solter, *The Aware Baby* (Goleta, CA: Shining Star Press, 1984).

28. Rudolf Steiner in a lecture given January 30, 1913, and quoted in *The Waldorf Kindergarten Newsletter*, Winter 1987, p. 15.

29. White, *op. cit.*, pp. 24-27.

30. For further information on the Pikler method, contact Resources for Infant Educarers, 1550 Murray Circle, Los Angeles, CA 90026.

## CHAPTER 3
# Growing Down & Waking Up

1. Jean Ayers, *Sensory Integration and Learning Disorders* (Los Angeles, CA: Western Psychological Services, 1973).

2. White, *op. cit.*, p. 60.

3. *Pediatric Notes*, March 26, 1987, p. 46, summarized in *Pediatrics for Parents*, Vol. 8, Issue 6, June 1987.

4. *Canadian Medical Association Journal*, January 1, 1987, p. 57, summarized in *Pediatrics for Parents*, ibid.

5. *Pediatric Notes, op. cit.*

6. White, *op. cit.*, p. 80.

7. Rudolf Steiner, lectures given in Dornach, Switzerland, April 15-22, 1923, reported by Albert Steffen in *Swiss Teachers' Course* (London: The Library of the Anthroposophical Society in Great Britain, na).

8. Rudolf Steiner, *Pneumatosophy*, "The Riddles of the Inner Human Being," lecture given in Berlin, May 23, 1923 (New York, NY: Anthroposophic Press, p. 2).

9. Rudolf Steiner, reported by Steffen, *loc. cit.*

10. Clyde Watson, *Catch Me & Kiss Me & Say It Again* (New York, NY: Philomel Books, 1978).

11. Rudolf *Steiner*, reported by Albert Steffen, *loc. cit.*

12. Karl König, *The First Three Years of the Child* (Spring Valley, NY: Anthroposophic Press, 1969, p. 24).

13. Daniel Udo de Haes, *The Young Child* (Spring Valley, NY: Anthroposophic Press, 1986, p. 24).

14. *Ibid.*

15. Steiner, *Pneumatosophy, op. cit.*, p. 3.

16. Reprinted from page 19 of the *Waldorf Parenting Handbook* by Lois Cusick by permission of the publishers, St. George Publications, Spring Valley, NY 10977.

17. White, *op. cit.*, p. 157.


CHAPTER 4
# *Helping Your Baby's Development in the First Year*

1. References quoted in Robert B. McCall, "Support Thy Wife," *Parents*, July 1987, pp. 168-169.

2. See illustration in White, *op. cit.*, p. 74.

3. See work by Audrey McAllen, available through the Remedial Research Group, 9200 Fair Oaks Blvd., Fair Oaks, CA 95628.

4. Joseph Chilton Pearce, *The Magical Child* (New York, NY: E. P. Dutton, 1977).

5. White, *op. cit.*, p. 102.

6. *Ibid.*, p. 88.

7. *Ibid.*, p. 106.

8. *Ibid.*, p. 91.

9. Anne Scott, *The Laughing Baby* (South Hadley, MA: Bergin & Garvey, 1987).

10. White, *op. cit.*, pp. 282-294 and write for further information from The Center for Parent Education, 55 Chapel St., Newton, MA 02160.

## CHAPTER 5
# Helping Your Toddler's Development

1. Elkind, *op. cit.*
2. White, *op. cit.*, p. 176.
3. *Ibid.*, p. 151.
4. *Ibid.*, p. 181.
5. Udo de Haes, *op. cit.*
6. *Ibid.*, p. 61.
7. *Ibid.*
8. *Ibid.*, p. 65.
9. *Ibid.*, p. 72.
10. Steiner, *The Education of the Child, op. cit.*, p. 26.
11. Heidi Britz-Crecelius, *Children at Play* (New York, NY: Inner Traditions International, 1986, pp. 94-96).
12. Steiner, *op. cit.*, pp. 25-26.
13. For detailed directions on making knot dolls, see Susan Smith, *Echoes of a Dream* (London, Ontario: Waldorf School Association of London, 1982) or Freya Jaffke, *Making Soft Toys* (Millbrae, CA: Celestial Arts, 1981).
14. Watson, *op. cit.*

## CHAPTER 6
# Parenting Issues of the First Three Years

1. Rudolf Steiner, *Knowledge of Higher Worlds: How is It Achieved?* (London, England: Rudolf Steiner Press, 1969).
2. Thoman and Browder, *op. cit.*
3. Tine Thevenin, *The Family Bed* (Garden City Park, NY: Avery, 1987).
4. Norbert Glas, *Conception, Birth and Early Childhood* (Spring Valley, NY: Anthroposophic Press, 1972).
5. Wilhelm zur Linden, *When A Child is Born* (New York, NY: Thorsons Publishers, Inc., 1984).
6. Wendy Cook, *Foodways* (Glouscestershire, England: Hawthorn Press, 1988). Write to St. George Book Service or Anthroposophic Press (see Appendix A) for titles by Steiner on nutrition.
7. Aletha Jauch Solter, "Exercises in Self-Awareness for New Parents" (Goleta, CA: Shining Star Press, 1984).
8. Aletha Jauch Solter, *The Aware Baby op. cit.*
9. Vimala Schneider, "Crying," *Mothering,* Spring 1987, p. 23.
10. David Sobel, "Waldorf Teacher Training Newsletter," Spring 1987, p. 5.
11. T. Berry Brazelton, *Working and Caring* (Reading, MA: Addison-Wesley, 1985).
12. White, *op. cit.*, p. 267.

13. *Ibid.*
14. Elkind, *op. cit.*
15. White, *op. cit.*, p. 272.
16. Rahima Baldwin and Terra Palmarini, *Pregnant Feelings* (Berkeley, CA: Celestial Arts, 1986).
17. White, *op. cit.*, p. 182.
18. T. Berry Brazelton, *Infants and Mothers: Differences in Development* (New York, NY: Dell, 1986).
19. Rudolf Steiner, *The Four Temperaments* (Hudson, New York: Anthroposophic Press, 1987).

## CHAPTER 7
# The Development of Fantasy & Creative Play

1. Caroline von Heydebrand, *Childhood: A Study of the Growing Soul* (London: Anthroposophical Publishing Company, 1946, p. 60).
2. Britz-Crecelius, *op. cit.*, p. 7.
3. Caroline von Heydebrand, "The Child at Play," in Paul M. Allen (Ed.), *Education as an Art: Rudolf Steiner and Other Writers* (Blauvelt, NY: Steinerbooks/Multimedia Publishing Corp., 1970, p. 89).
4. Britz-Crecelius, *op. cit.*, p. 32.
5. *Ibid.*, p. 40.
6. Bruno Bettelheim, *The Uses of Enchantment* (New York, NY: Alfred A. Knopf, 1975, p. 46).
7. von Heydebrand, *op. cit.*, p. 95.
8. Britz-Crecelius, *op. cit.*, pp. 79-101.
9. *Ibid.*, p. 92.
10. Bruno Bettelheim, "The Importance of Play," *The Atlantic Monthly*, March 1987, p. 40.
11. Britz-Crecelius, *op. cit.*, p. 97.
12. *Ibid.*
13. Bettelheim, *op. cit.*, p. 37.
14. *Ibid.*, p. 36.
15. *Ibid.*, p. 37.
16. Quoted in Britz-Crecelius, *op. cit.*, p. 81.
17. Karin Neuschütz, *The Doll Book* (Burdett, NY: Larson Publications, 1982).

## CHAPTER 8
# Nourishing Your Child's Imagination

1. Dr. Karen N. Olness, "Little People, Images and Child Health," *Amer J of Clinical Hypnosis*, Vol. 27, No. 3, January 1985.

2. Rudolf Steiner, *The Arts and Their Mission*. Lectures given in Oslo, May 27-June 9, 1923 (New York: Anthroposophic Press, 1964, p. 108).

3. Rudolf Steiner, course of lectures delivered at Ilkey, Yorkshire, England, August 1923 and quoted in Grunelius, *op. cit.*, pp. 42-43.

4. Olness, *op. cit.*

5. Margret Meyerkort, "The Hidden Treasure in Fairy Tales," in Gudrun Davy and Bons Voors (eds.), *Lifeways* (Glouscestershire, England: Hawthorn Press, 1983, p. 246).

6. Olness, *op. cit.*, p. 173.

7. Udo de Haes, *op. cit.*, p. 32.

8. Eileen Hutchins, "The Value of Fairy Tales and Nursery Rhymes," *Child and Man Extracts* (Sussex, England: Steiner Schools Fellowship, na, p. 173).

9. Joan Almon, "Choosing Fairy Tales for Young Children," *Waldorf Kindergarten Newsletter*, Fall 1985, p. 7.

10. Quoted by Mary Jo Kochakian in "Fairy tales allow kids to grapple with good and evil, says psychologist," *Ann Arbor News*, July 5, 1987.

11. Kornei Chukovsky, *From Two to Five* (Berkeley, CA: University of California Press, 1963).

12. See Helmut von Kügelgen, "Fairy Tale Language and the Image of Man," *Waldorf Kindergarten Newsletter*, Fall 1986 and Rudolf Steiner, *The Interpretation of Fairy Tales* (Spring Valley, NY: Anthroposophic Press, 1943).

13. Miriam Whitfield, *Fairy Stories . . . Why, When, How* (Boulder, CO: The Juniper Tree, 1986).

14. *Ibid.*, p. 22.

15. *Ibid.*, p. 23.

16. Diana Hughes, "Fairy Tales: A Basis for Moral Education," *Ethics in Education*, Vol. 6, No. 4, March 1987, p. 11.

17. *Ibid.*, p. 12.

18. Bettelheim, *Uses of Enchantment*, *op. cit.*, p. 9

19. Hughes, *op. cit.*, p. 11.

20. *Kochakian, loc. cit.*

21. Neil Postman, *The Disappearance of Childhood* (New York, NY: Dell Publishing, 1982, pp. 93-94).

22. Udo de Haes, *op. cit.*, p. 49.

23. Almon, *op. cit.*

24. *Ibid.*

25. Udo de Haes, *op. cit.*, p. 52.

26. Bronja Zahlingen, *Plays for Puppets and Marionettes* (Silver Spring, MD: Acorn Hill Children's Center, 1983).

27. Bronja Zahlingen, "The Pedagogical Value of Marionette and Table Puppet Shows for the Small Child," *Waldorf Kindergarten Newsletter*, Fall 1982.

28. Helmut von Kügelgen, "Marionette Theaters: Posing a Task for Socially Oriented Education," *Waldorf Kindergarten Newsletter*, Fall-Winter 1982.

29. *Ibid.*

## CHAPTER 9
# Developing Your Child's Artistic Ability

1. Rauld Russell, "Wet-on-Wet Watercolor Painting," *Mothering,* Summer 1987, p. 89.
2. Rudolf Steiner, *The Education of the Child, op. cit.,* p. 27.
3. Johann Wolfgang von Goethe, *Theory of Colours* (Totowa, NJ: Biblio Distribution Center, 1967).
4. Rudolf Steiner, *Practical Advice for Teachers* (London, England: Rudolf Steiner Press, 1970, p. 11).
5. Brunhild Müller, *Painting with Children* (Edinburgh, UK: Floris Books, 1987, p. 11).
6. Russell, *op. cit.,* p. 90.
7. *Ibid.,* p. 89.
8. Caroline von Heydebrand, "The Child When He Paints," in Allen (ed.) *op. cit.,* p. 86.
9. Freya Jaffke, "About Painting and Human Development Through Art" translated from *Plan und Praxis des Waldorfkindergartens* for the *Waldorf Kindergarten Newsletter,* Fall 1984.
10. *Ibid.*
11. *Ibid.*
12. Michaela Strauss, *Understanding Children's Drawings* (London, England: Rudolf Steiner Press, 1978).
13. *Ibid.,* pp. 22 and 29.
14. *Ibid.,* p. 47.
15. *Ibid.,* p. 62.
16. Isabel Wyatt, *Seven-Year-Old Wonder-Book* (San Rafael, CA: Dawn-Leigh Publications, 1978).
17. Smith, *op. cit.,* p. 62.

## CHAPTER 10
# Your Child's Musical Ability

1. Julius Knierim, *Quintenlieder* (Echzell, Germany: Verlag Das Seelenpflegebedürftige Kind, 1982, pp. 3-4).
2. Rudolf Steiner, *Practical Course for Teachers* (London: Rudolf Steiner Press, 1937, pp. 18-19).
3. Knierim, *loc. cit.*
4. See Chapter 2.
5. Rudolf Steiner, *The Kingdom of Childhood, op. cit.,* p. 110.
6. Knierim, *loc. cit.*
7. Hutchins, *op. cit.,* p. 44.
8. Rosemary Gebert, in a lecture at the Waldorf Institute, Oct. 1981.

9. Jane Winslow Eliot, *From Ring Around the Roses to London Bridge is Falling Down: Some Incarnating Games* (New York, NY: Rudolf Steiner School Press, 1982, p. 1).

10. Hutchins, *loc. cit.*

11. Steiner, *Education of the Child, op. cit.*, p. 29.

12. "Mood of the Fifth" is a special kind of pentatonic music which is discussed in Julius Knierim's book *Quintenlieder: Songs in the Mood of the Fifth*, being translated by Karen and Peter Klaveness. Readers interested in the healing and other esoteric aspects of music are referred to Rudolf Steiner's work *The Inner Nature of Music and the Experience of Tone* (Spring Valley, NY: Anthroposophic Press, 1983).

13. Rudolf Steiner, course of lectures delivered at the foundation of the Waldorf School in Stuttgart, August 21-September 5, 1919, and quoted in Grunelius, *op. cit.*, p. 45.

14. Elkin, *op. cit.*

## CHAPTER 11
# *Rhythm and Discipline in Home Life*

1. Margret Meyerkort, "Creative Discipline" in Davy and Voors (eds.), *op. cit.*, pp. 214-223.

2. Rudolf Steiner, *Soul Economy and Waldorf Education* (Spring Valley, NY: Anthroposophic Press, 1986, p. 121).

3. *Ibid.*, p. 115.

4. Grunelius, *op. cit.*, p. 29.

5. *Ibid.*, p. 28.

6. Rudolf Steiner, *Signs and Symbols of the Christmas Festival* (Spring Valley, NY: Anthroposophic Press, 1969).

7. Grunelius, *op. cit.*, p. 27.

8. *Ibid.*

9. Andrea Gambardella, "Rhythm in Home Life," *Waldorf Kindergarten Newsletter*, Fall 1984, p. 10.

10. Bons Voors, "Family Meals," in Davy and Voors (eds.), *op. cit.*, pp. 154-160.

11. Margret Meyerkort, "Sleeping and Waking," in *ibid.*, pp. 142-153.

12. *Ibid.*, p. 150.

13. Rudolf Steiner, *Prayers for Mothers and Children* (London: Rudolf Steiner Press, 1983, p. 50 (translated from the German).

14. Michael Strassfeld, *The Jewish Holidays* (New York, NY: Harper & Row, 1985).

15. Richard Siegel, et al., *The First Jewish Catalog* (Philadelphia, PA: The Jewish Publication Society of America, na).

16. Friedel Lenz, *Celebrating Festivals with Children* (Spring Valley, NY: Anthroposophic Press, 1986).

17. Diana Carey & Judy Large, *Festivals, Family & Food* (Gloucester, UK: Hawthorn Press, 1982).

18. Margret Meyerkort, (ed.), *Spring* (Gloucester, U.K.: Wynstone's Press, 1983). Available from the Rudolf Steiner College, 9200 Fair Oaks Blvd., Fair Oaks, CA 95628.

## CHAPTER 12
# Cognitive Development &
# Early-Childhood Education

1. Elkind, *Miseducation, op. cit.*, pp. 119-122.
2. Grunelius, *op. cit.*, p. 26.
3. Steiner, *Education of the Child, op. cit.*, p. 21.
4. "Kids Need Time to be Kids," *Newsweek*, Feb. 2, 1987, p. 58.
5. *Ibid.*, p. 56.
6. *Ibid.*, pp. 57-58.
7. *Ibid.*, p. 57.
8. Steiner, *op. cit.*, pp. 28-29.


## CHAPTER 13
# Readiness for First Grade

1. Diana Loercher Pazicky, "Just because a child is the right age doesn't mean he's ready for school," *Philadelphia Inquirer*, April 22, 1984.
2. James K. Uphoff and June Gilmore, "Pupil Age at School Entrance—How Many are Ready for Success?" *Educational Leadership*, September 1985, pp. 86-90.
3. *Ibid.*, p. 86.
4. Pazicky, *op. cit.*
5. Audrey McAllen, "On First Grade Readiness: An Interview with Margret Meyerkort," *Bulletin of the Remedial Research Group*, No. 5, Autumn 1986 (Fair Oaks, CA: Remedial Research Group at the Rudolf Steiner College, pp. 12-15).
6. Raymond S. and Dorothy N. Moore, *Better Late Than Early* (New York: Reader's Digest Press, 1975) and *School Can Wait* (Provo, UT: Brigham Young University Press, 1979).
7. Bruno Bettelheim and Karen Zelan, "Why Children Don't Like to Read," *Atlantic Monthly*, November 1981.
8. *Ibid.*
9. *Ibid.*


## CHAPTER 14
# More Parenting Issues

1. Elkind, *The Hurried Child* and *Miseducation, op. cit.*
2. Rudolf Steiner, from a course of lectures delivered in Oxford, England, in the summer of 1922, quoted in Grunelius, *op. cit.*, p. 43.

3. Rudolf Steiner, *Human Values in Education*, lectures given in Arnheim, Switzerland, July 17-24, 1924 (London: Rudolf Steiner Press, 1971, p. 55).

4. John Rosemond, "Children and Television," *Boston Globe*, Jan. 3, 1984.

5. Audrey McAllen, "Movement or Television," Bulletin of the Remedial Research Group (Fair Oaks, CA: Rudolf Steiner College, na).

6. *Ibid.*

7. *Ibid.*

8. Rosemond, *op. cit.*

9. Dr. Walter Buhler, "TV and the Growing Child," translated by P. Sagal from "Soziale Hygiene: Merkblätter zur Gesundheitspflege im persönlichen und sozialen Leben," Nr. 27 (Bad Liebenzell, West Germany: Verein fur ein erweitertes Heilwesen).

10. J. Gerhartz-Franck, Leipzig, 1955, quoted in *ibid.*, p. 9.

11. Interview with Joseph Chilton Pearce in *Mothering*, Spring 1985.

12. Marie Winn, *The Plug-In Drug* (New York, NY: Viking, 1985).

13. Jane Brody, "Concerned parents should think twice before allowing television in the home," *Ann Arbor News*, Jan. 28, 1987.

14. Elkind, *Miseducation, op. cit.*

15. Quoted in *Mothering*, No. 44, Summer 1987, p. 80.

16. *Pediatrics*, 78:369.

17. Marshall Klaus, at a lecture in Denver, 1979.

18. Jane Brody, "An open approach helps children deal with the death of a loved one," *Ann Arbor News*, Feb. 5, 1988.

19. Nancy C. Dodge, *Thumpy's Story*, available from Prairie Lark Press, P.O. Box 699, Springfield, IL 62705. And Elisabeth Kübler-Ross, *Remember the Secret* (Berkeley, CA: Celestial Arts).

20. Bettelheim, *The Uses of Enchantment, op. cit.*, p. 50.

21. See Otto Wolff, "Childhood Diseases as a Source of Development," *Weleda News*, Vol. 4, 1983, pp. 14-15.

22. Dr. Uwe Stave, "Reflections on Fever in Childhood," *Journal for Anthroposophy*, No. 42, Autumn 1985, p. 9.

23. *Ibid.*, p. 10.

24. In addition to Western allopathic medicine, other systems such as homeopathy, naturopathy, anthroposophical or ayurvedic medicine also can provide helpful approaches.

25. Zur Linden, *op. cit.*, pp. 163-164.

26. Dr. Alvin N. Eden, "Visit with a Pediatrician," *American Baby*, March 1987, pp. 42-45.

27. *Ibid.*, p. 42.

28. *Ibid.*

29. *Ibid.*

30. *American Journal of Diseases for Children*, quoted in *The Compleat Mother*, Summer 1987, p. 6.

31. Tineke van Bentheim, et al., *Caring for the Sick at Home* (Edinburgh, UK: Floris Books, 1987, pp. 76-77).

32. Davy and Voors, *op. cit.*, p. 269.

33. J. G. Bennett, et al., *The Spiritual Hunger of the Modern Child* (Charles Town, WV: Claymont Communications, 1984).

34. Rene Knight-Weiler, *Spiritual Mothering Journal*, pp. 28-29.

35. *Ibid.*
36. Joseph Chilton Pearce, *The Magical Child Matures* (New York: Bantam, 1986).
37. Herbert Hahn, *From the Well-Springs of the Soul: Religious Instruction for the Child* (Forest Row, England: Rudolf Steiner Schools Fellowship, 1966).
38. Friedel Lenz, *Celebrating the Festivals with Children* (Hudson, NY: Anthroposophic Press, 1986).
39. Rudolf Steiner, *Study of Man* (London: Anthroposophic Press, 1947, p. 138).
40. Rudolf Steiner, *The Roots of Education* (London: Rudolf Steiner Press, 1968, pp. 37-38).
41. Rudolf Steiner, *The Essentials of Education* (London: Rudolf Steiner Press, 1948, p. 29).
42. Steiner, *Human Values in Education, op. cit.*, p. 125.
43. Rudolf Steiner, *The Renewal of Education* (Forest Row, UK: Steiner Schools Fellowship Publications, 1981, p. 65).
44. Peggy O'Mara McMahon, "An Ethic of Parenting," *Mothering*, No. 47, Spring 1988, p. 6.
45. *Ibid.*, p. 7.

# BIBLIOGRAPHY

Almon, Joan. "Choosing Fairy Tales for Young Children." *Waldorf Kindergarten Newsletter*, Fall, 1985.

Baker, Jeannine, et al. *Conscious Conception*. (Monroe, UT: Freestone Publishing Company, 1986).

Baldwin, Rahima. *Special Delivery*. (Berkeley, CA: Celestial Arts, 1986).

Baldwin, Rahima and Palmarini, Terra. *Pregnant Feelings*. (Berkeley, CA: Celestial Arts, 1986).

Bennett, John et al. *The Spiritual Hunger of the Modern Child*. (Charles Town, WV: Claymont Communications, 1984).

Bettelheim, Bruno. *The Uses of Enchantment*. (New York, NY: Alfred A. Knopf, 1975).

———— "The Importance of Play." *The Atlantic Monthly*, March 1987.

Bettelheim, Bruno and Zelan, Karen. "Why Children Don't Like to Read." *Atlantic Monthly*, November, 1981.

Brazelton, T. Berry. *Infants and Mothers: Differences in Development*. (New York, NY: Dell, 1986).

———— *Working and Caring*. (Reading, MA: Addison-Wesley, 1985).

Britz-Crecelius. *Children at Play*. (New York NY: Inner Traditions International, 1986).

Carey, Diana and Large, Judy. *Festivals, Family & Food*. (Gloucester, UK· Hawthorn Press, 1982).

Carlgren, Frans. *Education Towards Freedom*. (East Grinstead, UK: Lanthorn Press, 1976).

Chukovsky, Kornei. *From Two to Five*. (Berkeley, CA: University of California Press, 1963).

Cook, Wendy. *Foodways*. (Gloucester, UK: Hawthorn Press, 1988).

Cooper, Stephanie, et al. *The Children's Year*. (Gloucester, UK: Hawthorn Press, 1987).

Corda, Murshida Vera Justin. *Cradle of Heaven*. (Lebanon Springs, NY: Omega Press, 1987).

Cusick, Lois. *Waldorf Parenting Handbook*. (Spring Valley, NY: St. George Publications, 1984).

Davy, Gudrun and Voors, Bons (Eds). *Lifeways*. (Glous., UK: Hawthorn Press, 1983).

Dodge, Nancy C. *Thumpy's Story*. (Springfield, IL: Prairie Lark Press, 1986).

Eden, Dr. Alvin N. "Visit with a Pediatrician." *American Baby*, March 1987.

Edmunds, L. Francis. *Rudolf Steiner Education*. (Hudson, NY: Anthroposophic Press, 1987).

Eliot, Jane Winslow. *From Ring Around the Roses to London Bridge is Falling Down*. (New York, NY: Rudolf Steiner School Press, 1982).

Elkind, David. *The Hurried Child*. (New York, NY: Alfred A. Knopf, 1984).

———— *Miseducation: Preschoolers at Risk* (New York, NY: Alfred A. Knopf, 1987).

Gabert, Erich. *Punishment in Self-Education and the Education of the Child*. (Forest Row, UK: Steiner Schools Fellowship Publications, 1972).

Gaskin, Ina May. *Spiritual Midwifery*. (Summertown, TN: The Book Publishing Company, 1987).

———— *Babies, Breastfeeding and Bonding*. (South Hadley, MA: Bergin & Garvey, 1987).

Glas, Norbert. *Conception, Birth and Early Childhood*. (Spring Valley, NY: Anthroposophic Press, 1972).

Grunelius, Elizabeth. *Early Childhood Education and the Waldorf School Plan* (Engelwood, NJ: Waldorf School Monographs, 1974).

Hahn, Herbert. *From the Well-Springs of the Soul*. (Forest Row, UK: Rudolf Steiner Schools Fellowship, 1966).

Harwood, A.C. *The Recovery of Man in Childhood*. (Spring Valley, NY: Anthroposophic Press, 1958).

Hassauer, Werner. *Die Geburt der Individualität*. (Stuttgart, Germany: Verlag Urachhaus Johannes M. Mayer GmbH, 1984).

Hughes, Diana. 'Fairy Tales: A Basis for Moral Education." *Ethics in Education*, Vol. 6. No. 4, March 1987.

Hutchins, Eileen "The Value of Fairy Tales and Nursery Rhymes." *Child and Man Extracts*. (Sussex, UK: Steiner Schools Fellowship, na).

Jaffke, Freya. *Making Soft Toys*. (Millbrae, CA: Celestial Arts, 1981).

———— "About Painting and Human Development through Art." *Waldorf Kindergarten Newsletter*, Fall, 1984.

Knierim, Julius. *Quintenlieder*. (Echzell, Germany: Verlag Das Seelenflegebedruftige Kind, 1982).

König, Karl. *The First Three Years of the Child*. (Spring Valley, NY: Anthroposophic Press, 1969).

Lagercrantz, Hugo and Slotkin, Theodore. "The 'Stress' of Being Born," *Scientific American*, April 1986, pp. 100-107.

Leboyer, Frederick. *Birth Without Violence*. (New York, NY: Alfred A. Knopf, 1975).

Lebret, Elisabeth. *Pentatonic Songs*. (Toronto, Ontario: Waldorf School Association of Ontario, 1985).

Lenz, Freidel. *Celebrating the Festivals with Children*. (Hudson, NY: Anthroposophic Press, 1986).

Masters, Brien, Ed. *Rudolf Steiner Waldorf Education*. (Spring Valley, NY: Steiner Schools Fellowship, 1986).

Meyer, Rudolf. *The Wisdom of Fairy Tales*. (Edinburgh, UK: Floris Books, 1987).

Montagu, Ashley. *Touching*. (New York, NY: Columbia University Press, 1971).

Moore, Raymond, and Moore, Dorothy. *Better Late Than Early*. (New York: Reader's Digest Press, 1975).

———— *School Can Wait*. (Provo, UT: Brigham Young University Press, 1979).

Müller, Brunhild. *Painting with Children* (Edinburgh, UK: Floris Books, 1987).

Neuschütz, Karin. *The Doll Book*. (Burdett, NY: Larson Publications, 1982).

Olness, Karen N. "Little People, Images and Child Health," *American Journal of Clinical Hypnosis*, Vol. 27, No. 3, January 1985.

O'Mara McMahon, Peggy. "An Ethic of Parenting." *Mothering*, No. 47, Spring 1988.

Pearce, Joseph Chilton. *The Magical Child*. (New York, NY: E.P. Dutton, 1977).

———— *The Magical Child Matures* (New York, NY: Bantam, 1986).

Querido, René. *Creativity in Education: The Waldorf Approach.* (San Francisco, CA: H.S. Dakin Company, 1985).

Russell, Rauld. "Wet-on-Wet Watercolor Painting." *Mothering,* Summer 1987.

————— *How to Do Wet-on-Wet Watercolor Painting and Teach Your Children.* (Coos Bay, OR: The Iris, 1987).

Russ, Johanne. *Clump-a-Dump and Snickle-Snack.* (Spring Valley, NY: Mercury Press, na).

Salter, Joan. *The Incarnating Child.* (Gloucester, UK: Hawthorn Press, 1987).

Scott, Anne. *The Laughing Baby.* (South Hadley, MA: Bergin & Garvey, 1987).

Segal, Marilyn. *Your Child at Play: Birth to One Year.* (New York: Newmarket Press, 1985).

Segal, Marilyn and Adcock, Don. *Your Child at Play: One to Two Years.* (New York: Newmarket Press, 1985).

Siegel, Richard. *The First Jewish Catalog.* (Philadelphia, PA: The Jewish Publication Society of America, na).

Smith, Susan. *Echoes of a Dream.* (London, Ontario: Waldorf School Association of London, 1982).

Solter, Aletha Jauch. *The Aware Baby.* (Goleta, CA: Shining Star Press, 1984). "Exercises in Self-Awareness for New Parents" (Goleta, CA: Shining Star Press, 1984).

Stave, Uwe. "Reflections on Fever in Childhood." *Journal for Anthroposophy,* No. 42, Autumn 1985.

Steiner, Rudolf. *The Arts and Their Mission.* (New York: Anthroposophic Press, 1964).

————— *The Cycle of the Year.* (Spring Valley, NY: Anthroposophic Press, 1984).

————— *The Education of The Child.* (London, UK: Rudolf Steiner Press, 1965).

————— *The Essentials of Education.* (London, UK: Rudolf Steiner Press, 1948).

————— *The Four Temperaments.* (Hudson, NY: Anthroposophic Press, 1987).

———— *Human Values in Education.* (London, UK: Rudolf Steiner Press, 1971).

———— "The Interpretation of Fairy Tales" (New York: Anthroposophic Press, 1943).

———— *An Introduction to Waldorf Education.* (Spring Valley, NY: Anthroposophic Press, 1985).

———— *The Kingdom of Childhood.* (London, UK: Rudolf Steiner Press, 1974).

———— *Lectures to Teachers.* (London, UK: The Library of the Anthroposophical Society in Great Britain, 1948).

———— *Pneumatosophy.* (New York: Anthroposophic Press, na).

———— *Practical Advice for Teachers.* (London, UK: Rudolf Steiner Press, 1970).

———— *Practical Course for Teachers.* (London, UK: Rudolf Steiner Press, 1937).

———— *Prayers for Mothers and Children.* (London, UK: Rudolf Steiner Press, 1983).

———— *The Renewal of Educaton.* (Forest Row, UK: Steiner Schools Fellowship Publications, 1981).

———— *The Roots of Education.* (London, UK: Rudolf Steiner Press, 1968).

———— *Signs and Symbols of the Christmas Festival.* (Spring Valley, NY: Anthroposophic Press. 1969).

———— *Soul Economy and Waldorf Education.* (Spring Valley, NY: Anthroposophic Press, 1986).

———— *The Spiritual Ground of Education.* (London, UK: Rudolf Steiner Press, 1947).

———— *Study of Man.* (London, UK: Anthroposophic Press, 1947).

———— *Swiss Teachers' Course.* (London, UK: The Library of the Anthroposophical Society in Great Britain, na).

Strassford, Michael. *The Jewish Holidays.* (New York, NY: Harper & Row, 1985).

Strauss, Michaela. *Understanding Children's Drawings.* (London, UK: Rudolf Steiner Press, 1978).

Thoman, Evelyn and Browder, Sue. *Born Dancing.* (New York, NY: Harper and Row 1987).

Udo de Haes, Daniel. *The Young Child*. (Spring Valley, NY: Anthroposophic Press, 1986).

Uphoff, James and Gilmore, June, "Pupil Age at School Entrance—How Many are Ready for Success?" *Educational Leadership*, September, 1985, pp. 86-90.

van Bentheim, Tineke, et al. *Caring for the Sick at Home*. (Edinburgh, UK: Floris Books, 1987).

von Heydebrand, Caroline. "The Child at Play" and "The Child When He Paints" in Allen, Paul (Ed.). *Education as an Art. Rudolf Steiner and Other Writers*. (Blauvelt, NY: Steinerbooks, 1970).

———— *Childhood, A Study of the Growing Soul*. (London, UK: Anthroposophical Publishing Co., 1946).

van Kügelgen, Helmut. "Fairy Tale Language and the Image of Man." *Waldorf Kindergarten Newsletter*, Fall, 1986.

———— "Marionette Theaters. Posing a Task for Socially Oriented Education." *Waldorf Kindergarten Newsletter*, Fall 1982.

Watson, Clyde. *Catch Me and Kiss Me and Say It Again*. (New York, NY: Philomel Books, 1978).

White, Burton L. *Educating the Infant and Toddler*. (Lexington, MA: D.C. Heath and Co., 1988).

———— *The First Three Years of Life* (New York, NY: Prentice Hall, 1986).

Whitfield, Miriam. *Fairy Stories . . . Why, When, How*. (Boulder, CO: The Juniper Tree, 1986).

Winn, Marie. *The Plug-In Drug*. (New York, NY: Viking, 1985).

Zahlingen, Bronja. "The Pedagogical Value of Marionette and Table Puppet Shows for the Small Child." *Waldorf Kindergarten Newsletter*, Fall, 1982.

———— *Plays for Puppets and Marionettes* (Silver Spring, MD: Acorn Hill Children's Center, 1983).

zur Linden, Wilhelm. *When A Child Is Born*. (New York, NY: Thorsons Publishers, 1984).

# INDEX

Four-year-olds
  abstract concepts and, 255
  drawings of, 201, 202–203
  fairy tales and, 175, 181, 182
  preschool and, 258
  singing and, 212
  Waldorf early-childhood education
      program and, 269
  watercolor painting and, 198
  *See also* Preschoolers
Free play. *See* Play
*From Ring Around the Roses to London
      Bridge is Falling Down: Some
      Incarnating Games* (Eliot), 222
*From the Well-Springs of the Soul: Religious
      Instruction for the Child* (Hahn),
      318, 326
*From Two to Five* (Chukovsky), 176, 188
Funerals, children attending, 308

**G**

Gabert, Erich, 252
Gallico, Paul, 161
Gambardella, Andrea, 236
Games
  circle, 215–216
  for infants, 90, 92–93
  for one-year-olds, 90
  for toddlers, 107–108, 113–114, 216
  of toddlers, 146–147
Garnet Hill, 54
Gaskin, Ina May, 45, 46, 53
*Gateways* (Meyerkort), 221
Gesell Institute of Human Development,
      276–227
Gesell Readiness Test, 279
Gifted children
  balanced development of, 285, 294–295
  Waldorf approach to, 284–285
GI Joe dolls, 154
Gilmore, June, 275–276, 287
Glas, Norbert, 21, 53, 75
Goethe, 193
"Go In and Out the Windows", 216
Grasping reflex, 40
Gratitude, fostering, in young children,
      320
Gravity
  fetus's experience of, 26, 27
  newborn's experience of, 27
*Grimm's Fairy Tales*, 175, 176, 180, 188
*Growing Without Schooling*, 288
Grunelius, Elizabeth, 230, 234, 235, 256,
      271
Guardian angels, 309

Guessing games, five- to seven-year-olds
      and, 278
Guilt
  letting go of, 20
  negative effect of, 295
  from separation of mother and child
      at birth, 44
  sibling rivalry and parental, 133
Guns (toy), 301
Gymnastics classes
  infants/toddlers and, 92, 99
  preschoolers/kindergartners and, 219

**H**

Hahn, Herbert, 318, 326
Hands, control of, in newborns/infants,
      58–59, 61
*Hanky Panky* (Burns), 162
Hanna Anderson, 54
Hannukkah, 248
"Hansel and Gretel", meaning of, 177–
      178, 179
Hans Schumm Woodworks, 164
*The Hardy Boys* books, 157
Harps. *See* Kinderharps
Harps of Lorien, 222
Harwood, A. C., 22, 272
Hats
  for imaginative play, 160
  for newborns, 38–39
Hauschka, Rudolf, 325
Head
  control of, in newborns/infants, 58–59
  covering in newborns, 38–39
  pubescent children centered in, 12
Head Start Program, 1–2
Health
  books on, 325
  early intellectual awakening and, 294–
      295
*Health and Illness* (Steiner), 325
Hearing
  disorders of, watching for, 66, 79
  stimulating/protecting sense of, in
      newborns, 37–38
Heartbeat
  elementary-school-aged children and,
      12
  holding infants and, 34
Hearth Song, 54, 159, 162, 165, 205, 206,
      222
Heart/lung/rhythmic system (Steiner),
      146
  singing and, 212–213
Heart Wood Arts, 164

crawling development in, 60–61, 82
"babyproofing" the home and, 82–83
critical learning period of, 1–3
crying of, 43, 46–47, 85–86, 125–126
daycare and, 21, 77–78, 127–129
demanding nature of, prior to crawling, 86–87
development of,
parental assistance in, 77–94
regressions in, 82
disciplining, 226
dropping objects by, 84–85
emotional development in, 62, 85–87
environment of, 83, 132
equipment for, 90–92
etheric energy field of mother and, 117, 128
exercise courses for, 79
experience of being with, 61–63
eye-hand coordination in, 59
failure to thrive by, 43–44
flash cards and, 84, 258
games for, 90, 92–93
gymnastics classes and, 92, 99
hands of, control of, 58–59, 61
head of, control of, 58–59
holding, 34
imitation and, 111
immunizations and, 130–131, 310–311
incarnation process of, 11, 62–63, 64, 73, 74
intellectual development in, 83–85, 255
language development in, 49, 65–66, 87–89
learning process of, 14, 84
legs of, control of, 58, 60–61
love's healing power for, 316
memory development in, 71, 83–84
movement and, 83, 146
music and, 37–38, 89
pacifiers and, 48, 91
parents' importance for, 1–3
parents' self-development and, 132, 318, 319–322
personalities in, 134
physical development in, 58–61, 79–83
playpens and, 81, 83, 92
problem-solving ability in, 70
psychic connection between mother and, 128
quality time and, 78
reaching by, development of, 59
regressions in development of, 82
rhythmic lifestyle for, introducing, 119–121

self sense of, 11, 62–63, 64, 73, 74
senses of, stimulating/protecting, 33–39, 131–132
sick, 315, 316
sight development in, 58–59
singing to, 37–38, 66, 88–89, 212
skill development in, 58–61
sleeping with parents, 121–123
sleep patterns of, 61
smiling in, 42, 62
solid foods and, 124–125
sound exploration and, 85, 88, 89
sound quality and, 37–38, 88
space experience of, 149–150
spoiling, 86–87
stair gates and, 82, 91
stranger anxiety in, 62–63
strollers and, 81
swimming classes and, 92, 99
tape-recorded sounds and, 37–38, 48, 212
teething in, 61–62
throwing objects by, 83–84
tickle response of, 62
torso of, control of, 59–60
toys for, 80, 81, 83, 85, 89–92
sources of, 93–94
transitional nature of first six weeks for, 40
walking development in, 61, 63–65
weaning, 123–125
will of, 62
See also Children; Early childhood; Newborns
Infants and Toddlers: Differences in Development (Brazelton), 134
Infant walkers. See Walkers
Informed Birth & Parenting Books, 327
Inner life
development of,
in parents, 318, 319–320
in young children, 68–70, 319–320
See also Spiritual world
Inquisitiveness, of toddlers, 97–98
Intellectual development
advanced, in childhood, 285, 294–295
developmental age and, 275, 277
in early childhood, 255–257, 284
emotional development and, 294
from five to seven, 278, 280–281, 284
imagination and, 168, 279
of infants, 83–85, 255
of newborns, 83–85, 255
physical development and, 256–257, 294–295
television and, 298

of toddlers, 97, 99, 104–107
Waldorf early-childhood education
program and, 264
*See also* Brain development; Thinking
Intellectual stimulation, for mothers, 141
International Association of Infant
Massage Instructors, 126
"The Interpretation of Fairy Tales"
(Steiner), 188
*An Introduction to Waldorf Education*
(Steiner), 287
Invisible companions, 154

## J

Jaffke, Freya, 115, 164, 186, 200, 208
Jewish festivals
celebrating, 248, 249–250
*See also* Religious instruction
*The Jewish Holidays* (Strassfeld), 249, 252
Judgment, imagination and, 279
Jung, Carl, on fairy tales, 176
Junior first grade, 277
Junior-high-school-aged children. *See*
Adolescents

## K

Kennell, 44
Kick toy, 80, 91
Kidnapping, educating children about,
301–303
Kindergarten
development occurring in, 277–278,
279–281
eurythmy in, 330
evaluating, 258–260, 261–268
pre-kindergarten, 277
purpose of, 156
readiness for, 275–276
reading in, Waldorf approach to, 283
Waldorf early-childhood program for,
260–268
home-based, 268–271
Kindergartners
abstract concepts and, 255–257
dance lessons and, 219–220
disciplining, 226, 227, 229
drawings of, 201, 202, 203–204
fairy tales for, 183
first graders different from, 6
gymnastics classes and, 219
intellectual development in, 255–257
music lessons and, 220, 221
nap/quiet times and, 241–242
passive nature of modern, 297
pentatonic music and, 217
pretend as form of play in, 149

reasoning with, 10, 71, 227
sports and, 219–220
swimming classes and, 219
watercolor painting and, 194, 198–199
*See also* Children; Early childhood;
Five-year-olds; Imitation
Kinderharps
bedtime and, 89, 218, 243
described, 89, 218
musical ability development and, 218
nap/quiet times and, 89, 218, 242
sources of, 94, 222
Kitchen-type toys, 158–159
Klaus, Marshall, 44, 306
Knierim, Julius, 212, 213
Knight-Weiler, René, 317–318
*Knowledge of Higher Worlds* (Steiner), 118
Kolisko, Eugen, 325
König, Karl, 68
Kübler-Ross, Elizabeth, 308

## L

La Leche League, 45, 123, 124
Language development
in newborns/infants, 49, 65–66, 87–89
rhymes and, 66, 88
singing and, 66
in toddlers, 57, 65–70, 97, 104–107
walking/movement and, 67–68
Large, Judy, 208
Large, Martin, 326
*The Laughing Baby: Remembering Nursery
Rhymes and Reasons* (Scott), 88,
93, 115, 222
Leadership abilities, and age
kindergarten entered, 276
Learning disabled
inappropriateness of label, 6
television and, 296–297
Learning process
from birth to seven years, 14–16, 84
of newborns/infants, 14, 84
of toddlers, aids to, 99–101
Leboyer, Frederick, 25, 42, 53
Lebret, Elizabeth, 221
Legs, control of, in infants, 58, 60–61
Leidloff, Jean, 123
Lemon wrap, for fever, 314
Lenz, Friedel, 188, 252, 318, 326
Life, preparing children for, 291–293,
301–303
Life energy field, of mother and young
child, 117, 128
*Lifeways* (Davy and Voors), 143, 188, 252,
271
Lighting, newborns and, 36–37

Movies
adverse effects of, 157, 171, 185
educational, 298
*See also* Cartoons; Television
Müller, Brunhild, 193, 194, 208
Mumps, 310, 311
Music, for newborns/infants, 37–38, 89
Musical ability development, 211–222
eurythmy and, 331
fingerplays and, 215–217
imitation and, 220
kinderharps and, 218
movement games and, 215–217
music/dance lessons and, 219–221
pentatonic instrument sources for, 222
pentatonic music and, 217–218
percussion instruments and, 218
performing and, 220
reading music and, 220
rock music and, 218
singing with children and, 212–214
songbooks for, 221–222
*See also* Singing

# N

Nagy, Maria, 307
*Nancy Drew* books, 157
Nap times, 241–242
The Natural Baby Company, 54
Natural childbirth, misnomer of, 4
Natural fiber clothing/bedding
newborns and, 35
sources of, 54
Natural fiber toys, sources of, 94
Nature
color and, 191–192
experiencing through play, 150–152, 163
seasonal celebrations and, 250
toddlers and, 113
Negative behavior, disciplining, 231–233
Negativism
in elementary-school-aged children/
adolescents, 73
in toddlers, 73, 101–104, 108
Neighbor children, playing with, 301
Nerve/sense/head system (Steiner), 146
Nervous children, rhythm in home life
and, 235
Neuschütz, Karen, 162, 164
Newborns
arrhythmic lifestyle of, 120
baby-care products for, sources of, 54

baby talk and, 49, 65
bathing,
consoling nature of, 27
treatment of baby during, 49
birth experience of, 25–26
body control in, 41–42
bonding with, 43–44
books on, 53
breastfeeding, 45–46, 119–121, 124
breath experience of, 28–29
carriers for, cautions about, 34
colic and, 46–47, 125
colors soothing for, 47–48
comfort provision for, 42
consciousness of, 11–12, 13–14, 29–31,
57, 62
crying of, 32, 43, 46–47, 85–86, 125–
126
daycare and, 21, 127–129
demanding nature of, 49–50
development of, parental assistance
in, 77–94
diapering, treatment of baby during,
49
diapers and, 35
environment of, 47–48
equipment for, 90–92
etheric energy field of mother and,
117, 128
experience of being with, 49–52
eye-hand coordination in, 59
eyes of, control of, 42, 58
gravity experience of, 27
hands of, control of, 58–59
head of,
control of, 58
covering for, 38–39
hearing sense, stimulating/protecting,
37–38
incarnation process of, 13–14, 29–31,
62
intellectual development in, 83–85, 255
language development in, 49, 87–89
learning process of, 14
lighting and, 36–37
loving, 43–44
lullaby bears and, 48
massaging, 45
mobiles and, 48, 80
mood changes in, 39
music and, 37–38, 89
natural fibers and, 35
sources of, 54
noise and, 37–38

toys for, 161–162, 163
  sources of, 164–165
  in Waldorf early-childhood
    education program, 261–262
  ways to encourage, 158–163, 169–
    170
  importance of, 149, 155–158
  invisible companions and, 154
  with neighbor children, 301
  stages of, 149
  See also Creativity; Fantasy;
    Imagination; Toys
Play areas, setting up, 158–159
Playdoh, 206
Play groups
  mothering support and, 141
  toddlers and, 99
  Waldorf early-childhood education
    (home-based) and, 268–271
Playpens, infants and, 81, 83, 92
Plays for Puppets and Marionettes
  (Zahlingen), 188
The Plug-In Drug (Winn), 298–299, 326
Postman, Neil, 179, 326
Postpartum period, 40
Postpartum support, importance of, 17–
  18, 50
Practical Course for Teachers (Steiner), 331
Prayers for Mothers and Children (Steiner),
  326
Pregnant Feelings (Baldwin and
  Palmarini), 40, 50, 53, 130
Pregnant women, Raphael's Sistine
  Madonna and, 48
Pre-kindergartens, 277
Premature babies
  love's healing power for, 316
  sensitivity of, 33
  wool sheets and, 35
Preschool
  computers and, 293
  evaluating, 258–260, 261–268
  value of, 257–258
  Waldorf early-childhood program for,
    260–268
  home-based, 268–271
Preschoolers
  abstract concepts and, 255–257
  bedtimes for, 243–244
  books on, 75
  centered in will and limbs, 11
  consciousness of, 11–12, 72, 74
  critical learning period of, 1–3
  dance classes and, 219–220

disciplining, 101–104, 136, 226, 227,
  228–229
drawings of, 201, 202
eurythmy and, 331
fairy tales and, 175, 179–184
fantasy and, 148
gymnastics classes and, 219
hot housing, 6, 259
incarnation process of, 11–12, 72, 74
intellectual development in, 255–257
learning process of, 14–16
making things with, 207
memory development in, 71–72
movement and, 11–12, 211, 212
musical activities and, 212
music lessons and, 220, 221
nap/quiet times and, 241–242
parents' importance for, 1–3
parents' self-development and, 100,
  318, 319–322
play of, imaginative, 147–148, 149
pretending as form of play in, 149
rational/scientific explanations and, 10,
  71, 102, 255
reasoning with, 10, 71, 227
self sense of, 11–12, 72, 74
space experience of, 150
sports and, 219–220
storytelling for, 172–174, 180
stranger danger education and, 302
swimming classes and, 219
thinking development in, 70–72
toys for, 110–111
verbal skills exceed conceptual
  knowledge in, 255
warmth maintenance in, 132
watercolor painting and, 197–198
See also Children; Early childhood;
  Four-year-olds; Imitation; Play;
  Three-year-olds
Pretending
  and invisible companions, 154
  preschoolers/kindergartners and, 149
Problems of Nutrition (Steiner), 325
Problem-solving ability development. See
  under Thinking
Protecting
  children from problems of adult
    world, 291–293, 301–303
  senses of newborns, 33–39, 47
Psychic connection, between mother and
  young child, 128
Pubescent children. See Adolescents
Punishing. See Disciplining

# S

Sabbath, 247
*See also* Religious festivals
St. George Book Service, 327
"Sally Go Round the Sun", 215
Salter, Joan, 22, 53, 75, 143, 325
Sandboxes, toddlers and, 110
Sanguine temperament, 135–136
Saturday Clubs, 270, 286
Scheduled breastfeeding, 119
Schneider, Vimala, 126
*School Can Wait* (Moore and Moore), 281, 287
Schooling, home. *See* Home schooling
School readiness
  books on, 287
  evaluating, 275–281
Scientific explanations, young children and, 10, 71, 102, 255
Scooting, 60
Scott, Anne, 88, 93, 115, 222
Seasons
  celebrating, 250
  rhythm of, 247–249
  Waldorf early-childhood education program and, 263–264, 265
Second grade
  reading in, Waldorf approach to, 282, 283
  Waldorf curriculum for, 329
  *See also* Elementary-school-aged children; Seven-year-olds
Security blanket, purpose of, 35
Seeger, Ruth Crawford, 222
Segal, Marilyn, 93, 115
Seizures, fever-induced, 312–313
Self-development of parents, importance of, 100, 132, 318, 319–322
Self sense
  of elementary-school-aged children, 11, 12
  incarnation process of, 11, 13–14, 31, 64
  of infants, 11, 62–63, 64, 73, 74
  of newborns, 29–31, 62
  of preschoolers, 11–12, 72, 74
  of toddlers, 11, 57, 64, 72–74
Sense impressions, from birth to seven years, 14–16
Senses, stimulating/protecting, in newborns/infants, 33–39, 47, 131–132
Sensitivity
  of newborns, 32
  in toddlers, teaching, 109

Sensorimotor intelligence, 70
Separation, of mother and child at birth, 44
Separation anxiety, 137–139
"Sesame Street", 100
"The Seven Ravens", 181
Seventeen-year-olds. *See* Adolescents
Seventh grade, Waldorf curriculum for, 330
Seven-year-olds
  developmental characteristics of, 277–279
  drawings of, 201, 202, 203–204, 278
  *See also* Elementary-school-aged children
*Seven-Year-Old-Wonder-Book*, 205
Sewing, preschoolers and, 207
Sibling rivalry, 133–134
Siblings, attendance of, at sibling's birth, 305–307
"A Sick Child in Hospital" (Westphal), 325
Sick children, caring for, 314–316
SIDS (Sudden Infant Death Syndrome), preventing, 122
Siegel, Richard, 252
Sight
  in newborns/infants, development of, 58–59
  stimulating/protecting sense of, 35–37
Silk, as baby fabric, 35
Silver nitrate, sense of sight and, 35
Singing
  to fetuses, 37, 212
  language development and, 66
  to newborns/infants, 37–38, 66, 88–89, 212
  songbooks for, 221–222
  to toddlers, 114, 173–174
  with young children, 212–214
  *See also* Musical ability development
Single parents
  rhythm in home life and, 305
  support systems for, importance of, 18, 119, 305
*Sistine Madonna* (Raphael), pregnant women and, 48
Sixteen-year-olds. *See* Adolescents
Sixth grade
  Waldorf curriculum for, 330
  *See also* Elementary-school-aged children
Six-year-olds
  drawings of, 201, 202, 203–204, 278

curative education of, 68
developmental stages of, 12–13, 145–146, 212–213
on difficult children, 31
on disciplining children, 226–227, 229
Ego concept of, 13–14
on emotions of infants, 62
on environment of newborns, 48
on environment of young children, 266
on etheric energy field of mother and young child, 117, 128
on eurythmy, 331
on fairy tales, 176, 179, 187, 188
on fingerplays, 215
on illness in later life, 294–295
on imagination, 167–168
on imitative nature of young children, 318–319
on immunization, 310
on infant nutrition, 124–125
on intellectual development in young children, 83, 84, 256–257, 293–295
on kinderharps, 218
on language development, 67, 70
major systems of, 145–146, 212–213
on meditation, 118
on musical ability, 212, 219
on natural fibers, 35
on natural processes of development, 7
on negativism in children, 73
on pentatonic music, 217
on puppet plays, 187
on Raphael's *Sistine Madonna* and pregnant women, 48
on reintegration of spirit and matter, 123
on religious nature of children, 318–319
on rhythm, 234–235
on rhythmical games, 216–217
on sense organ nature of young children, 32
on singing, 213
on soccer, 220
on soul life, 29
temperaments of, 134–136, 142
on toys for toddlers, 110, 112
Waldorf education and, 327
on weaning, 124
on will of infants, 62
Stepping reflex, 40
Stimulating/protecting senses of newborns, 33–39, 47

Stockinette caps, for newborns, 39
Stomachaches, 278
Storytelling
age to begin, 174–175
curative stories and, 184–185
imagination and, 172–174
methods of, 180–181
repetition in, 174, 180
times appropriate for, 181
value of, 172–174
in Waldorf early-childhood education program, 262, 267
Straddle toys, toddlers and, 110
Stranger anxiety, in infants, 62–63
Stranger danger, educating children about, 301–303
Strassfeld, Michael, 252
Strauss, Hans, 201
Strauss, Michaela, 201, 204, 208
Stresses of modern world, preparing children for, 291–293, 301–303
Strollers, 81
Stuffed animals
cautions about, 111, 152
making, 162
Sudden Infant Death Syndrome (SIDS), preventing, 122
Suicides (youth), and age kindergarten entered, 276
Super Baby syndrome, 258–259
Support
of mothers by fathers, 18, 118–119, 130
for parenting, importance of, 17–18, 50, 233
postpartum, importance of, 17–18, 50
for working mothers, 129
Support groups, for mothers, 141
Support systems, for single parents, importance of, 18, 119, 305
Sureway Trading Enterprises, 54, 165
Suzuki method, 220
Swaddling, consoling nature of, 27, 43
Swimming classes
infants and, 92, 99
preschoolers/kindergartners and, 219
Swings, toddlers and, 110
Synthetics, young children and, 131

## T

Talking, development of, 57, 67–68, 70–71
Tape-recorded sounds, young children and, 37–38, 48, 212

disciplining, 101–104
drawings of, 147, 200–202, 203
language development in, 57, 65–70,
    97, 104–107
memory development in, 71–72
negativism in, 73, 101–104, 108
play of, 153
    imaginative, 107–108, 147–148, 168
    books on, 115
    with other children, 153
rhythm in home life and, 235–236
self sense of, 11, 57, 72–74
storytelling for, 172–174
thinking process of, 70
toilet training and, 137
See also Toddlers

**U**

Udo de Haes, Daniel
    books of, 75, 115, 164, 189
    on gestures/facial expressions while
        storytelling, 181
    on language teaching, 104–105
    on soul language of objects, 68–69
    on toddlers hearing stories read to
        older children, 183–184
*Understanding Children's Drawings*
    (Strauss), 201, 204, 208
*Unplugging the Plug-In Drug* (Winn), 326
Uphoff, James, 275–276
*The Uses of Enchantment* (Bettelheim), 175

**V**

"The Value of Fairy Tales and Nursery
        Rhymes" (Hutchins), 173–174
Van Bentheim, Tineke, 325
Verbal skills, development of, 57, 67–68,
    70–71
Visual ability. *See* Sight
Von Heydebrand, Caroline, 146–147,
    149–150, 199
Von Sivers, Marie Steiner, 330
Voors, Bons, 143, 188, 252, 271

**W**

Wading pool, toddlers and, 110
Waking up children, 244–245
    spiritual world and, 243, 244
Waldorf early-childhood program, 260–
        268
    academic work in, 264
    activities in, 261–265
    books on, 271
    environment of, 265
    home-based, 268–271
        books on, 271–272

seminars on, 332
teacher's role in, 265–268
teacher training in, 268
Waldorf education
    books on, 333
    goal of, 328
    home schooling and, 286
    journals on, 271, 332–333
    Steiner, Rudolf, and, 327
Waldorf elementary schools
    academic work in, 281–285
    books in, 283
    books on, 287
    gifted children and, 284–285
    readiness for, 281
    teaching method in, 279
Waldorf Kindergarten Association of
        North America, 260
*Waldorf Kindergarten Newsletter*, 271, 333
*The Waldorf Parenting Handbook* (Cusick),
    72, 75, 271
Waldorf schools
    creative play and, 157–158
    curriculum of, 329–330
    eurythmy in, 330–331
    kinderharp and, 218
    lessons for young children and, 219
    list of, 329
    nondiscriminatory nature of, 270
    overview of, 328–330
Waldorf teacher training, 205, 268
    programs for, 331–332
Walkers
    crawling development and, 61, 92
    dangerous nature of, 92
    social/explorative behavior
        development and, 63
    walking development and, 63
Walking
    development of, 57, 61, 63–65
    language development and, 67–68
Warmth
    in newborns, stimulating/protecting
        sense of, 38–39
    in preschoolers, maintaining, 132
Water, experiencing through play, 151
Watercolor painting, 194–200
    books on, 208
    source of materials for, 208
    value of, 199–200
Watson, Clyde, 93, 115
*The Way of a Child* (Harwood), 272
Weaning, 123–125
*Welcome Home*, 22
Weleda Pharmacy, 54
West Earl Woolen Mill, 165

# Additional Resources

*THE BIRTH DISC,* by Harriette Hartigan, is a visual database of 9,000 color and black-and-white photographs illustrating the process of childbirth from pregnancy and labor through birth itself to post-partum and the newborn. The camera—accurate and immediate—documents the beauty and wonder of women giving birth and babies being born. It captures the emotions of fathers deeply caring and the joy of families celebrating new life.

To order *THE BIRTH DISC,* contact: Mikael Engebretson, Marketing Director; Image Premastering Services, Ltd.; 1781 Prior Avenue North; St. Paul, MN 55113; phone (612) 644-7802. Level I videodisc: $300.00.

# Also by Rahima Baldwin . . .

*Special Delivery: The Complete Guide to Informed Birth.* For couples who want to take greater responsibility for the birth of their babies at home, in a birth center, or in the hospital. Couples have come to see birth as a natural process. Any birth carried out with this awareness, with the focus on the people rather than on the technology, is a special delivery. This large-size book includes 30 photographs, bibliography, index, and black-and-white illustrations. $12.95.

*Pregnant Feelings* (Co-authored with Terra Palmarini). This book is unique in bringing a practical, self-help approach to the emotional and mental aspects of childbirth. Lovingly illustrated with black-and-white photographs by Harriette Hartigan. $10.95.

*Available at bookstores or by direct order from CELESTIAL ARTS, P.O. Box 7327, Berkeley CA 94707 (415) 524-1801.*

# More information from Rahima Baldwin . . .

* *Special Delivery Newsletter,* the quarterly publication of Informed Homebirth/Informed Birth and Parenting. $12 includes a year's membership (4 issues).

* The video *Special Delivery* shows three births, one in a hospital, one at home and one in a birth center. Discussions by couples include reasons behind their choices, the role of the father, different ways of meeting fear and pain. 40 minutes VHS or BETA. $44.95.

* *Informed Homebirth Tape Course* includes six cassettes by Rahima Baldwin covering all aspects of preparation for birth. $30.

*Write for further information or order directly by including a check or money order to Informed Homebirth/Informed Birth and Parenting, Box 3675, Ann Arbor, MI 48106, (313) 662-6857.*